Agram

A Quest for Substance

Ligia Luckhurst

éditions•出版社•ediciones

publishing•verlag•izdanja

For Peter O'Toole

CONTENTS

Acknowledgements

Many heartfelt thanks to Françoise Guillot and Neil Hack, without whose unflagging material, moral and practical support I wouldn't have found the means, the resolve and the discipline to bring this book out here and now.

Preface

Back in 1991, while I was running a tavern in the port of Ostend in Belgium, my home town which I left in 1983 but which still contained my mother, my aunt and uncle, my cousin and most of my best friends, got bombed in one of the opening moves of the war that erased Yugoslavia, the country I was born in, from the map and consigned it – to quote Leon Trotsky – "to the dustbin of history".

That is one hell of a long sentence. To continue:

Naturally, the media feasted on the gory corpse of Yugoslavia. I followed the reports, the editorials and the documentaries, at first with a kind of narcissistic fascination (as in "Look, we're on telly!"), then with bewilderment and finally with indignation. What annoyed me were the crude stereotypes – not because they were intended to offend but *because they weren't*. Naïve to the point of arrogance, they were nevertheless dished out blithely with confidence which brooked neither question nor doubt. In the end, I became very sad. *How can anyone hope to understand what is going on*, I thought, *if one is so ignorant? Let me help – let me explain a few things. I* remembered, reading the articles, how the people I met in the UK where I'd been living for the last 30 years used to ask me if there were telephones and motorways in Yugoslavia. Some of them asked questions of this kind even after having holidayed in Yugoslavia and used its telephones and motorways. That happens because we live in our heads more than in the world around us. I of course assumed that people in general *wanted* to understand what was going on because I, too, lived in my head more than in the world around me.

So I sat down in my tavern, between orders of mussels and chips, and started writing what I thought would be a pamphlet. After a page or two, however, I realised that anything I wrote would be distorted no less than the news, and that the veil of unknowing which covered Yugoslavia was impenetrable.

But, by the same token, I realised that the same veil of unknowing covered most things and not just Yugoslavia. And that I, too, could do with more insight into life, the universe and everything, but mostly into myself.

Last but not least, I had the bit between my teeth by then and couldn't give up my project even though it was, quite spontaneously, turning into a very different sort of project.

Writing on, I decided against documentary approach to what was now likely to be a sort of memoir, so much so that for a long time I wanted to call Yugoslavia 'Ruritania' (I'm still half convinced it would have been better to have stayed with that decision). Preconceived ideas dwell at a very deep level, so much so that the use of any Yugoslav names, I thought, would be full of dangerous pitfalls. If I wrote the word 'Belgrade', for example, the inevitable association with "Serbs"[1] and Milošević would immediately arise in the reader's mind, not to mention all the funny diacritical signs that would kick the whole text straight back into Balkan exotica where it would perish. Or am I imagining things? It could be that everyone here has forgotten

---

1 The Serbs of the media and the popular imagination, as distinct from the Serbs as a real, living people.

everything by now. Wars, like fads, come and go, unless you're in the middle of one.

Be that as it may, I changed most Yugoslav names into "Western" sounding ones either by directly translating them, or by trying to preserve in some other way their original meaning and mood, for there is a mood to any name. Where neither was possible, a name which would somehow contain the character of the person or the place in question was found. A similar technique was applied to certain concepts and other matters that could alienate the Western reader.

It goes without saying that I expected the reader to *know* that no Yugoslavs were *really* called Wilfrid Blake or Lillian Lagrange: a particular thrill can arise from being aware of that *reality gap*. Again, my expectations could be unfounded.

And Sean Feeney is really Peter O'Toole. The one who played Lawrence of Arabia. To make it more confusing, I mention Peter O'Toole once under his own name. "Sean Feeney" is the real name of the film director John Ford.

I decided to keep the language deceptively simple throughout the text, and to constantly invite the reader to a dialogue with the book.

Having thus set up the mode of my book, I had a whale of a time discussing everything under the sun in it: from slimming to "Star Wars", from moving flat to Macbeth, from dissecting corpses to dialectic materialism, from rock & pop to the Energy Flow of the Universe, all channelled through the story of growing up in socialist Yugoslavia. For reasons I cannot quite explain except perhaps by saying that the emotions I feel and the actions I take in dreaming count as much as the ones in waking life, I decided to structure my narrative around a number of dreams, recorded immediately on waking and preserved in a notebook. In addition, this gave me a twee aesthetic pleasure.

As I wrote, to my surprise, a set of neatly interconnected symbols emerged, such as the Green Clothes-Peg, the Demon Calf and the Socket. They were, to the best of my knowledge, completely original: I'd never seen any of them before anywhere. I did my best to give them time and space to work their magic. Because that's what symbols are really for: magic. I'm quite proud of myself for having done that.

I ended up with an intriguing blend of memoir, magic realism and blog that you see before you. But because I had an awful lot of mussels and chips to cook (this, too, is a symbol or a metaphor or something – I sold my tavern ages ago), the book took many, many years to write. And when I got near the end, I realised I couldn't finish it because I still hadn't found that fabled substance I'd been questing for.

Then my husband fell ill and, as he lay dying, gave me a helping hand. It's all there in the book, how he did that.

And then he died, and, a year later, I finished it.

Then I diddled with it from time to time, making changes. They were necessary, that's why I made them. Not because I had nothing better to do.

I've finished now. Dundiddling.

All yours now.

1. Alexandra

Farewell

Once upon a time in Europe there was a country called Yugoslavia, whose capital was Whiteburgh. I say "once upon a time" because it is no longer there.

It didn't go away, of course: countries don't. It was simply cancelled as a state, while its contents remained in place, more or less.

There were other cities in Yugoslavia, apart from Whiteburgh. Agram, my birthplace, was one of them. I lived in Agram and was five, I think, when I dreamt of Farewell. It is the first dream I remember, although there must have been other dreams, dreamt at the age of four, and at the age of three, and at all the ages in between.

Or I may have been seven. I started school when I was seven. The year before that, we — my parents and I — moved into a brand new flat. It was full of new furniture my parents had bought on credit. The year was nineteen fifty nine. Consequently, the furniture was bright and cheerful of design. Our curtains were Miroesque: black squiggles and geometric shapes in yellow, blue, red and green.

We lived with Mama's parents before we moved to our new flat. We were short of space but I enjoyed being crammed together with four people I loved. What grownups call discomfort or even squalor can be just right for kids. In the new flat I had a room all to myself. I inherited my parents' old double bed. I always expected fire to break out under the bed, God knows why. If I stuck my foot out over the edge, I could feel red-hot flames licking my heel. The door of my room had to be left ajar at night for the first six months in the flat.

I sleep in a different bedroom now, in another country. I've taken to leaving the bedroom door ajar at night again.

The flat was on the second floor of a medium-sized housing block, at right angle to another, larger block, both built by a big publishing and printing company to house the company's employees. My parents worked for the company. Mama worked in the accounts department. Papa was printer-compositor.

The two blocks formed an enclosure containing a spacious playground including a lawn planted with young weeping willows and poplars. There was a sandpit in the centre of the playground.

The playground was alive with children. Terror! Torment!

The only children I had known until then were Aspen and Maple, twin sisters the same age as me, who lived next door to my grandparents'. Our balconies were separated by a low wire fence. We used to play together. Aspen and Maple had toys from Italy, because their mother was Italian. They had Bambi, Lady and Tramp made of bath-sponge.

Now, all of a sudden, I had to meet many strange children and carry on seeing them day after day. That autumn I started going to school. School was easy. Playground was tough.

We did not have a television set. Nobody did except the very few, and they had to watch RAI Uno, the Italian first channel, because there was no Yugoslav television at the time. We bought our first black-and-white set some three years later, when I was ten. We watched RAI Uno a lot. I still remember a musical adventure series called 'Rinaldo Rinaldini', about a romantic highwayman, starring Domenico Modugno, a pop-singer. His greatest hit was 'Volare', the one that got recycled much later by the Gipsy Kings. Eventually, the Yugoslav Television – JRT – came into existence. Its identification sign showed a broadcasting tower with a dish aerial on top and the words *Yugoslav Radio-Television: Experimental Programme* written over the picture.

The set lived in my parents' bedroom where all three of us would sprawl on the large bed and watch Sjoukje Dijkstra win the ladies' world figure skating championship. We would also watch classic American films full of black cars and men in hats and trench coats, and series like 'The Naked City', 'The 87th Precinct', 'The Saint', 'Lost in Space', 'Lassie' and 'Fury'. Looking back at it now, it seems to me that I had spent my early schooldays in an imaginary America which blended seamlessly with the world around me.

I couldn't have been seven after all. I must've been at least ten when I dreamt of Farewell, because I remember the situation that brought about the dream, and it had to do with television.

It was a Saturday evening. I know that because Papa and I had had our baths. We bathed once a week and had never heard of anyone taking baths more often than that. It would have been very difficult to bathe daily. Our bathroom boiler, looking rather like Thomas the Tank Engine standing vertically, used wood and coal. The bath was made of enamelled cast iron. High above the bath, the shower was permanently fixed to the boiler. It could not be moved. That is important. Remember that.

The temperature of the shower could be adjusted by the taps on the mixer. To turn the taps, one had to stand under the shower or get out of the bath. Remember that, too.

So there we were, Papa and I, freshly bathed, with lovely clean underwear on, sprawling on the double bed and watching an American film about a tragic criminal hiding in an attic. He later ran down the staircase of an overground railway station, fired his gun once and was shot dead immediately afterwards. I was eating a slice of bread with goose liver pate spread thickly on it. I know it sounds extravagant, but it wasn't. It was not pâté de foie gras; it was just goose liver pate.

Mama was in the bath, taking a shower. It took her longer than usual — very long, in fact, but I only remember that in retrospect. Papa and I were totally engrossed in the film at the time, dead to the world.

"Paaaaapaaaa!" a faraway wail.

Mama called Papa 'Papa'. Papa referred to her as 'Mama'. Addressing her directly, he'd sometimes call her by her name, Patricia. Mostly he didn't call her anything at all.

The wail was coming from the bathroom. We became conscious of it only gradually. "Paaapaaaaa!" It rose and fell. "Go see what Mama wants", Papa said.

I got up and went, fuming. The film was about to end, and I was not going to see how. As I opened the bathroom door, Mama's wail became a scream. She stood in the bath, leaning against the wall — trying to melt into the wall — in a desperate effort to escape boiling hot water jetting out of the shower. The bathroom was full of steam. Mama's naked body was red — scalded. Her face was disfigured. Her mouth gaped: "Heeeelp!"

I reached for the hot water tap. It turned around until it went "click" but would not turn the water off. Mama screamed. To get out of the bath, she would have to step under the hot jet. She could not make herself do it. She must have been in agony! I panicked: "Paapaaa!" and ran away from Mama's screams.

Papa arrived, somewhat slowly. He tried the hot tap, then turned the cold one on and made the water cooler, so Mama could step out of the bath.

What had happened? The hot water tap had chewed through its washer. Mama did not know that. Standing under the shower, she used both hands to turn the water off simultaneously. The cold tap stopped running. The hot one went "click" and went on running and Mama flattened herself against the wall.

When all the hot water had run out of the tank, Papa changed the washer and that was that.

Mama was very angry, especially with Papa. She thought we hadn't come to her aid fast enough. "I could've died in there for all you care, you two," she said, but she was all right. There was no need to call the doctor or to apply an unguent. She had no burns. She trembled and cried a little. I was shattered. Mama in pain! Mama trembling! Mama crying!

I felt guilty. Papa did not. That made me think for a moment that we may not be guilty of anything after all, but it was only a passing thought. The wise part of me knew that Mama would withhold her love if I didn't feel guilty, so guilty I felt, and did not watch any more television that night. I sobbed myself to sleep instead.

I slept and I dreamt and here is my dream:

I've been out alone and now I've come back to my grandparents' flat. Nan is standing in the door, leaning against the door frame, wearing, as ever, a greasy apron over her dress and smoking a cigarette. Her hair is permed and blue-rinsed. Her face is sad and wise. "Where are Mama and Papa?" I ask. "They are gone," Nan replies, "they died. They won't be back." I start crying. I must find them at once.

Nan tells me where to look for them and I run, first down eight flights of stairs, then out of the house and down the lane to a deep well.

There is Mama — by the well. "How come?" I ask breathlessly. "Why?"

"Papa has killed himself into the well," comes the strange reply. "I must follow him down."

I beg Mama to reconsider, I plead, but Mama's mind is made up. The sadness of parting overcomes us both; it rises inside my body, an inner tide, reaching the throat where it explodes with a sharp pain, and the eyes through which it spills out. "Papa is calling me," says Mama. "Farewell." And she dives into the well.

I lean over the edge and peek in. "Can I come, too?" Mama's head emerges on the water surface, deep down in the well. "No," she says. "Farewell, daughter." I can hear Papa's voice too, from the depths of the well. "Farewell," he says, "farewell."

Papa is now going to die. I feel it, I know it. Mama's place is beside him. They belong together. They'll never be back. I'll never see them again.

I wake up choking on the tide of grief, and there they are, asleep in their bedroom, alive. They are together.

I have lived under the threat of farewells ever since, of people and things disappearing down a Farewell.

Alexandra, Desire and Forest Killed by a Bomb

Alexandra, Desiré and Forest are all alive and, for all I know, well. I see Alexandra occasionally but I have not seen Desiré and Forest for years.

Alexandra is my best friend. She and I are of an age. She is taller than I and used to be much slimmer. Even now, many years and two daughters later, she still appears slimmer. Her shoulders are broad. Her muscles are long and well defined. She looks very much like a woman in an El Greco painting. Her hands and feet are exquisite. Her head is an El Greco head: narrow, with a long nose, a weak chin, a full mouth, brown eyes and honey-coloured, straight, heavy hair. Alexandra is calm. She is not easily upset.

Alexandra was the first girl in town to wear hot pants. She taught me to paint my nails and colour my hair. She taught me to change my underwear regularly and take a shower daily. She taught me to use deodorant. Mama never bothered to make a woman of me, mainly because she was eccentric. She was a romantic, a bohemian type, a stern moralist and a masochist all rolled into one. She used to be stunningly beautiful but even then wore men's socks with court shoes and chain-smoked in the street. She was like a praying mantis in the way she treated men. Deodorants were the last thing on her mind.

I met Alexandra on my first day in secondary school. I was fifteen. By then my parents and I had moved yet again, as part of a flat exchange chain. It had been obvious for some time that Nan and Grandpa could not go on minding me and running our household while living in a separate flat about a mile away from ours. Grandpa would come round at seven in the morning to see me off to school. Nan would arrive later with the groceries. She'd cook lunch, hoover, dust, wash, iron and do whatever else was needed. My grandparents did all that because Papa and Mama both worked full time and Mama, who used to work more than full time, came home too tired to do anything but collapse into bed, often without taking her clothes off.

Papa worked from six in the morning to one in the afternoon. He would come home, have lunch, pick up a hold-all containing his swimming trunks, his Speedo cap, his Dunlop tennis balls and his Donnay racket and slip away to the sports centre where he'd spend the afternoon playing volley-ball, swimming or playing tennis. He moved in high circles because he could play tennis with either hand and was a sought-after opponent. He claimed he owed it to himself to spend all his free time in the fresh air because, being a printer, he worked with lead. He was given a free pint of milk daily by the firm. Milk was supposed to neutralise lead in the organism. Does it? I don't know.

When I was thirteen, my parents put their flat up for exchange and my grandparents put theirs up too. A chain of five exchanges was eventually organised. Five removal vans rolled away simultaneously, coordinated by telephone. At the end of the day, my parents, my grandparents and I found ourselves in a huge flat on the fourth floor of a grey thirties tenement comprising ten flats in all. It was owned by a housing association, which in Yugoslavia meant communal ownership. The flat could not be bought or sold to anyone. The rent it generated was ploughed back into communal housing. Our previous flat had been administered in the same way, although it had been built by the printing company, and my grandparents' flat was owned by a housing association, too. That is why we were able to exchange the two for the one.

Our new flat was equipped by a Moravia gas boiler which would come to life as one turned on any hot water tap in the flat. I did not avail myself of this luxury until I met Alexandra.

We used to sit at the same desk. Alexandra was between boyfriends. She was no longer a virgin. Many girls boasted of not being virgins. Alexandra did not boast, yet it was obvious that she was a woman. The boys knew that, oh yes. They swarmed around her although she was not glamorous or even beautiful by common standards. The boys teased her about her long nose and straight hair, using any excuse to touch her. Apart from that, they regarded her as one of the chaps because she'd smoke in the gents with them. One year later, after Alexandra had taught me to smoke, I became one of the chaps, too.

Alexandra had a cousin whose name was Forest. She was two, maybe three years older than Alexandra. Her father had been a guest-worker — a 'gastarbeiter' — in Germany for many years. Her mother had a lively social life and was seldom at home. There was also a brother, Aurel. The three of them lived a short walk away from my secondary school, in a flat which had originally been part of a much larger apartment. Their kitchen doubled as bathroom and one had to go out on the balcony in order to use the toilet. At night, Aurel slept in the kitchen, on a sofa.

Alexandra and I used to go there after school or simply truant and sit with Forest in her vast, warm multipurpose kitchen over innumerable cups of coffee, smoke and discuss life and death, art and philosophy, science and religion. We went there every day — sometimes twice a day. We could have gone to Alexandra's, but her parents were retired and always at home while Forest's mother wasn't. We'd often be joined by another girl of my age, Vicky, who knew Alexandra from primary school. Both Forest and Vicky were women, like Alexandra. Forest was petite, with long, rich, dark brown hair and kind black eyes in a heart-shaped little face. Her body was beautiful, with a narrow waist and generous, firm breasts. Unfortunately, as a little girl, she had had polio and one of her legs had remained shorter by an inch or so, stick-like and club-footed. She'd had multiple surgeries on it and did not need orthopaedic shoes.

Forest was good and compassionate. She was easily outraged. She had a special knack for understanding and undergoing suffering. She was very disciplined and used to be the only one in our circle able to sit and cram successfully. She thirsted for justice. She could sense a cold, calculating, sly spot in a human heart from miles away and would politely keep the person concerned at a distance.

I could never *really* love Forest. She and Alexandra were first and foremost to each other and I was, quite simply, jealous. Also, my heart was spot-ridden. I was not compassionate. I was too preoccupied with my own developing personality to pay much attention to other people. Forest did not like that, but nevertheless accepted me wholeheartedly because I was Alexandra's friend. In Forest's eyes — as in mine own — Alexandra's judgement was infallible.

About Desiré: he appeared on the scene during my second year of secondary school. He was Alexandra's new boyfriend. He may have been twenty-four at the time — a grownup.

Alexandra was going steady with a grownup! The boys at school hated Desiré. They said he was ugly and stupid and drew cartoons to prove it.

Desiré was tall and lean, with an interesting long face and a fine head of raven black hair. He was eloquent, cultured and witty. He was quick to take offence and to respond. He was vain. I don't know what he is like now.

Alexandra took pride in her womanhood and behaved like a

wife, visiting Desiré in his squalid flat where he lived without running water or television. She washed his clothes and occasionally cooked a meal for him.

I became aware of Desiré's existence only gradually. At first he was merely somebody with a claim on Alexandra's time and attention. Later, I fell in love with him. I was never interested in boys of my own age. Moreover, the fact that Desiré was Alexandra's boyfriend made him all the more attractive to me. And another thing: Desiré studied to be an actor. He had already appeared in public with a group of young actors who called themselves The Personality Scene and gave poetry readings.

I was fascinated by actors at the time. I had a steady crush on Sean Feeney, a famous Irish actor of whom more will be said later. I believed I could never love anyone but him. I was as good as married to him. That kept me away from boys. I experienced myself as slightly unnatural, which would not have worried me had not Alexandra and Forest and, of course, Desiré as well, felt that I was unnatural, too.

I thought I was ugly. My face, I thought, was broad and vulgar. I could not be as thin as Alexandra, Forest and Desiré, no matter how hard I tried. I did not understand Life as well as they did. I did not have Experience. My parents were not poor, divorced, drunken or violent. (Neither were Alexandra's, or Vicky's, for that matter.) I had no opportunity to suffer. I had migraines. My face twitched. I wept without cause. I had no idea I had fallen in love with Desiré.

One night, like any other night, I slept and I dreamt and here is my dream:

A war – the war – is raging in the world. It has been going on for some time and is not likely to end soon. Alexandra, Desiré, Forest and I are trying hard to live as if nothing were out of the ordinary. Among other ordinary things we do, we decide one fine day to take a walk in the country.

Blighted by the wanton destruction of war, Nature has

turned yellow. It has dried up. Also, it is summer: that could be a factor, too.

Once out of town, we divide our foursome in two: Alexandra and Desiré decide to walk in one direction and Forest and I in another. We are to meet up later in a garden café we all know, and have coffee there together.

Forest and I stroll along the yellow, blistering river bank, the space and time around us filled with raging war. We talk about the war and, more generally, about life. By and by, we arrive at the garden café with its red and white plastic chairs and tables covered with tablecloths which have seen better times. Alexandra and Desiré must already be there. We search for them, picking our way among tablefuls of holiday-makers. Forest is ahead of me.

At that moment, a bomb hits the café. The explosion is horrendous. Everything is blown to smithereens. When the pandemonium dies down, I get back on my feet, unhurt. Around me, the café lies in ruins. There can be no survivors.

I throw myself at the mountain of debris and start digging with my bare hands. Weeping, and screaming, I burrow among bits of furniture and pieces of human bodies. At last I begin to pull out pieces of Alexandra, Desiré, and, eventually, Forest.

They are dead. They are completely dismembered. I weep and in my despair wish I had died with them. How am I going to live? Why have I been spared? Why can't I get my share of the Crown of Thorns?

The House of Outcasts

It is absolutely true, I was *doomed to be spared*. Just listen to this.

One night I slept and I dreamt and here is my dream:

Somewhere on the outskirts of Agram, my home town, there is a huge yellow four-storey tenement. It resembles those run-down buildings in old Italian films like 'La Strada', 'Roma Citta Apperta' or 'The Walls of Malapaga', complete with crumbling plaster, mouse-holes, filthy toilets, ancient stinking cast-iron sinks in dark, dark corridors and washing hanging on clothes-lines outside windows.

The house is inhabited by a community of Outcasts. They are, to all intents and purposes, mad. They have been placed in isolation because their existence threatens the very structure of society. It has been explained to them that they will be better off inside, where they will be protected and in the company of their own kind.

The Outcasts are all exceptional people. They are free to live as they please, on condition that they never leave the house.

They make their own rules and police themselves, guarded only by their own personal ethics. They have more freedom in the house than they could ever have hoped to have outside and yet a heavy atmosphere of sadness and doom pervades the house.

The outcasts depend on public charity. In addition to that, each inmate has someone outside, a friend or a relative who visits and takes care of him or her.

One day, Alexandra receives the order to pack her belongings and enter the House. That is the way one gets there: one is ordered to go and one does, knowing full well it would be pointless to resist. In fact, one would have been expecting the order to come, perhaps, for years.

I accompany Alexandra to the House and help her settle there. I visit her often and bring as much food and money as I can. It is not a lot, as the whole world is steeped in miserable poverty.

Alexandra and her fellow inmates stroll along the corridors of the House, smoke, strum the guitar and sing together. Their song has no meaning because it cannot be shared with the outside world. It passes the time and that is all it does. The Outcasts cannot do anything that matters: they have been weeded out.

I feel that no matter what I do for Alexandra, it cannot have any significance. There can be no closeness or understanding between Alexandra and me. She is always cheerful and pleased to see me. Nevertheless, she seems to look down on me. Her eyes are those of a stranger: she is with 'them' and I am 'outside'.

I would give anything to enter the House as an Outcast, but it is impossible. Nobody can live there unless ordered to. "You mustn't despair," says Alexandra. "Somebody has to stay outside after all. We Outcasts couldn't live without you people." I don't look convinced. "It is no prize to be an Outcast, you know," says Alexandra.

I do know, only too well. If it were a prize, would there be suffering? And if there wasn't any suffering, would I want to share it? What a tangle! It's even silly.

But if I don't become an Outcast, I'll never be able to meet Alexandra on an equal footing! I'll never be together with her!

Alexandra still tries to cheer me up. She writes cheerful letters — in real life, that is, not in dreams. And I still haven't gone to live in the House of the Outcasts.

Or, to be absolutely truthful, I have — but only by proxy. It can be done by proxy. Exactly how and why it has been done, though, must remain a secret.

Anarchy

In the summer of nineteen seventy four, Alexandra, Forest and I went together on a camping holiday.

I was twenty two and studying 'Anglistics' — the English Language and Literature. Forest was preparing for her final exam in the subject we in Yugoslavia (and in all the states it has dissolved into since I've started writing this book) called Comparative Literature. She was going to graduate 'Indology' the following year. She was actually able to read texts in Sanskrit.

Alexandra had split with Desiré the year before. He had become difficult in a peevish, petty sort of way, and Alexandra had little time for peevishness and pettiness.

Her father had bought a car — a Fiat 1300 — and she had passed her driving test. We decided to take the car and an old tent and spend the summer camping along the Adriatic coast, just the three of us. Alexandra was the only one who could drive. She knew how to put distilled water in the cooler. She also knew how to top up the engine with oil. I'm not sure if she knew how to deal with a burst tyre, but we set off for the coast anyway.

Please note that Alexandra's father let us have his brand new car and did not bat an eyelid. Wasn't that grand?

Forest was in charge of cooking and washing. She was the Earth-Mother type, or so we all, including herself, believed. She packed a crate of cooking oil, flour, sugar, pasta and other provender, enough to last us a month. We had lots of luggage because we had to be self-sufficient. We did not expect camping sites to have any facilities.

The journey to the coast took one whole day, largely because we had chosen the wrong road. Eventually it got so bad that I had to walk in front of the Fiat and remove large stones from the carriageway. We reached our destination at sunset. Too tired to look for a camping site, we decided to spend the night by the road. Alexandra and Forest opted for sleeping in the open, on a blanket spread on the grass. I slept in the car. I was the cry-baby. I was the spoiled brat. I was afraid of insects.

In the morning, Alexandra's right arm was swollen to the armpit with insect bites. She was slightly feverish. In spite of that, she and Forest found an official camping site, checked us in, chose a good spot, erected the tent and did whatever else needed to be done. I don't remember doing anything. I believe I just fussed around, envious of Alexandra's leadership. I even envied her the insect bites. They were the price of freedom. Her swollen arm was a badge of courage.

The camping site was equipped with a café, a filthy toilet and — incredibly — a spring of sweet mountain water among the pebbles on the beach. We went to the spring daily with a jerry-can.

A gang of young lads, all of them our juniors, hung out at the cafe. They were secondary school students from middle class Bosnian families. And what did they do to pass the time? They stole car radios and cameras from parked cars and tents and sold them across the border in Albania, some hundred and fifty miles down the road. They removed our windscreen wipers and then gave them back to us just to let us know who was boss.

They were cocky and handsome. We became their molls and made love under the stars. In the back of our tent, I became a woman at last. Alexandra and Forest swapped their lovers. Those were the days! The lads borrowed our car to take the stolen goods to Albania and returned it with a tankful of petrol. Nothing was ever stolen from our tent.

My boyfriend, the leader of the gang, was the son of a prominent journalist from Sarajevo. He was going to study law. His grandmother, a formidable old Muslim lady, was also in the camp. She used to sit in front of her tent with her legs crossed and smoke a hookah. Cross my heart! My boyfriend, Sheriff, had to salaam formally and bow whenever he approached her.

One day a lad of sixteen came down from Sarajevo, lean and mean and snaggletoothed. His eyes were green, clear, cool. The contrast between those celestial eyes and the thug-like rest of his person made it obvious that the boy was as mad as the March Hare. He looked like he could kill a man at the drop of a hat.

He was the real leader of the gang. Sheriff was merely his deputy.

In the evening, after an incident I didn't see, the Mad Lad made a grownup, a tourist from the camp, crawl on his hands and knees and beg forgiveness. It was a disgusting scene. Nauseated as I was, I couldn't help feeling excited. That, I thought, had to be what Dostoevsky, Ingmar Bergman and Alexandra called the Real Life. I am now Alive and in Reality, I thought, and what remains of it will later be called Experience.

That night I slept and I dreamt and here is my dream:

Anarchy reigns in the world. All the laws and institutions have disappeared overnight. People have shaken off all their social and other habits which used to keep their true selves under control. Suddenly they are free to do as they please. All is permitted; all is good and can be done.

People live for the day. Leading a hand-to-mouth existence, they go wherever their whim takes them, do whatever they feel like doing there, and, when they've had enough of the place, they move on. If they fancy killing someone, they do so without a second thought. Civilisation as we know it has ceased to exist. Dead cars lie rusting along the curbs. There is no electricity. Dark windows of derelict houses look down on deserted streets without streetlights. Weeds are advancing. Jungle will follow.

Alexandra, Forest and I live in the back of a delivery van, moving on — always moving on. Whatever we need we take, untroubled by conscience, swift and efficient like animals.

On our travels we encounter a group of people squatting around a fire. We join them and realize that they are roasting a dead man on the spit. They cut slices off the roast and eat them without a twinge of disgust or remorse. We don't particularly like those people but we don't find them repulsive either.

The essence of the world, we feel, has been revealed. Human beings are finally free to be themselves. Truth reigns.

We like it that way.

When I dreamt the dream I was young and bolshy. I didn't mind seeing Ingrid Thulin cut her cunt with a piece of broken glass to spite her husband in "Cries and Whispers", if that represented the truth about human predicament. Today I think that decorum might well be more important than truth, at least occasionally.

Why?

Because decorum is human comment on truth. Decorum is our way of saying "Yes, but..." where animals only say "Yes".

Because they only say "Yes" and not "Yes, but...", animals are never confused. Because they are unconfused, they are beautiful, all of them, even the rhino and the warthog.

We are not as beautiful as the animals, but we are heroic.

My husband, whom I married many years later, worshipped animals because he preferred beauty to heroism. I married him because I preferred beauty to heroism, too.

Move on, my story.

Earthquake

How did we get rid of the gang? I don't remember. Why didn't they steal our money, our camera or our car to teach us a lesson? I don't remember that either.

Soon after the arrival of the Mad Lad, a mixed group of young people from Whiteburg, the capital of Yugoslavia, pitched their tents in our neighbourhood. Two boys shared one tent while a third boy and a beautiful girl — his fiancée — shared the other.

The two unattached boys, both seventeen going on eighteen, began visiting our tent and spending their evenings with us playing cards. One of them, a pimply, self-centred comedian, became interested in me. I was very careful not to encourage him. His unlovely, self-conscious way of attracting attention, I felt, resembled my own behaviour too closely for comfort.

The other boy, Eagerwill, was beautiful. It was typical of me not to notice until Alexandra said, "Eagerwill is simply exquisite. What eyes!" Then I woke up to Eagerwill's good looks, but it was too late.

One can find Eagerwill's face on many paintings, from medieval miniatures to Picasso's "Boy with a Pipe". He is dark, mercurial, green-eyed, proud-mouthed and very thin.

His heart is pure gold. Forest got on with him like a house on fire.

He has a tendency to walk slightly hunched and his wit stings. Under different circumstances he would have hunched still more and become like a beast of prey, crouching, ready to pounce. His acid remarks would have turned to venom. Thanks to Alexandra, this never happened.

One look at Alexandra was enough for Eagerwill. He saw where his salvation lay. He and Alexandra became lovers. Next summer Eagerwill came to stay with Alexandra in her parents' flat. They had, very conveniently, gone away for a month.

Forest and I moved in with Alexandra and Eagerwill. Alexandra's spirited, short-legged little bitch Liza was also with us, and so was a tom-cat. Likewise goldfish. Vicky and her boyfriend Romano, a student of philosophy, used to visit. Romano didn't suffer fools gladly and often punished them for being foolish. Eagerwill disapproved of that. He loved human beings, while Romano strove to improve them so that they could be loved. Many a night was spent discussing the subject, with Eagerwill and Romano sitting vis-à-vis, their shirt-sleeves rolled up, knocking back innumerable shots of grappa. The louder they spoke, the louder the canaries sang. Did I mention the canaries? There were caged canaries in the sitting room, I forget how many. There must have been at least three.

We played cards almost every evening, a game called 'Bela' or 'Belote'. Alexandra and Eagerwill were a team. Forest had no choice but to have me as a partner.

I was the worst player in the world. I couldn't muster enough attention to memorize the hands and plan a strategy. After a while I'd become so depressed I'd start playing against myself. Forest hated that. She accused me of seeking attention when I should be doing everything possible to make the month memorable for Alexandra and Eagerwill. Looking back, I know that she was right.

At that time Forest's own love affair with a man younger than herself was nearing its end. I was so self-centred I didn't even notice what was going on. I couldn't comprehend her moods. The whole world seemed to be in on something that was being kept secret from me.

In spite of that, I had a lovely time. Sometimes we'd stay up till seven in the morning and sleep till three in the afternoon. We went for long walks. We probed each other's souls until they hurt.

Mama and Papa were nonplussed when they heard that I was going to spend a month in Alexandra's flat, which was only a stroll away from our own. I stood by my decision, fluttering in the blast of Mama's anger. "If I'd gone to the seaside for a month," I said, "you wouldn't have minded at all. What's the difference?"

"You know very well what the difference is," Mama said.

"No, I don't" I said. "Tell me."

Did she explain the difference? I don't remember.

Papa was angry because, like Alexandra, I kept a zoo in my bedroom. I had a dog, a guinea-pig and fifty fish in a tank. In my absence, he had to walk the dog, change the guinea-pig's straw and feed the fish.

He also had to take care of Nan who was not feeling very well. Grandpa had been dead for some time.

Grandpa died at home early one morning. Papa was at work when it happened. Mama was on sick leave. She had a bad cold and was using the opportunity to lie in till late. I was in the kitchen, doing the previous night's dishes. I remember thinking, "It's time Grandpa took his pills; I'd better wake him up."

But I couldn't wake him up. I tried the mirror test and I tried the feather test. All the evidence was that Grandpa was dead.

Papa came home at once to take care of things. Grandpa had bequeathed his body to the Faculty of Medicine, for the students to dissect. Years later, he was buried in a mass grave, together with unidentified traffic accident victims. That was what he wanted.

On the day he died, Nan was in hospital having her eyes treated. Her eyes were damaged by diabetes. By the time she got home, Grandpa's body had already been taken away. In the end, the day turned out to be just like any other day.

Mama kept asking for lime blossom tea. She drank it, smoked and cried. "Poor little Grandpa," she kept saying over and over.

Papa did everything himself. He tied Grandpa's drooping jaw with a scarf, sponged off his body and dressed it in his Sunday best.

I came home to visit several times during that month at Alexandra's. Mama would never fail to give me the treatment. "How are things with you?" I'd ask, having made myself a cup of coffee. "What cheek," Mama would say, smoking. "What gall! You know full well how things are with us!" What hurt her most, I suppose, was that I was staying at Alexandra's. That added insult to injury. Mama was jealous of Alexandra. *She* wanted to be my First and Foremost.

That night I slept and I dreamt and here is my dream:

Alexandra, Eagerwill and I are living together in a flat on the third or perhaps the fourth floor of a huge yellow town house.

I come home carrying the shopping in a plastic bag. Alexandra and Eagerwill are having coffee in the kitchen. I help myself to some and sit down at the table.

"It's shaking a bit today," says Alexandra. "Might have a biggie later."

She is talking about an earthquake.

Indeed, there is a tremor. The old house groans, shaken in its foundations. Cracks appear along the walls.

At that moment the door opens and Mama comes in. She sits down next to me and starts a conversation about our mutual relationship. Just as the discussion begins to develop into a ponderous, heavy, overemotional affair, the *biggie* strikes. Rumble, bang, crash! The house breaks in two.

Through a cloud of dust I can see the crack in the floor dividing the kitchen in two halves. Alexandra and Eagerwill remain on one side while Mama sits petrified at the kitchen table on the other side of the crack.

I want to help Alexandra and Eagerwill. One of them may have been crushed — may be unconscious. For once it doesn't — cannot — matter whether my heart is pure or not, whether I'm self-centred or not. In an earthquake, people need each other. They can use any help they can get.

I'm about to step over the widening gap when Mama's hand closes around my wrist and holds it in an iron grip. Her face is frozen in a grotesque expression of terror.

"Let go," I wail, "let go, let go!"

Her mouth is a black hole with no scream coming out of it. She doesn't let go.

The gap is now too wide for me to jump over. The two halves of the flat sink away from one another. Alexandra and Eagerwill need me but they're not going to get me. Mama will not let go.

She never let go. Over the distance of over two thousand miles which I had eventually managed to put between us, she clung to me like ivy for as long as she could draw breath.

Earthquakes, by the way, are a common occurrence in Agram. It is not unusual for a person to dream about earthquakes, especially after experiencing a few.

I can remember quite a number of earthquake dreams. Strangely, though, what I knew to be a catastrophe by day appeared to be a boon by night. The dream earthquake would bring an end to life as I knew it. At one stroke it would remove all the obligations, habits and responsibilities and would place me free and whole in a world of fresh possibilities. It would change my reluctance to live into eagerness to make the most of it.

In waking life, I lived in mortal fear of earthquakes. I'd never lie in the bath for fear of a quake surprising me wet and naked. Every evening I'd put my papers — writings and drawings — together, so that I could grab them as I ran for safety. I always worried about whether I'd have time to save my dog Michael, and my guinea-pig. I practised standing in the door-frame holding Michael under my arm.

I was prepared to abandon my fish to their destiny. That is how it was.

Fred, Middle-aged and Ugly

Later that summer I went down to the coast all by myself. I went to the town of Vallegrande on the island of Korkyra. I had been holidaying in Vallegrande since the age of nine. I knew every stone in Vallegrande, and every blade of grass.

The town sits snugly at the far end of a deep natural harbour, all pines, olives and oleanders, sunbaked houses, children driving mini-tractors called 'cultivators', and boats, boats, boats. Sanders, coasters, trawlers, yachts from all over the world, hundreds of caïques and the daily ferry from the mainland.

There used to be donkeys in Vallegrande, and barefooted women in black, but that was long ago. Nowadays one can find smart cafés on every corner, and clubs full of young people dressed in Benetton, Robe di Kappa and Missoni. Men hop into their BMWs for a two hundred-yard drive to visit their neighbours.

Vallegrande is rich. There are more than three jobs per average family. On top of that, almost every family owns land and lets rooms to tourists.

When the Vallegrandians say "Shaaachaaa", it means "gone". When they say "Greencha", it means "I'm off". When two of them meet, one says "Hey" and the other one replies, "Aha". Their dialect is like a foreign language. In fact, the whole place is under a spell. The tourists either dislike it and flee or develop an attachment resembling addiction. The magic gets to them.

In the rich and happy town of Vallegrande, I had a poor boyfriend. His name was Fred Quail and he was two years younger than I. He looked Nordic: tall, blond, pale-eyed, slim. Vallegrandians often look like that when they're young.

I met Fred the year before. We happened to sit next to each other at a table in the company of mutual acquaintances. We glanced at each other frequently but never spoke a word. 'What a good-looking boy,' I thought, 'and how quiet he is!' At the end of the evening we found ourselves sitting there alone. Moreover, I was sitting on Fred Quail's knees. Gently, he began to fondle my breasts and tried to kiss me. I withdrew.

"Do we have to," I said, "like this... at once? Couldn't I just *look* at you?"

"Look all you want," said the Nordic Deity with a small, slightly derisive smile. Later I found out that his smile was always derisive: that was the way his face was built.

He spoke the heavy dialect of the more rural of Vallegrandian families, those with their roots in agriculture rather than in fishing. He was the only breadwinner in his family. He worked in the local shipyard doing two shifts a day. We could only meet in the evening. We'd go to what he called 'the Club': a small room at the back of a house belonging to one of his friends' parents. The room was decorated with amateurish erotic wall-paintings. It was fitted with red and green spotlights which could be turned on all together or separately. There was a bed with a bare mattress on it in the room, and an ashtray made of a tree stump. We'd go there to make love. That was what the room was for.

Fred's foreplay was token and he would come very quickly. I felt absolutely nothing. We'd wipe ourselves clean with

Kleenexes which we'd throw out of the window. I don't know where they ended up. Then we'd smoke a cigarette, sprawling naked on the mattress. More often than not, Fred would mount me again. Another wipe, another smoke. I was looking forward to the moment when I'd open the door and step into the night ablaze with gigantic stars and fragrant with jasmine, rosemary and pine. I was very much like the man who kept hitting himself on the head with a hammer because it felt so lovely when he stopped.

During the day I'd walk and swim and read and have espressos with a smug expression on my face. My neck was covered in love bites. I wanted everyone to know that I was being a woman night after night.

One Sunday we went swimming together. Fred snorkelled happily for hours, retrieving sea-urchins and starfish. He yelled and splashed about like a huge puppy-dog. In the afternoon he fell asleep in the sun. I carved his face in a bar of soap while he slept. I don't have that bar of soap any more. I must've thrown it away years ago.

In his own way Fred was beautiful. As a child he must have looked like an angel. He'd sometimes say strange things. "I'd like to go to the university and study philosophy," he'd say. That was not a joke. He meant it. "Only," he'd sigh, "I can't afford it."

Studying would have cost him nothing. What he could not afford was living away from home and not earning any wages. "Couldn't you get a grant?" I asked. "Yes, if I wanted to study medicine or engineering," he replied. "But you wouldn't like that?" "No," he said. "I'd like to study philosophy or nothing."

He opted for nothing.

Papa was livid when he learned that I had a boyfriend in Vallegrande. "I'll never be able to show my face there again," he thundered, "now that everyone knows my daughter's screwing around."

"What am I supposed to do," I said, hurt, "become a nun? Didn't you ever screw around?"

"Of course I did," Papa said grumpily, "but I did it in such a way that no one ever saw anything."

"No one has seen me either, Papa," I said. "Fred and I meet only at night."

"That's even worse!"

"No one knows."

"That's what you think." He left the room and returned a moment later. That was the way he discussed serious issues. He would leave the room, then come back. "What does he do?" he asked.

"Who?"

"He, he, damn him, he!"

"Fred?" I said. "He's a worker. He works in the shipyard."

"Wow, what a catch," said Papa with a wry smile. "An educated person like you should know better, but some people never learn."

"Papa, you're a worker yourself!" I cried, exasperated.

"And? Doesn't that prove my point?"

"What point?" I asked, on the brink of tears.

"I should've made you learn an honest trade," Papa said, "since all those books haven't taught you anything. Look at Mama and me."

"What about Mama and you?" A tear rolled down my flushed cheek.

"Mama's educated, right? She has two terms of nuclear physics under her belt, right?"

I nodded.

"Well, she can't discuss her stuff with me. I never had any education. Mama and I are not a good match. She would've been happier with someone else, someone more like her."

That was a new thought, and an unsettling one. Papa and Mama don't match? Yet they made *me*, snapping together like two pieces of a jigsaw puzzle. Was I made of two pieces of a jigsaw puzzle that didn't match?

"Nan warned Mama," Papa said. "She warned me, too. She never liked the idea of Mama and me getting married."

That was news indeed. I had never seen anything but

genuine friendship between Papa and Nan. "Doesn't Nan like you?" I said sheepishly.

"She likes me well enough," Papa said. "She likes me better than she likes Mama, I think, but Mama is her daughter and she has always wanted only the best for her, as is only natural."

"You are the best!" I said, throwing my arms around his short, muscular neck.

"Yes," Papa said, pushing me gently away, "for myself, I am the best. Not for Mama."

"But you *are*!"

"Bullshit." He left the room, came back again. "You," he said, "I don't want to know what you and that... Fred... are up to. Understood? If you want to discuss Fred, go talk to Mama. I don't want to know."

I discussed Fred Quail a lot, mostly with Alexandra and Forest. I was toying with the idea of getting married. Fred hadn't asked me, but I felt sure he was going to.

We seldom wrote. Fred was not terribly literate. In one of the two letters he wrote to me he said he missed me and I replied in the same vein, but the truth was, I didn't miss him at all. On the contrary, down there in Vallegrande, lying in Fred's arms, I missed Alexandra, Forest and Eagerwill.

With all the goodwill in the world, I could not imagine Fred Quail sitting opposite Eagerwill discussing Hegel while Alexandra, Forest and I discussed Dostoevsky.

Eagerwill, I forgot to say, was very much into philosophy.

Even while talking about getting married, deep down I must have known Fred was no Eagerwill.

We didn't see each other until the next summer when, after having spent a month at Alexandra's, I went down to Vallegrande for a month.

One may ask at this point who was paying for all this: for all the coffee and the cigarettes, for playing cards all night, for my trip to Vallegrande, for my stay there? This is how it was done: Alexandra's parents left her enough money to live on for a month. Forest's mother gave her a similar amount. Eagerwill, presumably, had come to an arrangement with his family. My expenses were paid for by my parents.

Mama gave me the money to stay at Alexandra's even though it hurt her deeply to do so. She could have made me stay at home just by refusing me the money but it didn't occur to her. Papa could have kept me away from Fred Quail by not paying for my holiday in Vallegrande but it did not occur to him either. Both Mama and Papa would have been outraged at the idea of influencing their daughter's moral choices by withdrawing from her the means to make them. They believed in the freedom of the individual and were ready to put their money where their mouths were.

Had I asked them, my parents would have been able to explain their point of view. Alexandra's parents, less sophisticated than Mama and less articulate than Papa, would have said, "We love Alexandra and we want her to have a good time while she can," but it would have meant the same thing.

Why didn't Papa and Mama demand that I use half of my holidays to earn the money for my vacation? Again, it did not occur to them. In their opinion I worked quite a lot and justified the money spent on me. I was a full-time student.

Could they afford it? Yes, they could. At that time in Yugoslavia, a printer-compositor and an accounts administrator could afford a full-time student daughter.

Was Fred there on the quay to embrace me as I got off the ferry in Vallegrande? No.

We met in the evening and made for the Club. On his way, he said "Hey!" and "Aha" as he passed by people he knew.

Thirty evenings later I went back home to Agram. During my stay in Vallegrande Fred had finally began to think about marriage but was careful not to commit himself to anything. One evening, in a cafe, we sat table to table with his parents, his sister and his brother-in-law. Fred never even said good evening to them! He whispered into my ear, "Don't look now, but my whole family is sitting next to us." I couldn't help feeling a bit cheap.

Fred had a cousin whose name was Grandy Andreis. He was a building contractor and was making a lot of money. His father, a rich, skinny, nasty man who owned land all over the island of Korkyra, had sent his other son, Alex, to the university, while Grandy, the younger of the two brothers, had to stay at home and learn a trade. That made Grandy very bitter. Alex was a failure. Grandy was hugely successful, but still remained bitter. He was a sickly young man with spindly arms and legs, a narrow but well padded body, curly brown hair, sideburns and a moustache which looked silly on his round, boyish face. His mind was medieval. He would have been at home in the thirteenth century. Compared with him, Fred Quail was a city slicker.

Grandy Andreis had made a virtue of his shortcomings. He grumbled at the evils of the modern world like an old, old man. He loved to sit in his front garden, drink wine from his own vineyard and preach on the sacred traditions of his family, his nation and his religion, which was Roman Catholic. At that time, Grandy was only twenty eight years old!

I don't remember how I got to know him, but we ended up spending a lot of time together. We'd sit in cafes or he'd take me out in his boat. We'd moor along one of his numerous plots of land, laze in the sun, smoke, talk, pick almonds and crack them between two flat stones. His dog Wookie was always with us. Wookee is dead now. He was very clever. He could steer Grandy's boat.

Grandy had an extremely poor opinion of Fred. He thought Fred was an irresponsible prat who was neglecting me. "Now, if I had me a fine woman like you," he'd say, "I'd marry her and take her to Paris and buy her cosmetics and fur coats because that's what a fine woman needs."

"Fred can't do that," I said. "He's poor."

"That's too bad."

"He has to work all day long. You can sit here with me because you can pay other people to work for you."

"I had nothing when I started," Grandy said.

"Anyway," I said, "I don't want cosmetics and fur coats."

I should have watched my mouth. Carelessly spoken words have the tendency to come true.

"What do you want, then?" said Grandy, drawing on his cigarette. I squatted by the sea, playing with pebbles. I was surprised at what my mouth said next. "I want to be a *witch*," it said. "I want to hide in the bushes, watch other people without being seen and throw pebbles at them."

I should've watched my mouth.

Grandy said, "Marry me."

I said, "No."

He said, "Please."

I said, "No."

He kissed me, rather better than Fred. I didn't respond. He was so ugly! He didn't look like a Nordic idol, nor did he resemble Picasso's "Boy with a Pipe". He smelled of sweat and had a foul temper.

He let go of me, hid behind a pine tree and wept. A few minutes later he reappeared, composed, with a fresh cigarette in his mouth. "Not to worry," he said.

Grandy Andreis married Irene, a blonde, long-faced, handsome Czech girl. Their marriage is an averagely happy one. They fight, then make up. Irene has to work very hard: Grandy is a real slave-driver. She doesn't have cosmetics or fur coats, although, to be absolutely fair, I must admit I've only ever seen her in the summer.

One night, back in Agram, I slept and I dreamt and here is my dream:

Fred and I meet in a restaurant. We sit facing each other at a table covered with a white tablecloth. The table is next to a window. The window is on my left — that is, on Fred's right. Remember that.

Fred is young and handsome. His voice is full of healthy metal. I look at him with love and hope.

Suddenly, Fred reaches for his forehead and begins to peel off his face like a thin rubber mask. An ugly, middle-aged man

appears from under the mask and I realize that he must be the
real Fred. His jowls hang limply and shake as he speaks. His
forehead and cheeks are wrinkled. His voice is dull. His
conversation is incredibly boring and insignificant.
I shrink from him in horror. Is that the man I'm going to
marry? How come I never noticed what he was really like? He's
been deceiving me all along!
If he's like that now, what is he going to be like in ten years'
time?
I wake up gasping for breath, immensely relieved that Fred
is not like that at all.

A fortnight later, Fred Quail came to Agram. We were to go
to the mountain resort of Bohin in Slovenia and spend three
days there together, just the two of us. I think it was my idea.
Fred and I had never spent a whole day together. I did not
know how he woke up in the morning, or brushed his teeth, or
anything. It was time I found out.
Papa forked out for my three days in Bohin, although he
knew I was going there with Fred. Wasn't that magnanimous?
When he got off the train in Agram, Fred gave me a peck
on the cheek and said, "Have you been faithful to me?"
"Yes'" I nodded enthusiastically. "And you to me?"
"What do you think?"
Next morning, on the coach to Bohin, Fred read the
"Sport" magazine. I said, "Haven't you got anything to ask
me?"
Fred said' "Like what?"
"Like, what have I been doing, am I well, do I love you?"
Fred never looked up from his paper. "What could you've
been doing? I can see that you're well. And I know you love
me."
When we got to Bohin, I chose the hotel: the 'Bellevue', a
chalet-style building overlooking Lake Bohin. I booked a room
and handed in our ID-cards. I did everything. Fred just sat in
an armchair and smoked. Once in the room, he flung himself
on the bed and said, "You'll make a lovely little wife once

you're properly trained."

An alarm-bell sounded somewhere inside me.

"Unpack my things, would you," Fred said, "and wash my socks."

I said, "No." I also said, "I'm going to freshen up and change. Then I'll go downstairs for a cup of coffee in the restaurant. Come with me, Fred, for we must talk."

In the restaurant, Fred and I sat down facing each other at a table covered with a white tablecloth. The table was next to a window. The window was on my left — that is, on Fred's right.

I noticed an ugly droop in the muscles which formed the corners of Fred's mouth. It must have been there all the time. There were crow's feet in the corners of Fred's eyes.

"Listen Fred," I said, "we're here to be together for three days. That we shall do, and we'll enjoy ourselves as best we can. We'll go for walks, we'll pick flowers and, when we go to bed, we'll make love. But when the three days are over and we return to Agram, that'll be it."

"*It?*"

"Yes. You'll go home to Vallegrande, I'll stay in Agram and that'll be it. I won't write to you and I hope you won't write to me either."

Ah, how lovely it felt! I didn't have to pretend any more! I wasn't going to be Mrs. Quail, ever!

And Papa knew what he was doing when he gave me the money for the trip.

Fred and I went for walks. He even picked flowers for me, in the pouring rain. He gave me long, forlorn looks. At night he made love to me. He said, "We must stay together."

I said, "Why? We don't love each other."

"With you," he said gravely, "I can always come, even twice in a row."

"I'm sorry," I said.

He'd get up in the middle of the night to cough and spit in the toilet. He smoked much too much.

What became of Fred Quail later? He married a girl from

Agram, having had acquired a taste for Agramians. She bore him a son. They were one of the poorest families in Vallegrande. Grandy Andreis occasionally gave Fred work on one building site or other, but Fred didn't seem to be able to work. He would stop in the middle of whatever he was doing and look at the sky. I saw him do it. Grandy said he was lazy but I think that Fred's mind was going. Never very fast, the wheels in his head were slowly grinding to a halt.

He is now quite fat and his face is flabby. He resembles the ugly, middle-aged man from my dream to a tee.

Grandy's health is very poor and he is more bitter than ever. I'm glad I didn't marry either of them

First Meditation: the World of Sunshine and Kittens

At the end of that summer of nineteen seventy six I was twenty four. I was nearing the end of my English studies.

I had known Alexandra and Forest for nine years and Eagerwill for a year and a half. I had known Vicky for almost as long as Alexandra, and Romano, too, for a number of years. My heart clung to all of them. I sought their company all the time, with the exception of Desiré, who had by then completely dropped out of the picture. (Eagerwill had in the meantime moved in permanently with Alexandra and her parents had taken him in with calm and good grace seldom to be found on Earth.) I worshipped Alexandra, regarded Forest with a curious blend of jealousy and warmth, adored Eagerwill and lived in constant fear of his rebukes. I was comfortable with Vicky because I sensed she was no better at it — whatever "it" was — than I. I feared and hated Romano but was at the same time attracted by his merciless irony and his capable mind.

They all expected something of me. They questioned

everything I said or did. I didn't question *them*; it was one-way traffic all the time. That, too, seemed to be my fault: I never had any questions to ask. Why?

I knew why: because I never thought about them, their personalities and their problems. I only thought about myself. I'd even sit down and say to myself, "I'll think about Alexandra now," or, "I'll think about Forest." Did any thoughts come? No. My mind would drone in an idle mode for a while and then I'd start thinking of something else, usually about their relationship with *me*. Why did they let me be their friend if so much about me was questionable? What was it they wanted from me?

It was something I lacked. A capacity. I lacked the capacity to share their experience...of what?

If one were to make a summary of what they used to say, it would go like this: I was self-centred: because self-centred, not interested in the world around me: because not interested, reluctant to leave my cocoon: because reluctant to leave my cocoon, have no experience of Life: because inexperienced, do not know people: because innocent of people, cannot share human togetherness: because unable to share human togetherness, I was self-centred.

This was my curse: a serpent biting its own tail.

In that chain of statements there was an imponderable that puzzled me: Life.

When they spoke of it, my friends would all have an identical knowing look in their eyes. For them, Life clearly had a meaning it didn't have for me.

For me, Life was a biological term. It was all about cell division, metabolism, decomposition. Life was the difference between organic and inorganic matter.

For my friends, Life had to do with Suffering. It had to do with Tragedy. It also had to do with the Absurd, whatever *that* was. One had to know Suffering and then actively seek Happiness. Seeking Happiness was connected with Love. One was also supposed to discover the Meaning and the Purpose of Life, or at least try to. The Meaning and the Purpose of Life had to be personal. Why? Because religions and ideologies were bankrupt and one's individuality was all one had in this world.

I could understand the bankruptcy of religions and ideologies. I could understand the importance of individuality, although I couldn't help thinking, "It's all right to cherish one's individuality if one looks like Alexandra and Eagerwill. Even Vicky, Romano and Desiré can bear to be themselves. Forest is deformed: that is almost beauty. But what about those who are fat, pimply and greasy-haired? What about *me*?"

It was the bit about suffering that worried me most. From all I'd heard and read, I was under the impression that suffering ennobled one. It made one look like Alexandra and Eagerwill and consequently enabled one to cherish one's individuality. (I totally failed to grasp the concept of suffering as the road to compassion.) Did Alexandra and Eagerwill suffer? I couldn't answer that.

One thing I did know, and knew it with a chilling certainty: I didn't suffer. Whatever troubles I may have been experiencing, they didn't seem to amount to real suffering. I was spared.

I think I already mentioned that.

I didn't have to seek happiness. Most mornings I woke up to it. Sunshine made me happy. My dog Michael made me happy. A film with Sean Feeney in it made me happy.

In my friends' eyes my happiness was of a lesser kind because it was the happiness of gratification — that is to say, the happiness of a child. I had not Eaten the Apple. Had I Eaten It and remained happy, that would have been an achievement.

Today I feel it does not matter all that much. Perhaps it is even better not to Eat the Apple. I've had proof that there is little dignity in suffering. Suffering is degrading. The happiness of gratification is better than no happiness at all. Unfortunately, though, the happiness of gratification is always under threat because it depends on external factors, i.e., sunshine or storm or the dog being alive and present. Remove that and what remains is want. Want results in suffering.

One can, of course, free oneself from want. All the great traditions teach us that and have developed techniques for eliminating want.

Without want there can be no gratification. Can there still be happiness? I don't know.

Back there in 'seventy six, all I wanted was to Eat the Apple. I wanted that like the Holy Grail.

Because, when one's happiness depends on the circumstances outside one's control, one is like a leaf in the wind. One lacks *substance*.

One night I slept and I dreamt, and here is my dream:

Once upon some future time a cosmic catastrophe will have taken place. The Earth's orbit will have shifted and a lot of other changes will have occurred, resulting in a deluge of colossal proportions, which will have covered most of the world with water. It will have happened before my dream begins.

And when it begins, there is no morning, no noon and no night. Blood-red, the sun is forever low on the western horizon. The atmosphere is hot and moist. Hot and moist it will remain, forever and ever and ever.

The sea has swallowed a lot of Vallegrande. The hills which once surrounded the harbour have turned into little islands, like so many green beads on a string, covered in lush tropical vegetation. The town itself is thriving. A road is being built. Lorries come and go. Tower blocks have mushroomed all over the place. With the change of climate, Vallegrande is changing its character. It is turning into Haiti, or, perhaps, Ceylon.

I still call Sri Lanka 'Ceylon'.

The ferry linking Vallegrande with the mainland is old, with low, rusty bulwarks. All ships seem to be like that. People keep repairing and converting them, coasters into ferries, ferries into lightships, lightships into tugs and so on. No new machinery will ever be constructed again. The genius of technology has forsaken mankind.

Many famous buildings are now under the sea. I remember visiting a gothic cathedral. Only a single spire can still be seen above the water. A small boat carrying tourists, myself among them, approaches the spire and the skipper, doubling as guide, ties it to a piece of masonry. Together with the other tourists, I descend a makeshift staircase through the spire into the nave which is completely under the sea.

It is a vast, murky, mouldy space illuminated by bare electric bulbs on a wire strung from pillar to pillar. The arches soar to meet at invisible points in the gloom. What an old, old place it is! The very air, motionless, encased in the nave under the sea, feels ancient. Water drips from the vault onto huge statues shapeless with age, looming in semi-darkness. They represent alien idols, remote and inscrutable.

London has changed beyond recognition. I know what I'm dreaming about because, previous to my dream, I visited London more than once. It has not been affected by the eternal sunset. Quite the opposite, it basks in sunshine under an azure sky with flocks of white, fluffy clouds all over it.

Sunny squares planted with flowers, brightly painted houses everywhere. The streets are not paved but covered with tiny, round, smooth, wet glistening pebbles. St. Paul's has metamorphosed into an architectural fantasy reminiscent of St. Basil in Moscow. In the city centre, whole streets have been roofed over with glass panels resting on Art Nouveau-style cast iron constructions. The streets are paved in marble, with cafes and restaurants on both sides. Only expensive materials have been used to decorate the cafés: leather, silk, Murano glass, teak and velvet. Bamboo, ficuses and philodendra grow in jardinières placed between the tables.

Roughly about that time, the Covent Garden Market got roofed over. I didn't know anything about it at the time. I only found out later.

In the London of my dream, all traffic has disappeared. There is not a car, a lorry, a van, a bus, a motorbike or a bicycle to be seen. Everyone walks. What has happened to the Underground? It doesn't run any more. I remember seeing an open-air tube station – like Moorgate, for example – overgrown with ivy. I remember a platform bench like the ones at Baron's

Court, all mossy and rotting away. A train engine sits on the rails in the mouth of the tunnel; an old, rusty steam engine. It is clear that no one has used the station for years.

Somewhere in the elegant town centre there is a tiny little theatre which one enters like one would enter a shop: one opens the door and steps in just like that, without a ticket. It is a theatre workshop.

Peter O'Toole and Richard Burton are staging a production of Anouilh's 'Becket' with the aid of anyone who cares to get involved. The workshop is full of passers-by who have wandered inside and stayed on. They all know the text. They're all acting and directing and designing sets.

It is not a rehearsal — it is the actual production. It is different each day because different people take part in it. Only O'Toole and Burton appear day after day in the leading roles.

Imagine children playing at Star Wars. "I'm Luke Skywalker," one would say. "No, I am," another. More likely than not, the two would fight over the issue. The winner would go on to be Skywalker.

"I'm Obi-Wan Kenobi," someone would claim and his claim would probably not be challenged. If one wants to be Obi-Wan, one probably knows what one's doing. "You," the children would say to a boy standing slightly outside the group — on the fringe, one could say — "you're Darth Vader."

"Why me?"

"You mean, you don't want to?"

'Vader' understands the boys would like him to refuse; they'd rather play without him. Unfortunately, that would also mean that one of them would have to be the villain. 'Vader' understands that as well. He understands much too much, his face is branded with understanding. That is what makes him such an obvious choice for Vader. "'Course I do," he says. He wants to be Vader quite passionately, in fact. He is about to experience the "tragic feeling of life"[1] which otherwise might

---

1 A term coined by Miguel de Unamuno

not have been available to such an ordinary, chubby, greasy-haired, pimply person like he. He imagines a black breathing-mask over his face, very like the helmet from the Ship Burial at Sutton Hoo. The imaginary mask gives him beauty and ennobles him for tragedy. Now he can cut off his son's right arm and offer him alliance without looking ridiculous. (Is there anyone who doesn't know the story of Star Wars? Luke Skywalker is Darth Vader's son. They fight on opposite sides in the Wars. Vader cuts his son's right hand off in a dramatic duel with light-sabres, then invites him to join him, Vader, in re-establishing order in the Galaxy. There's a lot more to it, but this should suffice to refresh the memory.) There would inevitably be a bespectacled, short boy with a Cheshire Cat grin on his face who'd take the part of Yoda because he can do funny voices. There would also be a girl there, one of those who like to hang around boys and play boyish games and are therefore called tomboys. She would be Princess Leia.

The children would step smoothly into their roles. They would say things like: "The Force is with you, young Skywalker, but you're not a Jedi yet," or, "Powerful Jedi was he — hmmmmmm — powerful Jedi." Skywalker would stage-direct Vader: "Now move towards me and strike," and Vader would say darkly, "I know." They'd all imitate the hissing of light-sabres and the roar of spaceship engines.

That is exactly how the visitors to the theatre workshop behave. They are all very cool about working with stars like O'Toole and Burton. The stars are excellent at play — it makes sense to play with them.

I also remember a quiet residential street in London (of my dream). It is a sunny summer afternoon. Front gardens of terraced houses are a riot of flowers. On the pavement, black and white kittens roll and tumble in the sun. A youth of about sixteen sits on the fence. He says, "Hello," and I say "Hello" to him; we then chat for a while.

Why don't we always live like this, I ask myself in my dream. (Like *what*, I ask myself today, awake, in retrospect. Like kittens?) I answer myself (in the dream), I believe, in the following fashion: we can live like this if we want to, and we can begin at once; it is purely a matter of rejecting the world of suffering we ourselves create for ourselves (and consequently no longer have a play to perform in our theatre workshop, because it is, like all plays, about suffering). The world of suffering is a false world anyway; the world of sunshine and kittens is the real one (for *kittens*). Deep in our hearts we know that, but we stubbornly maintain the illusion of suffering. Why? Because it is easier. It is easier because it is more difficult... or something.

To prevent any misunderstanding: I didn't dream the bit about the 'Star Wars'. I made it up as a model for the theatre workshop from my dream. Everything else is authentic dream-stuff, including the argument about the false world of suffering at the end (except the bits in brackets).

A year — or perhaps two years — after I dreamt of the deluge, a tidal wave came to Vallegrande. It was like a tsunami, only it wasn't one because it wasn't caused by an earthquake. In fact, scientists have not been able to establish its cause to this very day.

This is how it happened: one fine morning in June, the sea withdrew from the harbour. Out and away it went, leaving behind an expanse of mud, rock and stunned marine life.

The Vallegrandians began to gather. They climbed down to the exposed sea-bed to collect cockles and mussels, to look for long-lost possessions and to check their boats for damage. The sea stayed out for an hour, then returned. It came like a glistening wall surging forward and thundering as it surged.

The Vallegrandians scrambled up the slimy quayside and fled, screaming. The sea picked up their boats, carried them over the edge of the quay and hurled them into the town. Large fishing vessels ended up in the town park.

Everything along the seafront was flooded: shops, restaurants, houses and gardens. Those who found themselves above the flood line came out of their houses to watch their less fortunate neighbours salvage their furniture, their washing-machines and TV-sets, their barrels of wine and olive oil. They yelled advice and sniggered, but didn't help.. That was not very nice but that is what the Vallegrandians are like.

Grandy Andreis' dog Wookie rescued a drowning child. He dragged it out of the water by the hair. Wookie was trained to rescue people that way. Whenever he'd see someone swimming, he'd get excited and try to rescue the swimmer. The local newspaper, 'Free Dalmatia', carried an article about him.

The sea devoured one third of the town and sat on it for hours. Eventually it ebbed back to its normal level, leaving the town littered with boats.

The Vallegrandians rolled up their sleeves and set about repairing the damage. They made all the shops and cafes better than they were before. They built a whole new ferry-port. They even removed the salt-contaminated soil around the palm trees on the promenade and replaced it with fresh, sweet soil. They were more than ready for the next summer season.

I was not in Vallegrande when the deluge came. I only got there later, in August. I missed it by a month and a half.

The Vallegrandians still talk about the deluge. It was the most exciting thing that ever happened to them.

The deluge killed the biggest bougainvillea in town. I have photographs of that bougainvillea. It was a real giant.

2. Sean Feeney

Sean Feeney's Office

The time has come to speak of Sean Feeney.

In 1952, just before I was born, Mama bought the English-Croatian dictionary by Dr Rudolf Filipović. It was a huge volume bound in red canvas and printed on poor quality paper with slivers of wood still visible in it. In those days most books were printed on the same beige paper with slivers of wood in it and bound in red canvas. I have quite a few: 'And Quiet Flows the Don', for example, and 'A State in the Moon', a remarkable science-fiction novel by Manfred Langrenus, whose real name was Professor Friedrich Hecht, of Vienna, Austria. This superior novel is not, as far as I know, available in English. I still sometimes believe that everything that happens in it will come to pass.

'And Quiet Flows the Don', by Mikhail Sholokhov, is also brilliant. It has been translated into English.

Mama bought the English dictionary because she had decided that her unborn child would learn English one day. She also bought 'Webster's Illustrated Dictionary for Children'. It was full of pictures showing life in America in the fifties. There were gaily coloured cars with tailfins in it, pony-tailed cheerleaders and so on. I didn't notice any difference between the pictures in the dictionary and the real world around me. The only cars you could see in the streets of Agram at the time were Plymouths and Chevrolets, all tailfins and chrome. Little girls wore pony-tails. All the world was one.

Even before I could read I knew that the 'Illustrated Dictionary' was written in English. I knew I was going to speak that language one day.

In the meantime, Grandmother taught me German. I still remember jingles I used to learn by heart. For example:

"Auf dem Berge Si-na-i
Wohnt der Schneider Kikriki;
Seine Frau, die Margarete,
Saß auf dem Balkon und nähte.
Fiel herab, Fiel herab,
Und das linke Bein brach ab."

And so on. When I look at it now, this little poem seems a bit anti-Semitic, but it must have been fun at the time, or I would have forgotten it long ago. For the record, the poem came from a German primer printed in Germany *after* the war.

Nowadays I cannot say much more than "good morning", "a cup of coffee, please," and "thank you" in German, but I used to be quite fluent.

I learned my alphabet on Papa's knee. He would read 'Flash Gordon' aloud to me and I would gaze at the text while he read. It was, of course, in Croatian. I don't remember how it happened, but letters suddenly began making sense. One day I couldn't read, and the next day I could. I read 'Prince Valiant', 'Rip Kirby' and 'Dan Dare', all in Croatian.

There are so many beautiful comics hardly anyone in the UK and America has heard of. Who has, for example, heard of 'Johnny Hazard', 'Corto Maltese', 'Trigia', 'Jeremiah', or the comics – *tragics* would be a better word – by Enki Bilal? Not many.

Agram lies at the centre of the world. The proof of it can be found in Agram's newspapers, bookshops, radio and television. In Agram I had all Europe close to hand, and America as well.

Radio Agram played pop-songs in Italian, French and German, but mostly in English. The most popular ones could be heard every day. I memorized the lyrics like a parrot. To me they were clusters of sound without meaning, but no less thrilling for that. They were like 'Jabberwocky'.

I loved listening to Doris Day whom I called "Auntie Doris Day". I'd dance around the flat and sing, "Yormy liddel baybeebumblebee," or "kayse rasera, woteverwill bewillbe". Mama told me that 'bumblebee' meant 'bumbar'. 'Bumbar' is Croatian for 'bumblebee'. Thus 'bumblebee' became the first English word I ever learned. I also knew that people in English-speaking countries had names like Jim, Joe, Charlie, Jack, Harry, Tom and Bill. Those names often appeared in Westerns and in comic strips. Girls were called Mary, Nellie, Peggy, Dolly, Susan. I thought Jerry and Michael were names for dogs, because of Jack London's lovely books 'Jerry of the Islands' and 'Michael, Brother of Jerry'.

Many dogs in Agram were called Johnny. Why? I couldn't even begin to guess.

Once television came into the house, I was able to listen to spoken English — and spoken Italian and French and German. I'd listen to the rhythm of English, then go and stand in front of the mirror, making up "English" words. I'd imagine a tense situation and say bitter and tragic things to my non-existent partner in the scene. I did the same in "Italian", "French" and "German". It sounded like Chaplin's made-up German in 'The Great Dictator'.

I never pretended to speak Russian. I wasn't sure of how it sounded until much later. In 1948 the Yugoslav Communist Party quarrelled with the Soviet Union. Since then, things Russian were not exactly promoted. I knew little of the historic quarrel. Mama was very fond of Russians and worshipped the Soviet Union. It did not rub off. There were few Soviet films to be seen, so most of the time I forgot the place existed at all.

When I was twelve, or perhaps thirteen, I fell madly in love with Pat Boone. Does anyone remember him? I bought all his LPs and listened to them every day. I thought he was incredibly good-looking. I made it my business to know every detail about Pat Boone and to talk about him to anyone who would listen. To this very day I don't quite know what I read about him and what I made up. I wrote "novels" in which the hero would be thirteen or fourteen years old and would look like I imagined Pat Boone must have looked at that age. This is how one of those stories went:

Tennessee, eighteen sixty five.
My hero is very poor. His parents are ugly and uncouth. They neglect the hero, whose name is Pat.
Pat is an extremely good-looking boy, lively and intelligent. He excels at study but is equally good at sports. (Did they have that sort of school in Tennessee in eighteen sixty five? I never asked myself the question.) All the girls adore him. Boys hate him because they're envious of his perfection and despise him because he lives in a hovel at the end of the town.
Why Tennessee? Pat Boone hailed from there. Why that particular year? I had just read 'Gone With the Wind'.
The wealthiest and the most beautiful of the schoolgirls, Laura, loves Pat but her feelings are not returned. Why? Because she's bad. There is no kindness in her heart. Instead, Pat falls in love with Santina, a dark-haired, modest Plain Jane who is uncomplicated, honest and a bit of a tomboy. (I didn't even know that Santina was an Italian name. It means "little female saint".)
There is more than a drop of Cherokee blood in Pat's veins. He often spends his summer holidays with the Cherokee, living like an Indian. His Indian name is Sun Arrow. Childless, the old Chief wants Pat to become Chief after his death. Pat's best friend is an Indian boy. His name is Quanati's Feather. There is also a girl, Chuquelantu... (I had done a bit of research there. I had read 'Folktales of American Indians'.)
Pat — Sun Arrow — owns a beautiful bay stallion who walks

around unsaddled and unbridled. He lives with Pat by choice. They are friends and equals.

Where is the story? What happens? Pat and Santina discover a secret place, where a bandit by the name of Hobbs, the leader of a notorious gang, keeps his loot. Hobbs finds out that the children know about his treasure. He kidnaps Santina. Pat asks his Indian friends for help and sets out following the fresh trail made by Hobbs and his gang. He catches up with them but is spotted and overpowered by the bandits who treat him roughly.

I put great emphasis on suffering. I indulged in gruesome detail.

The bandits set Pat free in the middle of wilderness, certain that he will perish of hunger and exposure, but he doesn't. The Indians have taught him how to find food in the forest and to travel long distances on foot. He saves himself. I don't remember exactly how Santina gets home.

What happens next?

I didn't know at the time and I don't know now. I drew pictures of Pat's future adventures. In those drawings he was almost seventeen. At that age one can be involved in serious matters. Drama can come from within the person, not only from without. One can get married at seventeen. One can be jealous. One can become a traitor. One doesn't have to be caught by bandits in order to suffer.

The pictures showed Santina firing a pistol at someone. Who? They showed Laura, dressed like a lady from 'Gone with the Wind', her face contorted with insane anger. And Pat's sad, sad face... What was going on?

I didn't know. I was fourteen. I couldn't write about what my characters were experiencing. I knew what their faces would look like in moments of crisis, though. I'd seen such faces in films and comics. There were always crises in films and comics.

I made sure my characters were surrounded by horses and dogs. I understood dogs perfectly, having had just acquired a puppy, Michael.

I could only draw Pat's face in profile.

At the age of fourteen, I had been learning English for four years as part of my primary education. I knew the names of the colours, could tell the time, and could also recite little jingles like this one:

> In the merry month of May
> All the little birds are gay:
> They all laugh and sing and say,
> "Winter days are far away!
> Welcome, welcome, merry May!"

> In the merry month of May
> All the Pioneers are gay:
> They all laugh and sing and say,
> Winter days are far away!
> Welcome, welcome, merry May!"

Does anyone understand the second stanza? No. And why? Because the word "Pioneer"' makes no sense. Pioneers, as we all know, are people who blaze trails. They are the first to do things. The pioneers were the people who won the West for the USA. They all looked and spoke like Walter Brennan. They could have been gay in May but not in the way described in the poem.

The answer to this riddle is simple. The poem was written by a Yugoslav, probably a university professor of English. He used the word "Pioneers" (with a capital P) because Boy Scouts are — were — called Pioneers in socialist countries. The poem didn't sound strange to me then. I thought Pioneers were Pioneers everywhere.

I was beginning to understand the words that were coming out of Pat Boone's mouth. I still remember the triumph I felt when the jabberwocky noises fell together:

> Sometimes an April day
> Will suddenly bring showers,
> Rain to grow the flowers
> For her first bouquet.

Wow! Wow! Wow! Wow!

I found out that Pat Boone had written a book. I had to own it. It was a matter of life and death. An old Russian great-aunt, by the name of Tatiana Guliga, was contacted. She lived in San Francisco and must have been a very nice person because she found the book in a second-hand bookshop and sent it to me. It smelled of American books. American books have a peculiar smell. The Webster Illustrated Dictionary smelled like that, too. It must be the glue the American bookbinders use.

The book was called 'Twixt Twelve and Twenty'. I knew what "twelve" and "twenty" meant. I thought "twixt" was a funny way of saying "two". It was all about teenagers. I read it in a state of religious ecstasy. I could understand more than half of what I read. The other half I made up, unconsciously. I don't remember what I made up. I went from Mama to Papa, from Nan to Grandpa, from one classmate to another, pestering them all with the wisdom of the Book.

I began to keep a diary in English. It was all about Pat Boone and the beauty of nature.

I thought I was in love but I wasn't. I didn't mind Pat Boone being married. I thought it was wonderful. He had children — lovely girls, I don't remember how many. That was wonderful too. I boasted of his family as if it had been mine. I didn't want Pat, I wanted to be Pat. I projected myself onto him. That is how children love: they project themselves onto everything that catches their fancy. Until they stop doing that, they remain children, even if they're eighty.

Every night in bed, before going to sleep, I'd imagine myself as Pat, engaged in some wild adventure which involved suffering and deprivation. I was poor. I was hungry and cold. I was injured and bleeding. I was downtrodden. I was one with all suffering, downtrodden creatures, but my beauty shone like a star. Eventually, my heart would speed up and I'd get awfully hot and excited. I would, of course, be aroused by my fantasies, but I didn't know that. It was pleasant, and it was unpleasant as well.

One could say that my reveries were significant, even beautiful. They conformed to a well-known archetype. Here was religious eroticism in the making. Adonis, Osiris, Christ: a beautiful body taking upon itself all the suffering of the world — wailing women anointing the broken, emaciated limbs, washing blood off the milk-white skin with their tears, and so on.

And those who identify themselves with the milk-white, bleeding, naked sacrifice become flagellants.

Flagellants are people who whip themselves in order to mortify their flesh for the salvation of their soul and the greater glory of God.

Yes, and another thing: the milk-white, bleeding, naked sacrifice has definitely something feminine in his character, although he is — without exception — a man. Things are done to him, which he passively endures. He is helpless and exposed to violence. He is beautiful, in an abstract sort of way. One can find him in so many paintings, sculptures and literary descriptions that he need not be described yet again. Suffice it to say that Bruce Willis would not fit the role, nor would Daniel Craig.

That doesn't mean that all women passively endure things being done to them or that they are helpless and exposed to violence, or even that they are all beautiful. It means that passivity, helplessness and beauty are traditionally perceived as women's attributes.

What did it all signify? I was experiencing my first itch of womanhood identifying myself with the man who offered himself as a sacrifice to a violent Universe and could therefore be conventionally perceived as effeminate.

Why not simply imitate women and so become one?

I had no role model in my vicinity. When I met Alexandra, it was already too late — because of Sean Feeney, among other reasons. I really must get started on the subject of Sean Feeney. Here goes:

It was the summer of 1967. My family and I had completed our first year in the large flat to which we had moved in order to live together with Nan and Grandpa. My dog Michael was eleven months old. I was to begin secondary school in the autumn. It was a wonderful opportunity to start a new life with a clean slate. No one knew me in that part of town. My new classmates would have to believe anything I'd choose to tell them about myself. If I told them that I had been immensely popular in primary school they'd have to believe that, too. I decided to tell everyone that my nickname in my old school used to be Charlie. They'd have no reason to disbelieve me. They would call me Charlie. I very much wanted to be called Charlie. I thought it was cool.

Little did I know I was going to meet Alexandra there.

Opposite the block of flats where we lived there was a cinema. It was not an ordinary cinema. It was part of an institution called The Home of the Yugoslav People's Army — the Army Home for short.

The Army Home took up the entire opposite side of my street. It also occupied the entire side of another street, parallel to mine, and a good length of two other streets. It was a square structure consisting of four blocks with a sheltered courtyard within. There was a garden restaurant in the courtyard, and a low, rectangular building: the cinema. Both the restaurant and the cinema were open to the general public. Soldiers worked as waiters, cooks and ushers. I believe they were paid a nominal wage.

From my street, the courtyard and its delights could be reached through a lorry entrance. Inside the entrance there was a cubicle in the wall. A soldier would sit in the cubicle and sell cinema tickets.

The Army Home cinema was one of the best cinemas in town. It showed all the latest releases. It was also the most comfortable cinema in town, with nice chairs covered in red velvet instead of ordinary seats. One could move them around. I always bought an aisle seat. If I had a problem with the person in front of me, I just moved my chair into the aisle and enjoyed an unobstructed view of the screen.

I saw 'Spartacus' there, and 'Personna' and 'Dr Zhivago', mostly with Mama. In those days Mama still went to the *cinema*, and for walks.

It would not be long before she stopped doing that.

Everywhere around Agram the shows would begin at four in the afternoon, at six and at eight in the evening. In the Army Home cinema, they began at five-thirty and seven -thirty in the evening.

One afternoon, Mama, Nan and I went across the road to see 'Lord Jim' by Richard Brooks. 'Lord Jim' was a mediocre attempt to film Joseph Conrad's awkward novel. I had not read the novel previously nor heard of it. The story was completely new to me, as was the name of Joseph Conrad. It was Mama's idea to go and see the film. She had read the book many years before. "It takes place in Borneo," she said, and I became eager to see the film. I liked anything to do with exotic places: jungles, deserts and so on. I loved watching wildlife and strange customs of faraway tribes. I thought Europe was the pits. Any other place was better in my opinion.

'Lord Jim' didn't take place in Borneo. It began on board a Royal Navy training ship, and my eyes beheld Sean Feeney climbing up a mast.

My whole being experienced a profound shock. This is not a figure of speech. My being experienced a shock.

Sean Feeney looked like nothing on Earth. He looked like a Gothic sculpture. He looked like a painting. His face was straight out of the Book of Kells. I didn't know what Gothic sculpture or the Book of Kells looked like but was soon to become familiar with them, all because of Sean Feeney. His eyes were bright blue, with tiny pupils. The intensity of their blue glare rendered them expressionless, almost unseeing. They seemed to be forever focused on a scene of confusion and torment somewhere inside Sean Feeney's head.

The story of 'Lord Jim' was all about making moral choices and standing by them, even when it meant certain death. The hero had pledged his life, forfeited the pledge and willingly gone to his death. Instead of walking away to live another sunny day and then another and another and many more thereafter, he willingly bared his chest to his executioner's bullet.

Had he chosen to walk away, no one would have done anything to him or said a word. His hands and feet were not tied. His house wasn't guarded. Moreover, no one outside the remote Thai village where his drama took place knew or cared about his disgrace. He could have gone anywhere with his beautiful girlfriend who loved him. He could have become a farmer. He could have had children and raised horses and dogs. He could have grown fruit.

Yet he went and had himself shot. He even handed the loaded rifle to the man who wanted his death. Why?

Because he had a set of moral standards which he believed had been established by God. This belief he shared with most people brought up within the bounds of Western civilisation (and beyond). He judged himself by that set of moral standards even though he may have lost his religion, and decided that he could not let himself off. He preferred paying for his mistake to living another sunny day, or a billion of sunny days.

That I found completely incomprehensible and profoundly distressing. My normal reaction would have been to dismiss the problem by calling the hero a bloody idiot.

The trouble was, no one who looked like Sean Feeney could be a bloody idiot. He was made to suffer. His body was designed to contain a tormented soul. Like Alexandra — whom I was yet to meet — he had the hands of an El Greco saint. If he were to lay on the ground dead and bleeding, he would not look like a victim of an armed robbery. He would look like Jesus Christ.

I was soon to discover El Greco and Jesus Christ, thanks to Sean Feeney.

There was no way out of it; I had to roll up my sleeves and try to understand.

Today I've come full circle. I am perfectly happy to call Lord Jim a bloody idiot and his moral dilemma an exercise in self-importance. So what if he would have found it difficult to live in dishonour? His girlfriend would have preferred him alive. One could say, of course, that, feeling unworthy, he would have become impossible to live with, which would have eventually hurt his girlfriend more than his honourable death. But it would have been up to him, wouldn't it, not to allow that to happen? Had he been able to curb his self-importance, he would have been able to give and to receive joy for years to come in spite of the smear on his soul. Others have done it. It is not easy, but life, as the saying goes, is not a bed of roses.

When the film ended, I dissolved in tears and had to be led home like an invalid. "Ah, Papa," I sobbed while Papa regarded me with a puzzled expression, "ah, Papa, how the audience wept! I've never seen anything like it. Tears were flowing in the aisles, the floor was all wet, honest!" I believed what I said. To this very day I hold the mental image of the Army Home cinema flooded with tears.

Papa and Mama sat down to supper. I ran to my room, threw myself on the bed and cried. I kept it up until Mama came in to see how I was. By that time I had nearly cried myself dry.

"Kitten," Mama said, stroking my hair. She called me Kitten. Most of the time I called her Cat or Kitty. We referred to Papa as Tomcat and to our family unit as The Pussycats. "Dear Kitten, what's up?"

"I'm soo saaaad!" I bawled.

"It'll pass."

"It woooon't! It can't! He got shot! Nothing can change that!"

"It's only a story."

"So whaaat!"

Mama cuddled me.

I pulled myself together, sat up and dried my face. It twitched. I had a headache.

"What's his name?" I said.

"Whose name?"

"His, his."

"Jim."

"No, no, the actor's name."

"Sean Feeney," Mother said. She was still interested in trivia back then in 'sixty seven.

For the next few days I went around pale and wan, collecting all I could find about Sean Feeney. I searched through my collection of movie magazines which I initially bought because of Pat Boone and later out of habit. I found a lot of material about Sean Feeney, and many photographs, too. He seemed to be a major star. I cut out everything of interest and surrounded myself with clippings. I examined every inch of Sean Feeney's face. In the beginning, the image in my mind refused to fall together, but in a day or two his face and its expressions solidified. I read all his interviews and all the articles about him over and over and over.

In a week, I knew Sean Feeney like I knew the back of my hand. I understood that the stories he repeatedly told in his interviews, although probably true, served as a protective wall to hide the day-to-day Sean Feeney, the one who brushed his teeth, had colds, stared at the wall in the small hours of the morning and so on — in a word, the Sean Feeney that mattered.

I respected his attitude. I learned the stories by heart and went from Mama to Papa and from Nan to Grandpa, boring them with Feeney-lore. I never thought about the day-to-day Feeney but I knew his essence. His face was transparent. I could see the essence inside, writhing. I felt I could not quite project myself onto that particular essence, nor did I want to.

After a week or two of that, I said to Mama, "I'm in love."

"With whom?" she said.

"With Sean Feeney."

"What about Pat Boone, then?"

I blushed. "That's childish nonsense," I said. "This is serious."

"My lovely, serious Kitten."

I went to the library, borrowed 'Lord Jim' by Joseph

Conrad, in Croatian, and dived in. The book was full of drama coming from within the person, not caused by bandits kidnapping heroines. To be sure, the hero's difficult moral decisions were prompted by outside events, but in between sinking ships and battles in the jungle, there were pages and pages of tortured self-examination for me to devour. Then came the end, and that terrible, painful passage, telling how "Jim waited a while before Doramin, and then said gently, 'I am come in sorrow.' He waited again. 'I am come ready and unarmed,' he repeated. ... Doramin, struggling to his feet, made with his two supporters a swaying, tottering group; his little eyes stared with an expression of mad pain, of rage, with a ferocious glitter, which the bystanders noticed, and then, while Jim stood stiffened and with bared head in the light of torches, looking him straight in the face, he clung heavily with his left arm round the neck of a bowed youth, and lifting deliberately his right, shot his son's friend through the chest. The crowd, which had fallen apart behind Jim as soon as Doramin had raised his hand, rushed tumultuously forward after the shot. They said that the white man sent right and left at all those faces a proud and unflinching glance. Then with his hand over his lips he fell forward, dead.[1]"

I ran to my room, buried my face among the pillows and howled.

"My Kitten! What's wrong?"

"This!" I wailed. "Listen, Mama." And I read the passage aloud. I couldn't finish. "Why? Why must it be so?"

Mother couldn't give me an off-hand answer. She knew I was asking about the meaning and purpose of Human Existence. Why must it be that way it is? There are no off-hand answers to that.

I went on to read most of the books by Joseph Conrad. I felt close to Sean Feeney when I read them. He had to have read them too. He was serious about his work. I knew that.

---

1 Joseph Conrad: 'Lord Jim', Collins 1957 – p 348

Sean Feeney was an Irishman. What did that mean? In what way was Ireland different from England, or from my country, or from my home town? I had forgotten most of what I'd learned about it in geography lessons. My knowledge of Ireland was limited to a Walt Disney film, 'Darby O'Gill and the Little People', a charming fairy-tale involving Brian, the King of Leprechauns, Banshee the phantom wailer who appeared whenever someone was about to die, a black coach driven by a headless coachman which descended from the clouds to collect the dead, a cnoc with a ruin on top of it, a dog-cart, a young couple courting under the eye of a chaperone, a village pub and a lot of people being called O'This and O'That.

A multitude of things was there to discover and to understand. What, for example, was a cnoc? It looked just like a hill to me. Perhaps it was a hill? (It was.) Why not call it a hill, then? After all, the conversation in the film was in English. And Sean Feeney spoke English at home and lived in London.

I searched through books and found out about the Irish language. The Irish were Celts. Who were the Celts? Long, long ago, I discovered, the Celts had inhabited my country, too. I went wild with joy. If we traced our ancestry back a few score of generations, Sean Feeney and I could be related!

I bought the Aer Lingus Red Guide to Ireland, with detailed maps, and the 'Teach Yourself Irish' book, both easily obtainable in Agram. The 'Teach Yourself Irish' abounded in words looking and probably sounding like nothing on Earth.

Inch by inch, I crept nearer to Sean Feeney and his world.

I hardly left my room that summer and in September, entering my new classroom, I walked straight into Alexandra. "Hi," I said cheerfully, "can I sit at your desk?" "But of course," she said. She wore the shortest mini-skirt I'd ever seen. Her hair was very long and straight as was the fashion of the day. She looked a bit like Barbara Streisand and also a bit like Mama Michelle of the 'Mamas and Papas'.

"Call me Charlie," I said.

"Alexandra," said Alexandra and shook my hand.

Some time before that memorable day I slept and I dreamt and here is my dream:

I'm watching TV, colour TV. In those days we didn't have one, but I'm watching it anyway. I'm watching a programme called 'Sunday Afternoon' which contains a little bit of everything: a bit of sport, a bit of pop-music, an interview, then more sport and pop music, then perhaps a cartoon and so on. The presenter says that there's been a change of schedule: instead of the announced programme, we shall be shown a documentary about "Sean Feeney's Office".

One can see a landscape speeding past the window of a car. The voiceover says, "On an island in Beverly Hills (!) in the villa that once belonged to Marilyn Monroe (!!) Sean Feeney has his office." The "island" comes into view. It is crammed with factories and tall chimneys belching smoke. Pan to a cluster of Georgian brick houses forming a square with gravel-covered pavements, planted with delicate-looking deciduous trees — lime trees, perhaps. It is autumn and the trees are shedding their leaves. The overall mood is one of melancholy severity.

That is the outside of Sean Feeney's Office. Inside, there is a press conference going on. Sean Feeney sits at the head of a very long table with journalists on both sides. He looks extremely pale and thin. His hair is grey. His face is smooth and, I believe, made up. He is dressed in an elegant grey suit with a tie the colour of moss and slate.

Next to Sean Feeney sits a French journalist, a brazen, stupid, vulgar man whose name seems to be Cheval.[2] "Wotar yoo doon now," he asks Sean Feeney, "ayoo doon somefin at the moment?"

Sean Feeney hates the situation and is very nervous. He lights a cigarette and holds it with his right hand as he smokes. His left hand appears to be deformed: it can only be moved

2 'Horse' in French

jerkily and resembles the hand of someone with cerebral palsy, or a claw. "I'm not doing anything at the moment, my dear Cheval," he replies with an effort to contain his fear and revulsion, "but I have plans." "Wot plans?" Cheval insists. "Wot plans can yoo 'ave?"

Sean Feeney's secretary, a fat, furious, black-haired lady, springs up from her seat. "Merde[3]," she shouts at Cheval, "merde, merde!"

Where have I seen Georgian buildings before dreaming about them? In photographs and films. Did I know at the time that they were called Georgian? No. Agram and Central Europe didn't have Georgian architecture. At that time, we in Europe had Classicism. In Agram, Classicist buildings are all situated in the Old Town, on a hill, and can be reached by funicular railway. They come into their own in the autumn, when they sprawl in the golden haze of weary sunshine, floating cobwebs and leaves turning red. They go well with Mozart and a dish of plum dumplings in plum sauce and cream.

How different the Georgian mood of melancholy severity! It goes well with stormy skies, cawing crows, single malt whisky, and the echo of sea shanties.

Why did I dream that Sean Feeney's left hand was deformed? Why was he so full of fear and revulsion? Could it be that he was branded in some strange way, singled out? Was it because he understood Life? Did he belong to the House of the Outcasts?

----

3 'Shit' in French

Meeting Sean Feeney in a Place Called Farrington

Does anyone remember Mireille Mathieu? She used to be very popular back then in Agram. She was a French pop-singer specialising in the kind of songs that Edith Piaf used to sing. For those who don't know of her, Edith Piaf's best known recordings are 'Je ne regrette rien' and 'Milord'. Mireille Mathieu wore her hair bobbed short, with a peculiar V-shaped fringe which shortened towards the temples, forming a sharp point just above the nose. I thought her hairstyle was radical. I went to the hairdresser and had my own fringe cut that way.

I weighed just over eleven stone at the time. My arms and legs were hairy. I wore a black, long-sleeved protective cotton dress to school. We all did. The boys wore jackets of a similar type. We were allowed to vary the style of our dresses. Some of us wore them buttoned, while others preferred zippers. The school dresses could be navy as well as black. They weren't school uniforms. Their purpose was to make the rich and the poor children look exactly the same. The poor children were supposed to feel less self-conscious that way. The theory was noble in spirit but didn't work: we never did our school dresses and jackets up and wore our own clothes underneath. There was no rule against that.

Alexandra's school dress was a racy black mini number. She wore black fishnet tights with it and elegant pumps which were almost courts. Her nails were long and almond-shaped. She owned a leatherette handbag. She carried all her schoolbooks loose in the crook of her arm.

I hid my satchel at the bottom of the wardrobe and grew my nails long. One day, at Forest's, I painted them with pale pink pearl polish. I hadn't felt as feminine before or since. Papa saw my talons and remarked, "You'll be painting your face next."

I was indeed contemplating trying on Alexandra's cake mascara. I'd have already done it had I not been put off by the fact that one had to spit on the cake before working the brush over it. I was going to try wetting the brush under the tap.

"What's wrong with wearing eye makeup?"

"That's what whores do," Papa said, "and if you do what whores do, what are you but a whore?"

Papa was not a Christian, nor was he a Muslim. He thought nothing of small crimes. Once, on a holiday in Vallegrande, he stole a set of cutlery from a hotel. We — that is, Papa, Mama and I — were staying in private accommodation, but took pre-paid lunches at the hotel which, by the way, was not a proper hotel. It was a 'working people's holiday home'. Major companies used to build such holiday homes along the Adriatic coast. Their employees could holiday there very cheaply. Thanks to that system I had my first experience of the sea at the age of two. If they were not fully booked, the 'holiday homes' could accept outside trade and charge hotel prices for their services. The one in Vallegrande offered real home cooking: balmy clear soups, heaps of fresh tomato and cucumber salad with onions and garlic, escalopes to die for. The average wait between courses was half an hour.

Papa thought that was too long, as it probably was. Had I been his age, I would've thought it too long, too. He felt cheated. One day, he stole a knife, a fork, a spoon and a desert-spoon as compensation.

Mama was furious. "I will not have stolen property in my house," she said. "In any case, I won't use those pieces of cutlery, ever." She was true to her word and remained so to the end of her days, even when Papa, who had become an urnful of ashes long before Mama died, couldn't benefit from her upright moral stance any more.

Papa used that set of cutlery three times a day every day, relishing the fact that he had stolen it. Yet, when it came to make-up, he was a real puritan.

How come companies could afford to build holiday homes for their workers and run them so cheaply? They didn't have to pay dividends to shareholders. They didn't belong to shareholders or, indeed, anyone. They could use any profit they made to improve the lot of their employees. In fact, they were not companies at all. They were called "organisations of associated labour".

But that was long ago, in the fifties and the sixties.

I promised Papa I wouldn't use eye makeup for the time being.

I wanted nylons, though, and ladies' shoes, not childish ribbed tights and lace-up brogues I wore (ribbed tights and brogues had gone in and out of fashion several times since). I even bought black fishnets which looked awkward in combination with a brown corduroy skirt and ankle-high boots. I felt that the overall look was wrong but could not give up separate items which had become talismans.

Alexandra wore fishnets.

Sean Feeney, I was told, wore corduroy a lot.

I wanted to be Sean Feeney like I wanted to be Pat Boone before. (I knew it was silly but old habits die hard.) I also wanted to be a woman Sean Feeney could love. I wanted to be two different persons permanently busy seducing one another. It was also terribly important that Alexandra should approve of both. Had I been a man, she would have been the woman I would want to love. But I was a woman, and in my heart of hearts, I wanted to be just like Alexandra, so that the male part of my being could love myself. For want of a better name, this unbelievable muddle must be called friendship. Is every really loving friendship a bit like that? Possibly. I don't know.

I had two pairs of brown corduroy trousers made by a tailor called 'Bespoke'. It is true. He called himself 'Bespoke'. People addressed him as 'Mr Bespoke' and did not burst out laughing.

I couldn't buy ready-made trousers because my thighs and my bottom were too broad in proportion to my wasp-like waist. In fact, I had most of my clothes made for me. They were usually designed by myself and made by Madame Kollosa, a moonlighting pensioner. My designs were based on whatever film I had seen last. They also depended on whatever piece of fabric Mama would discover in the depths of her wardrobe. They had nothing to do with the fashion of the day.

When Mr Bespoke finished my trousers, I put them on and turned this way and that in front of the mirror. Any resemblance to either Sean Feeney or Alexandra was out of the question. My reflection spoke of overindulgence in peace and plenty.

We had always eaten well in my family. When Grandfather Ludwig married Nan Josephine, she did not know how to fry an egg or warm up a bowl of milk. She could just about do her shoelaces up. She was brought up by a bunch of older sisters who doted on her and spoiled her until she was virtually incapable of looking after herself, never mind about looking after others. (There were thirteen of them in all and they were dirt-poor, but that did not prevent them turning their pet sibling into an insufferable little miss.) When she got her first teaching job, she had to leave home and move to another town. She became anorexic and would walk about in the wind and the rain shivering with cold while carrying her coat over her arm and weeping bitterly because there was no one about to tell her to put it on. That was how she was.

75

Grandpa Ludwig married her shortly after he had become the manager of a vast estate which included fields of grain and corn, orchards, vineyards, meadows and forests teeming with game. The estate belonged to the state — whatever the state meant in the days before the Second World War. Grandpa was given the use of the Manager's Cottage, a large house surrounded by a large garden and sporting three levels of cellars. He had a coach-and-pair at his disposal and a coachman-cum-groom to drive the horses and odd-job. Nan was given a maid but soon discovered she couldn't give her orders because she didn't know anything at all about running a household. Fortunately she had the good sense to befriend an old peasant-woman whom everyone called Staller-Neni. 'Neni' means 'auntie' in Hungarian. Staller-Neni was Hungarian. Many Hungarians lived on and around the estate because it lay next to the Hungarian border.

Staller-Neni taught my Nan how to wash clothes, how to sweep and how to iron, but most important of all, she taught Nan how to cook.

What did they cook, Nan and Staller-Neni? The food they prepared has been described in Central-European cook-books and some of it — goulash, for example — has found its way into the Cordon Bleu menu. Yet, were one to make those dishes from the recipes, one would never arrive at the ancient, savoury archetypes Staller-Neni made. Most of them had a common base of chopped onions fried in oil, diced speck, white roux and sweet paprika powder. To this one could add almost any boiled vegetable: Savoy cabbage, leeks, beans and so on, and season it with salt and pepper and, perhaps, parsley. There was also plenty of roast chicken on the menu, boiled beef, Wiener schnitzel, veal escalope, roast suckling piglets, suckling lamb, many varieties of home-made sausages and famous dishes of the Panonian region: sarma, which is meatballs wrapped in sauerkraut leaves, paprikash, Szekely-goulash and so on.

What is the Panonian region? Once upon a time, many millions of years ago, brand-new mountain ranges — the Alps, the Dinarides, the Carpathians, the Tatras — began rising from the bottom of the Ocean which covered most of Europe. They rose and rose, thrusting sea-shells and dead corals towards the stars, and as they rose, a huge sea was cut off from the Ocean and left there to evaporate and die. It was the Panonian Sea.

I often wander who gave it that name. There were no human beings on our planet then. There were no dinosaurs either. Plants one could find, perhaps, and insects, and fish.

The Panonian Sea evaporated from its bed which is now called the Panonian Plain. It includes parts of former Yugoslavia, almost the whole of Hungary and bits and pieces of other countries. Lake Balaton in Hungary is all that is left of the once great Panonian Sea.

Nan in her turn taught Mama everything she had learned from Staller-Neni. Mama had no desire to learn. She picked things up as she needed them. In the early post-war years she wanted to be a nuclear physicist. She completed one term at the Faculty of Mathematics and Physics and then something happened. What? I never managed to get an entirely satisfactory answer to that question. She divorced her first husband whom she'd married at the age of eighteen. I would have been infinitely better looking had I been his daughter. His name was Ladislas. He was tall, lean, dry and wry. I don't know whether he is still alive. I'd prefer him not to be.

Mama and Ladislas ended up living in two cities three hundred and ninety three kilometres apart. There was an episode involving her running away from her parents' flat and throwing the keys of the flat into the Sava from a bridge at midnight. In connection with all that, Mama — Patricia Prochazka at that time — abandoned her study of nuclear physics and got herself a job in a factory called "Ventilator".

Then came the flowing dresses, the lipstick and the Crawford look.

With Mama, any dance was a tango.

Her favourite film was 'The Black Orpheus'.

Her favourite city was Rio De Janeiro, a place she would never visit.

Later, when she married my father Emanuel and had me, she had to cook Sundays (the rest of the week's cooking was done by Nan). Mama made excellent deep-fried potatoes and roast chicken. She also made very decent beef consommé followed by boiled beef, new potatoes with crème fraîche and horseradish sauce. She made delicious carp in breadcrumbs and excelled at simple salads.

Some years after we'd moved flat and had Grandpa and Nan with us once more, Nan became ill. Mama was still in full time work. I had to do the cooking for the family. I was already in charge of washing and ironing because Mama would do it neither well nor often enough.

I learned all about doing the family laundry at Alexandra's mother's knee. She taught me how to use fabric softener and how to iron shirts. Papa made it all easy by never wearing collar-and-tie. He only wore polo-necks, jeans and cords. He owned one black suit and was cremated in it. I would've had him cremated in white 501s and a white polo-neck, but Mama thought it best not to upset the undertakers.

Anyway, by-and-by, the tradition of Staller-Neni passed into my keeping, down to making apple strudel and dobosz-torta.

In his prime, Papa could eat six stuffed peppers for lunch, along with a pound of bread. At the age of fourteen I was known to put away half a roast chicken, a plateful of potatoes and two slices of bread, all followed by six bananas as pudding. If I bought a watermelon, I expected four pounds in weight of it for myself. One must bear in mind, though, that we seldom bought one weighing less than sixteen pounds.

Nothing could have been further removed from the sphere in which Sean Feeney lived and breathed.

One evening I went to the local grocery shop, bought several jars of frozen chestnut purée with whipped cream on top and, while queuing at the checkout, made a silent, solemn vow: this was to be my last supper. I was to have very little in the way of breakfast and lunch either. I was to become as slim as a reed. I wanted to discover what my bone structure looked like.

Those were, after all, the early seventies. You were not human if you didn't look emaciated. You were guilty of unawareness. No one, it was believed, could be aware of the Human Condition and remain healthy and happy. You had to do lots of things which were bad for you if you desired the friendship of your aware peers.

I didn't understand why. No one could offer me a plausible explanation. One thing was clear, though: my very asking "why" marked me as an outsider.

I badly wanted to know "why". I had a feeling that therein lay the key to Sean Feeney's character.

We used to say "personality" in those days. It was Desiré's favourite concept. We discussed Individuality which could only be bought at the price of essential aloneness of human beings. We discussed the impossibility of communication. We watched films like 'Personna' and 'The Face' by Ingmar Bergman.

I could never really understand why Liv Ulmann refused to speak in 'Personna'. The film would have me believe that she, or, rather, the character she played — a famous actress called Elisabet Vogler — suddenly realised that in real life she did for nothing what she did on stage for a living, namely, lied and play-acted. Furthermore, she discovered that everybody did the same and that it was not possible to open one's mouth without lying and play-acting. Filled with revulsion, Elisabet stopped speaking and would not utter another word.

Would it not have been simpler to stop lying and play-acting and to speak the truth even if it was antisocial? Refusing to speak was equally antisocial. People got hurt by Elisabet's silence. She didn't seem to mind. Would it have been more painful for them if she spoke what she felt was the truth? I doubt it. It would have been more painful for Elisabet, perhaps.

And yes, I know the assumption was that there was no truth, that all those things we could communicate about our personalities added up to no more than a handful of trifles, no matter how hard and how earnestly we tried. Only in silence there was truth.

That is what everybody said and wrote about 'Personna'. That was what we talked about with smiles of bitter understanding on our lips which drew on cigarettes.

Nonetheless, in my innermost self — yes, there *is* an innermost self — I felt it was crap.

I think that Bergman's film is about something entirely different: it is a classical vampire movie. Elisabet Vogler is an artist — an actress. Her face and body are there to incarnate other people's ideas and emotions. She, her Self, is merely an empty shell, without a feeling to call her own.

She is not dead, yet not alive. The day she realises her own emptiness, she stops speaking. She has nothing to say; consequently, she will say nothing.

Elisabet's lot is a hard one. She suffers; her soul hungers. In her despair she preys on other people and feeds on their emotions. She gobbles other people up. She sucks them dry. In one scene she literally sucks her nurse's blood. What could be more explicit?

Who are the lucky people who have their own emotions? They are the "ordinary people", the "beautiful blond people" as Thomas Mann called them. They don't actually have to be blond, but they are all non-artists. They don't create, they live.

Art is ersatz life.

The artists are the Undead, the Nosferatu.[1]

What else is new?

There is a grain of truth in what Bergman says. I vouch for it. However, artists tend to blow it out of all proportion. It becomes an excuse for absolutely everything and lets them get away with murder. They walk around looking wan; they drink and smoke to excess and behave outrageously. They think they're the only people who've Eaten the Apple. They think

---

1 Romanian term for vampires, meaning 'the undead' There is a film by Murnau called 'Nosferatu', and a remake by Werner Herzog.

everybody else still lives in Paradise, while they've been cast out of it.

When I say "artists", I use the word in the sense in which it is used on the Continent: I mean painters, sculptors, writers, composers, musicians, conductors, dancers, poets, actors, film and theatre directors, architects.

In the late sixties and the early seventies, an entire generation of young people identified themselves with the Artists whose destiny they saw as paradigmatic of the Human Situation in the Universe. For fairness' sake, I must also mention that the young people in question were mainly well educated and not hard up. There were other young people in Agram who got up at four-thirty to be at work at five-thirty. The mills and the plants of the industrial zones on the outskirts of Agram would swallow them up in the morning and disgorge them at lunchtime, only to devour the next shift which finished at ten in the evening. Those young people were weary to death of the Human Situation and would have enjoyed being healthy and looking happy if only they could.

Together with soldiers on leave, they watched Danish sex comedies rather than Bergman. They also watched Kung-Fu movies and Spaghetti westerns. That goes to prove that, left to their own devices, the People, the Mass, the Crowd, the Mob[2], have an excellent feeling for quality.

I mean this to be taken literally. Forget Danish sex comedies, but Spaghetti westerns and Kung-Fu films are, by and large, excellent. But I digress.

The Artists — the Nosferatu — are Singers. The Handsome Blond People are their Song. The Singers — if they are genuine — would, in most cases, give anything to be the Song: to mind their own business and let someone else do the singing.

Sean Feeney was an actor, thus eminently an Artist. Desiré,

2 Siegfried Sassoon: "I am the People, the Mob, the Crowd, the Mass…"

Alexandra's boyfriend, was an actor. Being an actor was as artistic as could be, so long as one was an actor in a theatre. Strictly film actors like John Wayne, Henry Fonda and James Stewart did not qualify.

Sean Feeney had done all the right things: not only films but Shakespeare, not only Shakespeare but Brecht and Beckett. And the films he'd done were 'serious' films. (Like 'Lord Jim'? As compared, say, to 'My Darling Clementine'? But we were young and didn't know better.)

The very idea of serious as opposed to cheap entertainment came to me through watching Sean Feeney's films. (Until then I was perfectly happy, as I am again, to tell everyone that I enjoyed 'South Pacific' and 'The Sound of Music'.) In one aspect at least they were all like 'Lord Jim': the central character was on a journey of self-discovery, questioning the Meaning of Life and his own ability to cope with Life's challenges. More often than not, he'd find himself on the road to despair. It was possible, with a modicum of effort, to find a link between this troubled character and the anti-heroes of modern literature. Sean Feeney liked Camus. He smoked Gauloises. He used a cigarette holder. He wore glasses! His driving licence had been withdrawn. He stayed up late boozing and discussing philosophy. He should've been the coolest of cool cats but he wasn't. Everybody around him was cool, but he wasn't.

He is a Song who has mistaken himself for a Singer.

He isn't willing to be an instrument which plays a Shakespeare score. There is not a self-denying bone in his body. Moreover, from what I've heard, he is very good at everyday life. He is as good at it as a woman. He is better at everyday life than at his art.

Believing oneself to be a Singer when one is in fact a Song is one of the worst mistakes a human being can make. One worries about matters that do not really concern him or her but does not devote enough attention to the ones that do, like children, friends, decorating, local politics, spouse's health and so on. One does not enjoy everyday life as much as one could because it takes up time and energy one feels ought to be spent on art and art alone. One develops weird patterns of behaviour which are excusable in Singers because they compensate for the lost delights of everyday life but are unnecessarily damaging and very unseemly for Songs.

Whatever Sean Feeney did in the way of artistic behaviour got noticed and talked about because it was unseemly. Some genuine Singers did far worse things, yet no one thought they were uncool. But Sean Feeney had a lifetime of embarrassment.

Back in the early sixties, I knew none of this. I was yet to reach for my first Thomas Mann book. I was merely aware that Sean Feeney existed. I was desperate to penetrate the sphere of his existence. That was all I knew.

Had it not been so, I would have known Alexandra better. I would have been a better friend to Forest. I would have seen into their hearts like they saw into mine.

I scribbled "Sean Feeney" on anything that could be scribbled on.

"It's not possible to be in love with a picture," Alexandra said. "When you're in love, you're in love all over, not just in your head. And for that you need flesh and blood."

"Sean *is* flesh and blood," I said, "only he lives in London and doesn't know me."

"You don't know him either."

"Yes, I do. I know all about him."

"That's not the same."

"I know how he moves. I know how he speaks."

"In a movie. What is he like at home?"

"The same."

"How do you know?"

"I know."

Alexandra shook her head. "It isn't possible. A person is such a complex thing... and he's never seen you. You've never exchanged a word... or even a glance."

"You're saying it's impossible to fall in love with someone who's never seen you?"

"It is possible."

"Aha. And then, suppose one daren't speak out? Could one not remain in love like that for years and long from afar?"

Alexandra thought it over. "It is possible. To be *in love*, that is, although it'd be a grim affair if it were to go on for years. But it wouldn't be *love*, uh-huh."

"Why?"

"Because you need two for love, like I said before."

"You mean there's no such thing as unrequited love?"

Alexandra thought that over, too. "I'd like to say there wasn't," she said, "but I'm not sure. There just might be."

"There you are! I love Sean Feeney and, for now, my love is unrequited."

"No." Alexandra shook her head. "It isn't possible."

"Aaaargh!" I said. I had to have Alexandra's blessing. Without it, I felt, not only my love for Sean Feeney but my very personality had no substance.

"Aargh all you want. It is not possible to love a picture. If you'd as much as seen him cross the road... if you'd seen him in theatre, say... then..."

I didn't expect Alexandra to concede even that much. I was grateful. But then, "As the matter stands, you're not in love at all," said Alexandra. "You're simply protecting yourself from real life, that's all. Sean Feeney is safe for you. He can't hurt you like a flesh-and-blood lover could."

"But I hurt all over," I moaned, eager to claim the crown of thorns. "Just not being with him hurts."

"Find a man... Better still, allow a man to find you, and the hurting will stop."

"You think I wouldn't like to?" I cried. "I can't get interested in anyone! I tried, but I can't! There's no room inside me for anyone! I'm full of Sean Feeney!"

"You mean," said Alexandra, "that real men around you don't speak English and may have smelly feet, while the picture of Sean Feeney doesn't."

Believe it or not, she was ninety percent right. I know that now.

But the remaining ten per cent, the remaining ten percent of it was genuine mystery.

The evening I had my last chestnut purée I slept and I dreamt, and here is my dream:

I seem to be staying in London when I happen to find out that Sean Feeney will, on a certain date, be in a place called Farrington. It is easy to get there by train, so I decide to ambush Sean.

It is winter, must be, because I remember a thin layer of snow on the ground. Yet, oddly, I travel without an overcoat. I have not taken any food with me or money either. I am wearing a pair of lived-in jeans and an old pullover. It is obvious that I intend to return the same day.

Yet why do I have my dog Michael with me? Just in case I... just in case I what?

In Farrington, I look for a hotel described to me by whom? It turns out to be a cluster of genuine Tudor buildings – a stable and a barn with a hayloft — restored and joined together to make a hotel. In the hayloft, bales of hay have been treated with some kind of preserving liquid and kept as a feature. I distinctly remember dreaming about those bales of hay.

I take a room in the hotel. Why? I'm, after all, supposed to return to London that night! So why do I take a room? Just in case I... in case I what?

The room is tiny and sparsely furnished. There appears to be perpetual evening in it.

Now I must look for Sean Feeney in the building where he is, according to my information, to recite poetry and later attend a cocktail-party.

I enter a large, entirely crimson hall, empty but for two men lounging on the carpet. I know that one of them must be Sean Feeney, but I keep my cool and approach the other one, who turns out to be JB, Sean's best friend, a man of spectacular ugliness. I speak to JB, introducing myself with more cheek than I ever believed I could muster. JB is surprised that I've managed to find them in this obscure place, but agrees to introduce me to Sean Feeney who sprawls on the carpet beside him.

Sean seems to have aged considerably and to have become somehow ordinary. He and JB exchange bored comments about me: about my daring, my appearance, my character, my intelligence or the lack of it. "*Isn't* she?" they keep saying, and, "Yes, *rather.*"

Am I *what?*

JB and Sean Feeney finally decide that, for that one evening only, I can be in their company. I am to be an instant, throwaway friend. The three of us settle down to a serious conversation about important issues, like the meaning of life, and so on.

I feel I could spend my entire life with Sean Feeney. Our relationship, I feel, could be unbelievably rich. We were made for each other, I feel. He doesn't seem to notice. He is going to miss the opportunity of a lifetime. He could have perfect happiness but he is not going to have it.

By and by, the audience for his poetry reading arrives. I offer suggestions and he heeds them. People look at me and envy me. Little do they know that our cosy closeness is to last but one night.

After the show, I suddenly think of my dog Michael back there in the dusky hotel room. He must be hungry, poor thing! I'm pretty hungry myself but there is no food at the cocktail-party. I remember a packet of biscuits I've brought along from London and dash to the hotel where Michael and I have it between us.

Back to the cocktail party, and it's over. The night fades out. Nothing has happened. Should something have happened? If yes, what?

Sean Feeney and JB are politely surprised when they notice that I have apparently been expecting something of them. What were my expectations based upon? What right do I have to look so disappointed?

Stormy clouds gather on Sean Feeney's brow. "Right, he's

going to scream now," says JB: a friendly warning.

And Sean Feeney shouts. He orders me out of his sight.

I leave, dragging my feet, crushed by the enormity of my loss — and his! How could he not have noticed who I was? My only hope of meaningful life rested on his knowing who I was.

Hurried footsteps behind me: JB "Sean has calmed down, I think he'd like you to come back."

Need I say I woke up just then?

And who on earth is JB?

Many years later I married an Englishman and came to live near London. My husband Edward became a director of a tiny, ill-starred shipping company with an office just off St John's Square in Clerkenwell. The tube station nearest to the office was Farringdon. I used it almost every day.

The Decline of Sean Feeney

In the early seventies, young people hung out together, just as they do now. They weren't in a hurry to grow up, and the youth of the nineties was exactly the same. The motive behind the behaviour of the seventies' kids and the nineties' kids, however, couldn't have been more different.

The children of the nineties refused to make the effort to join the grown-up society because they didn't believe it would meet their expectations. They didn't believe they had a chance to make it to the top and they were brought up to want to be at the top. They had nothing against the society they lived in, as long as they could be at its top, but the top was so hard to reach and would accommodate so few that they didn't want to bother. (I'm not even taking into consideration here the vast numbers of kids who don't understand the idea of society, accommodation or effort. The idea of being at the top, of course, is understood by everyone.)

We are now in the noughties, and the Millennium has indeed brought a change in the zeitgeist. The young now want to be grown up *now*, and assume that being at the top is their birthright. If it doesn't happen – and mostly it doesn't – they whinge, scream, throw petrol over people and set them alight. And stuff like that.

In the seventies, young people believed they had every chance of joining the grownup society and even making it to the top — indeed, they feared they might not be able to avoid making it good in the world of their parents, if they became like them. But to become like them was anathema. They wanted to abandon the existing social systems and set up one based on their own values. They argued about their values all the time and thus never got around to setting up the system. I should know, I was one of them. I vowed never to live like my parents.

I still keep my vow, although, again, I wish I'd kept my big mouth shut. I have no family. I have difficulties finding and keeping nine-to-five jobs. I don't do anything a person of my age ought to do, even though I do have a mortgage. My parents did not have one. They lived in a council flat, exactly like I used to before I exercised my Right to Buy. But that was in another time, in another place and cannot be compared.

If I carry on the way I do, I might succeed in staying a misfit for the rest of my life, but I no longer relish the prospect.

It is high time this book got published: the passage of time keeps interfering with what I want to say.

Forest doesn't live like her parents, either. She is in her late forties and single. (In her flipping *sixties* now! *Hell!* I wish this book was out of the way!) In her early forties she still enjoyed sitting together with Alexandra and Eagerwill, talking, smoking and sipping coffee. She liked singing old folk-songs. She was waiting for a Mitya Karamazov to come by. Some years ago, and quite unexpectedly, she went off her mind. I have no idea of what she's up to these days or where she can be found. Alexandra does not know where to look for her, and neither does Forest's brother Aurel.

Alexandra does and doesn't live like her parents. She believes that there are certain ways of life which are close to perfection and should therefore be preserved, whether they've been inherited from our parents or not (Alexandra is a pragmatist). Few things, in her opinion, can beat the union of lovers blessed by children. She has been married to Eagerwill for twenty years now. (*Thirty five! Aaargh!*) They have two daughters, Melita and Nelly, lots of flower pots, a bowl with goldfish, three dogs, and a tame sparrow. Alexandra's mother lived with them. She was a widow and a very fed-up person. Eventually she began to miss the point of getting up in the morning, and in consequence became ill, ageing fast. She died nearly ten years ago. Alexandra had her hands full then, and has them full now, and you'd better believe it.

But she handles her family in a way very different from the way her mother handled hers. She has two tenets: active pursuit of happiness and giving people what they really need, not what one believes they ought to need.

Most people think she's just another housewife.

Vicky definitely does not live like her parents. She has taken up anthroposophy and works in a Steiner school in Agram. Her story is terrifying and not a little weird.

Vicky was the first of us to marry. She married Romano, her philosopher boyfriend. Soon after they married, they separated. Romano went to live with his grandparents, his books, his grand piano and his bicycle. Vicky had an affair with Romano's secondary school classmate, Allbright. The affair took a serious turn and Allbright moved in with Vicky. She had a flat of her own.

Vicky and Allbright went on living together for years, but they never married. They had quite a few rows. Their rows were about principles, never about another man or another woman.

Allbright was a philosophy graduate. He was anxious for his life to reflect his convictions. He read a lot and did not pursue material wealth. Freedom was his favourite concept. He'd spend hours discussing its many aspects and definitions. He resented even the slightest infringement of his personal freedom to the point where he'd turn bitter and start ranting and spiting venom. He was, among other things, an honest-to-God macho bloke who liked his food and, more particularly, his drink, and was a DIY enthusiast. He liked hiking in the countryside. He enjoyed talking to the "wise old men of the people" and took pride in knowing how that was done. Well built and muscular, he had an attractive manly face framed with a soft, tidy beard. His hair and eyes were dark. He made one think of Emerson, Thoreau and, perhaps, of Whitman.

Vicky was trying hard to be like Alexandra in every way, without much success. She wore her lustreless hair long, never touched alcohol, cherished Life but forgot to water her plants and never managed to be friendly with her parents' pet dog.

Her soul hungered for glamour, inward and outward. Her femininity was feline and aggressive, not soothing like Alexandra's. She liked moving among famous people. She would have liked to have had a religious revelation.

When Vicky and Allbright started living together I was already a graduate of 'Anglistics' and had started to study painting, having given in to Alexandra's enthusiastic persuasions. Vicky had graduated philosophy (yes, she too) and had taken a job teaching Marxism at one of Agram's secondary schools. She was not a Marxist but it was a job and it gave her an opportunity to practise the art of disciplined thought exchange.

Allbright didn't have a job. He'd occasionally translate from English, mainly modern American authors. He was an expert on Bernard Malamud.

Vicky was the wage-earner. She was the bread-winner.

Allbright shopped, hoovered and even cooked. He seldom went out and devoted a lot of his time to home improvements. He made and painted all the furniture in the flat. He customized the washing-machine with bicycle paint and covered all the walls in shelving. He by-passed the electricity meter and connected the flat directly onto the grid.

In a few years, Vicky's flat attained such a state of completeness that even the smallest object within it had its own specially designed and lovingly made niche from which it could not be moved. The sum total of the niches and the objects inside them made one large niche, most carefully designed to contain Allbright.

It was a bit scary.

It got so bad with Allbright that he only went out in the morning for bread and newspapers.

He and Vicky didn't have a TV-set. They didn't have a telephone. It was partly because Alexandra and Eagerwill didn't have a TV-set or a telephone at the time.

They kept an open house. Vicky made conscious effort to keep in touch with all the latest cultural trends. Young intellectuals, most of them former school or university colleagues, came to eat pasta, drink grappa and converse. They were all Vicky's guests. Allbright would take part in their spirited discussion but kept his distance. He'd get up to change the record or turn up the heater or fetch more booze. Each time he'd glance ironically at Vicky from the corner of his eye.

Vicky used a cigarette-holder when she smoked, a quirk she picked up from Alexandra, who had dropped it years before.

There was a time when I used to use a cigarette-holder, too: first a long, thin, wooden one like Alexandra did, and later a short, black Bakelite one, like Sean Feeney's. That was my favourite cigarette-holder. I lost it long ago.

Sean Feeney still uses his.

Allbright and Eagerwill got on together extremely well. Eagerwill liked Allbright much better than he'd liked Romano, Vicky's ex-husband. In his opinion Allbright was a full-blooded human being with, perhaps, more than his fair share of human weaknesses. Eagerwill loved human beings for their weaknesses as well as for their strength.

With Eagerwill, it is not merely an excuse to patronise other people. He genuinely loves human beings for their weaknesses.

But Allbright grew *terribly* bitter. He felt he was being strangled to death. He should have, of course, got up and gone — but gone where, to do what? It was becoming increasingly difficult for a thirty-year old graduate philosopher to get a job. Also, he was deeply entrenched in his comfortable habits. Last but not least, he still loved Vicky although he also hated her for allowing him to remain her lapdog.

What should she have done with Allbright? She loved him, too. Perhaps she should have thrown him out to fend for himself, at least temporarily, until he regained some of his self-respect. But it's easy to be general after the battle.

Allbright went on and on about freedom.

One evening, in 1982, Alexandra, Eagerwill and I stayed at Vicky's after her other guests had departed. Allbright was in a particularly bad mood and had had too much to drink. At one point he turned to Eagerwill and said, "Let's go out, you and I, and have a drink somewhere."

"Thanks," Eagerwill replied, "but I'd rather not."

"Oh?" Allbright smiled. "You mean, you daren't, because of Alexandra."

Alexandra, who was talking to Vicky, glanced at Allbright and smiled.

"Why do you have to say such rubbish?" said Eagerwill. "Alex, time to go home. We'll miss the last tram."

"Let me finish my cigarette."

"Yeah, yeah, okay, but do get on with it," Eagerwill said, frowning, sensing trouble.

"Why go home at all?" said Allbright.

"Oh, hell," said Vicky, got up and went to the kitchen.

"Because it makes sense," Alexandra explained, smiling. "Eagerwill must go to work in the morning and so must I. So must Vicky, come to think of it. It makes sense to have a sleep before one goes to work."

"That's it," Allbright said and lit a cigarette. "You've had it, Eagerwill my lad. Once you're married, you must do the sensible thing and it's always *she* who decides what's sensible."

"It was Eagerwill who told Alexandra it was time to go," I remarked.

"That's what you *heard*," said Allbright, "but in fact it was the other way round."

"That's clever but untrue," said Eagerwill. "I want to go

93

home. *I* want to."

"Because that's what Alexandra wants."

"Allbright," Alexandra put in, "you don't get it. Eagerwill *wants* to want what I want. It's called love."

"The fact is, he can't go out and have a midnight drink — sorry, he can't want to have a midnight drink. His free will has been surgically removed."

"Midnight!!" I cried. "I should've been home ages ago!"

"Why?" Allbright asked. "Who's in charge of *your* free will?"

"No one," I replied, bristling. "I should've been home because it's sensible. Why is it immediately assumed that anything sensible must be imposed upon us? Is it not possible for something sensible to be pleasant and desirable as well? Why should only drinking and lack of sleep be desirable?"

Why indeed?

It appears, God knows why, that, once we begin finding healthy and sensible behaviour desirable, we stop being young and become middle-aged. It is just as well, because at middle age, vice looks seedy rather than daring. On the other hand, why should one give a damn?

When I and my friends were young, the cry was, "Sex and drugs and rock-'n-roll!" (Very few made the word flesh but all of us wanted to.) "Satisfaction" was the anthem of my generation. Every DJ would open and/or close his session with it.

I thought it all boring and uncomfortable at the time but today, gasping in the airless, terminally cute environment which is the noughties for the middle aged, I feel I should've been a bit less sensible while there still was time.

Because the available thrills in the noughties all come pre-digested and packaged. Read Slavoj Žižek. He'll tell you all about the real meaning of decaffeinated coffee.

To return to the story: "Apart from it being sensible," said Alexandra, putting out her cigarette and stretching, "do you have to go home at once?"

"No," I said. "I don't have to be home at any particular time." At that time I could stay out as late as I liked. It had taken me years to battle out that right.

"Well, in that case," said Alexandra and got up from where she was sitting, "I say — let's all go out and have a drink."

"You don't drink," Allbright remarked.

"You're *so* right, but I can have an espresso."

"You've left it too long. Everything's closed."

"Oh no it isn't. What about the Rubber Strip?"

The Rubber Strip was a cafe at the Agram Central Coach Station. It stayed open round the clock. I don't know what's become of it now that the Coach Station has moved to another building.

"Oh, come on," said Allbright, "you'd never go to the Rubber Strip — and at this hour!"

"I'll come, too," I said happily, looking forward to sharing an adventure with Alexandra.

"That's all stuff and nonsense." Eagerwill got up angrily. "We're going home, Alex. Come, take your handbag; we're off."

"Go home if you like," said Alexandra, "but I'm going to the Rubber Strip — alone, if I must."

The Rubber Strip was not the place for a woman on her own — or for accompanied women, either. Or for anyone, really. It was full of dirty, smelly winos, of itinerant casual labourers, of National Servicemen on leave and cheap, bedraggled prostitutes. The barmaids looked bleary-eyed and washed out, with drooping mouths and dragging feet.

"If you're trying to prove something, you'll only disprove it," said Allbright cleverly.

"Never mind that now. I fancy going to the Rubber Strip. Coming along? Or have you got cold feet?"

Allbright got up.

"Count me out," said Vicky, yawning. "I've got to go to work in the morning. "Night."

And off we went.

The Rubber Strip was as ghastly as could be expected. Alexandra had an espresso and chatted cheerfully. I had an espresso and a grappa with Eagerwill and Allbright. There was vomit on the floor.

After half an hour Allbright began to look very displeased with himself. "Have you had enough?" said Alexandra, finishing her coffee and picking up her handbag composedly. "I knew it would be a waste of time. Eagerwill knew, too. We could've told you, but you would've accused us of being each other's slaves or something."

"Home, Alex, and I mean it," said Eagerwill.

"Yes, o Bwana[1]."

Next year I went to London where I met my future husband and fell in love with him. I didn't return to Agram for some time. When I did, I visited, among other people, Vicky and Allbright.

Allbright was worse. He insisted on washing his and Vicky's dirty linen in front of other people. Nothing could please him. He could approve of nothing and there was nothing he could embrace.

He so wanted to embrace something! He so wanted to step out into the world and walk among *his* people, work with them to create a better, more beautiful, more meaningful world — or simply be happy among his own kind.

But who were *his own* people? Where could they be found?

Allbright thought they were somewhere else, in some other place, other than the one it was his lot to inhabit.

I have recently found out that they are all over the place, just outside the door (or inside, for that matter), wherever one is. The problem is in opening the door, stepping out and joining them, because one finds them appalling while fearing their ridicule. Moreover, one knows there is very little to be gained from them and, perhaps, if one wants to be honest, very little one can give them in return, because one is like them in

---

1 'Master' in Swahili. As in 'big Bwana', 'the white Bwana…'

every way — because, yea verily, one *is* one of them. Having admitted that to oneself, one can step out.

What is the object of the exercise? It doesn't look like a big deal, and with good reason, too: it *is* no big deal to be a human being among other human beings. It should be as natural as breathing and to most people it does come naturally: to everyone in the Third World, for example. To Allbright, who, like most of us young people of Agram, never had to limit his inner life nor have his moral choices influenced by material needs, it had become almost impossible to be a man among men.

Vicky took it all with calm and cool that was, perhaps, uncalled for. She was trying to behave like Alexandra would have done.

Alexandra would have behaved quite differently.

Alexandra would have challenged Allbright. She would have supplied unambiguous choices for him to make. She would have exercised his will until he either regained some self-respect and walked tall again or broke under the treatment, in which case she would have sent him packing, because, as she has been sometimes known to say, she is no Mother Theresa.

The evening I visited Allbright Vicky was not at home. I don't remember where she'd gone. Allbright and I downed a grappa each. He made coffee, then we had more grappa. He seemed to have had some before I'd arrived.

His beard was tidy. His shirt had been freshly laundered. Every little thing in the flat was in its Designated Place.

He and Vicky had just returned from a trip to London, so Allbright delivered a soliloquy on Anglo-Saxon culture. He told me how arrogant and preposterous they were, those Anglo-Saxons who were mere savages at the time when what is today known as (flipping *former*) Yugoslavia was part of the Roman Empire, full of thriving cities with temples of Jupiter and Apollo, buzzing with commerce and art.

He said, "The English language is truly the world language now. Everyone speaks it. Those who don't, shall. Yet, believe it or not, in the seventh century, when we, the Croats, came down to the Adriatic Sea, there was no such thing as the English language! It didn't exist! Not a soul on this planet spoke English!"

I said, "That's right. There existed a sort of proto-English. I think it was called Frisian, but it was as different from the Old English as Danish is from German, and more."

"And more," Allbright sighed, knocking back a grappa. "When we, the Croats, reached the sea, we had a fully developed, sophisticated language. We have enough documents to prove it. You and I can read those documents. So can Steve the waiter down in the cafe. The language hasn't changed much. Great literature exists in it." He downed another grappa. "No one speaks Croatian except Croats, damn it! Why?"

"That's the way the cookie crumbles?" I offered.

"They don't come and live down here in Agram! We go and live up there, in London!"

"And in other places."

"The arrogance! The sheer, damned arrogance of the English! They have all the money *and* all the Shakespeare too!"

"Precious few Englishmen have any money, it's all credit cards now" I said by way of consolation.

"They don't translate *my* books," he said, "I translate *theirs*. Why?"

I thought, "perhaps because you haven't written any," but I knew that that was not the way he meant it.

"The arrogance!" he cried. "The cheek!"

Then he looked away from me. He looked hard at the carpet. "Any job," he said.

"What?"

"Any job you can get me. Anything at all. I'd be ever so grateful. Tell... them... I'll sweep the streets... anything at all."

"Tell whom?"

"*Them*... How do I know? Them, the English."

I told him he was being silly. I told him the UK was the last place on the planet for him to look for a job. I told him there was little I could do about it. Nothing I'd said reached him: I could see it in his eyes. At the end of the day I was going to board a plane in Agram and disembark at Heathrow. That much he knew and that, for him, was enough.

My generation grew up learning English. It was the language of rock and pop.

When I began learning English, I firmly believed I was going to live in America one day. I had seen so many American films that I felt I knew America like I knew Agram. I thought there was nothing I didn't know about New York. I had never seen it in colour, but I knew that, whatever colour New York was, it was black and white underneath. I liked it that way. I liked the strong-featured men speaking from the corners of their mouths. I liked women wearing black lipstick and peeling off rather than taking off their nylons.

I read "The Manhattan Transfer" by John Dos Passos when I was seventeen. Sean Feeney once said that he liked Dos Passos, so I had no choice but to read his novels. I loved the atmosphere of moody modernity and the terribly artificial writing technique Dos Passos used. (I experimented with it myself.) I thought I could tune into the New York vibe.

I don't know if I'd dare visit New York today. I've seen many more films, most of them in colour, but I confess I haven't a clue of what New York is like. Its architecture is awesome, that's all I know.

What is the Manhattan Transfer? I know what Manhattan is, but what is its *Transfer*? Does it have something to do with the public transport?

All I remember about that book now is that its heroine is called Maisie. I also remember the description of the New York Docks in the early morning. Someone is sitting there on a bollard watching the Docks wake up, or maybe I've mixed it all up with Otis Redding's song 'Dock of the Bay'.

In my mind it all looked very much like an Adriatic port with its blue sea and white stone quays. I never saw any real docks until the winter of 1984 in Hull.

I also thought I might live in San Francisco one day. Jack London used to live there. I had read 'East of Eden' by John

Steinbeck. The story took place in and around Salinas, California. I could understand everything that went on between the characters in the story. Their motivations were crystal-clear to me. Consequently, Sonoma Valley seemed to be an old haunt. I would be at home there, I felt. I never thought about what I'd *do* in America.

Young people of my generation in Yugoslavia knew what they wanted. They seldom thought about what they should *do* in order to get what they wanted. They felt their desire was enough. Doing things to make our wishes come true was not our way. We expected to somehow grow into achievement. If I wanted to live in America, I only had to go on living as I did, day in and day out, and one day I'd get there.

I never wanted to live in America because it was a rich capitalist country. It was because of the books and the films. I swear it. I wanted to live in the places the books told about.

All my favourite books were translations. Their stories all took place in foreign countries, mostly America or Britain. All the films I saw were foreign, subtitled films, mainly American.

Once I heard Sean Feeney speak, I changed my hitherto American pronunciation of English and turned my attention to Britain.

I had read 'The Pickwick Papers' at the age of twelve and knew that there was a Goswell Road in London, and a Holborn, and that lawyers, for reasons best known to themselves, lived in Inns. According to 'The Pickwick Papers', Londoners, among other things, ate pork trotters.

Papa was enormously fond of pork trotters, and so was I.

It dawned on me that in London one could see Sean Feeney on stage. One might run into him in the street. One could pass by his house. Sean Feeney lived in London! He was not a mirage, he was a man of flesh and blood and one could, if one tried hard enough, be in the same place at the same time as he. One could see and hear and smell London and know that the sensations one felt would be the same ones that filed Sean Feeney's eyes and ears and nose. One could share an experience with Sean Feeney, and that is what one wants when one is in love.

I made up my mind to go and live in London one day. I was not in a hurry because Sean Feeney was married and had children. His wife was real. His children were real. They all breathed and moved as I thought about them. I had to take them into account if I was to take my own feelings seriously.

My resolution must have been made very firmly because, by and by, I did move to the UK.

I never met Sean Feeney. The chances of that happening, I found out, had always been slight. I was not aware of how slight until the UK became a real place where one wakes up every morning and brushes one's teeth and pays bills. Once that happened, everything fell into perspective.

Also, I love my husband. I think I've got over Sean Feeney. Still, if I were ever to run into him, I don't know how I would react. Sean Feeney is real. My husband is real. He could resent my running into Sean Feeney. After all, I married him because I fell in love with Sean Feeney many years ago! He might not like being reminded of that. Because both of them are real men and exist. (My husband is dead now, but I still love him and he still somehow exists.)

I remember how odd it felt when I first understood the reality of Sean Feeney – when my mind grasped the fact that he'd age and die one day. Somewhere in a drawer in his house there must be a few photographs from his childhood. It felt odder than odd to think about those things.

One night I slept and I dreamt, and here is my dream:

In order to help a friend of his, a small metalware manufacturer, Sean Feeney takes a stall at the local fair, selling his friend's products: cute little badges. Sean is dressed very informally in something halfway between a bathrobe and a monk's habit. The bathrobe, otherwise of expensive silk, appears to be crumpled and stained with greasy spots. There is something almost indecently laid back about his whole person. He seems to have aged in an ugly way and put on weight. Even his voice has lost its edge. He greets the punters cheerfully, perfectly aware that they are more interested in the badges than in the great Sean Feeney.

I have, for the umpteenth time, come to meet him. To use the opportunity, if there be one.

"May I embrace you?" I say urgently and throw my arms around his neck, hugging him as I would hug Mama or Papa. Everything I ever wanted to tell him I try to compress into that single hug.

As I do so, I can hear him chat with someone over my head. I let go. On the whole, it seems to be the best thing to do.

Oh! I've dropped my shopping bag full of just purchased books of Elizabethan and Jacobean plays: 'The Duchess of Malfi', 'The Jew of Malta' and so on. The books are lying scattered all over the floor. I kneel down to gather them when Sean Feeney says, "Let me see your books."

Blessed books! We talk about them, question — answer. I feel I'm being tested but I could be wrong: Sean Feeney takes my words in thirstily, visibly reviving, remoulding himself into his true image, reclaiming the sphere he once used to inhabit, long before his decline. When did he step down from lofty heights to don the greasy bathrobe? Why? I don't know.

Sean Feeney wants to continue the conversation but he is too busy to give it the attention it merits. He gives me the keys of his house: I am to leave my books there and drop in whenever I feel like it. He might be in too, and we could then carry on from where we broke off.

I make off with the keys, legs pumping madly down the road. I know the house. I've always known it. A brick wall surrounds the front garden. The door is made of steel. But I am already inside.[2]

When I woke up, I dug among my papers for a recent photograph of Sean Feeney and gazed at it, looking for the signs of decay I'd seen in my dream. I didn't find them and the

---

2 Many years later, when he no longer lived there, I saw Sean Feeney's house on the internet. It was exactly as in my dream, iron door and all.

relief I felt was almost sweeter than the keys of Sean Feeney's house in my hand.

To return to my visit to Allbright.

Before I left, I said to him, "If I'm allowed a non-sequitur, I must tell you that your flat is not a flat at all: it is a suicide machine. It'll get you if you're not careful." Cross my heart and hope to die, those were the words I said. I was speaking from experience.

Had I not been careful, my own flat would've got me.

Just listen to this:

One evening in the winter of 1985 I phoned Alexandra from my home in the UK as I sometimes do, just to say "hello" and "how are things with you".

"Hello," she said. "We're all fine, but Vicky's flat has burned down."

"Whaaaat?" I cried.

"You heard," Alexandra said icily.

Yes, I'd heard what she said and yes, it was stupid to yell "whaaat" just for effect when real people had been struck by real misfortune, only it was the sort of thing that always happened to others, never to people of one's own.

"When?" I asked.

"New Year's Eve."

Crikey! Holy smoke!

"Anything left?"

"The place was gutted."

I suppressed the exclamations announcing my horror and amazement. Authentic horror and amazement are mute. One's jaw drops and one cannot utter a peep. Alexandra knew that. She also knew that I knew that she knew and had remained silent to impress her with the authenticity of my emotion. Whom was I trying to kid?

"And *they*?"

"Vicky was not at home when it happened. Allbright is in hospital."

"How is he?"

"Third degree burns on two thirds of his skin surface. He's not going to live."

"Perhaps he is!" I yelled into the telephone, trying hard to grasp the reality of what I'd just heard.

"He cannot live," Alexandra said. "It is a medical impossibility. You need a certain amount of skin to live — otherwise you die."

"Is he conscious?"

"Very much so. Eagerwill is with him at this moment."

At this point my emotion became genuine and my jaw dropped as I tried to imagine Eagerwill talking to a man with two thirds of his skin burned away, the man who was, but would soon cease to be, my friend Allbright.

"How long can he live like that?"

"The doctor said a week."

"Does he know?"

"Of course he knows."

I could not utter a peep.

What could Allbright and Eagerwill be talking about? Were they smoking and swilling grappa, or was that forbidden to a healthy thirty-four year old man who was going to die in less than a week's time? Had Vicky been to see him?

"Has Vicky been to see him?"

"Yes."

What could have transpired between them?

I suddenly remembered what I'd said to Allbright about the flat. I remembered how, many years ago, in Vallegrande, I said to Grandy Andreis that I wanted to be a witch so I could sit invisible, watch other people and throw pebbles at them.

I should've kept my big mouth *shut*.

"Coming to Agram?" said Alexandra.

"I won't be able to make it in a week," I said glumly and hung up. It was true. In order to get an air ticket I could afford I had to book an apex a fortnight in advance. I had no one to borrow from in order to buy the more expensive ordinary return. And even if I could borrow the money, I would not be able to repay it.

I wasn't going to see Allbright again. I wasn't going to share his and Eagerwill's sojourn at Death's door. Whatever Allbright had to say to me, if anything, would remain unsaid.

Allbright held out for ten full days. He was young and strong. His body wanted to live. Well anaesthetised, he was not in pain. He read, received visitors, ate, drank and smoked, and felt, I imagine, ready to get up and leave the hospital, only he had far too little skin. Then his kidneys failed, and his liver, and Allbright died.

I don't think it was my doing, whatever I might have said in Vallegrande. I'm not as conceited as that. Only, I still should have kept my big mouth shut. Just *because*.

This is how it happened: Allbright and Vicky had one of their rows which had in their later years become less and less abstract. Vicky grew weary of rowing and nipped out to wish her parents and her younger sister a happy New Year. Allbright stayed at home with his anger and some bottles of wine. He felt self-righteous and, consequently, hurt. He got drunk. Not blindly drunk. Quite simply, plainly drunk.

His generous, handsome soul which had attracted Eagerwill's friendship emerged from its hiding-place and spread out throughout Allbright's person. Denied foothold, the Demon of Peevishness fled.

Allbright relaxed, drew himself a bath and undressed. Then he noticed that the hot tap was running cold: the gas bottle needed changing.

Still naked, a burning cigarette in his mouth, Allbright bent over the gas bottles and began changing them. The next minute he was enveloped in flames.

By the time Vicky arrived home, the neighbours had already called the fire-brigade. Allbright had been taken to hospital, freed forever from making choices, no longer under an obligation to go out and walk tall among all the ordinary people he was supposed to resemble. He was not an ordinary man any more. He was a man with a week to live.

He could do as he pleased. He could say whatever came to his mind.

The funny thing is, we're all dying people. Yet we seldom do as we please and almost never say what comes to our minds: the very state of affairs which drove Elisabet Vogler to silence. If she'd only remembered that she was dying, she would've, perhaps, broken the deadlock and spoken what was on her mind, if there, indeed, was anything on her mind to be said.

How did Allbright use his ten days of total freedom? I don't know. Remember? I had no money to fly to Agram and visit him. Or, to rephrase, I didn't have what it took to visit him.

Was his mind worth speaking? Was there anything on it? I don't know.

I once asked Eagerwill, "What did you and Allbright talk about when you visited him in hospital?"

"I'm not telling you," Eagerwill replied. "You would've found out for yourself had you been there with us."

"But I didn't have what it took to be with you," I said.

"But you didn't have what it took."

This may sound unfair, but it isn't, not really. In my shoes, Eagerwill would have found the way to fly to Agram, if he had to rob a bank. He respects me. He wouldn't allow me excuses he would not allow himself.

In a world of responsible equals, if one wishes to be let off the hook, one has to pay for it.

Once Allbright's funeral was over, Vicky went for a short holiday to recuperate her strength. She then had the flat re-decorated and went on living in it. She might have preferred to live somewhere else but flats all of one's own are not easily got in Agram (or anywhere).

Next time I saw her, at Forest's, she wore black lycra leggings over claret coloured tights and a black mini-skirt over the leggings. She declined coffee and asked for a hibiscus infusion instead. She sat there hunched, not looking Agramian at all. We in Agram tend to go for the Italian style in fashion, more tailored and dressy. Agramians are not into health food and herbal teas.

Vicky looked like a Londoner.

She had never been interested in anything English. Allbright had tried to involve her in his obsession, without success. When he had finally managed to persuade her to visit London with him, Vicky was unimpressed. She spoke very little English, but that didn't worry her. She shopped, ordered food in cafes and bought railway tickets for Allbright who trudged at her heels, tongue-tied and painfully self-conscious, although it was his second visit to his heart's capital.

On his first visit there he had been like fish in water. He used to give me tips on how to get along in London painlessly.

Back in Agram, Vicky decided that London was nice but that she could easily do without it. Allbright was jealous. How dared she manage so well in his beloved city when he had fallen out of the groove? How dared London embrace her and reject him? How dared she not care for the favours London had lavished on her, when he, who had come bearing his heart on the palm of his hand, had found the gate shut?

That gate never opened for Allbright.

But *Vicky*, Vicky went to live in Britain. She lived there for some months while she trained as a Steiner teacher, somewhere in Kent. It sort of happened to her.

Had Allbright lived, I would've acquired enough experience of life in the West to answer his question of "Why English and not Croatian." Let me now enlighten anyone who still remembers the question and is interested in the answer. And Allbright, if he somehow happens to get the word.

Listen carefully, Allbright, my friend. That is *not* the way the cookie crumbles.

Never mind English being the language of rock and pop in Agram and in Kuala Lumpur. Sod 'Satisfaction' and your translations of Malamud.

English is the language of *money*. It is the language of big business and of small business too. The Anglo-Saxon world moves money around and tells it where to go. Everybody wants money. That is why everybody speaks English. It has been so, probably, since the Industrial Revolution. It has something to do with the Protestant ethics. God will mark his favourites by blessing them with wealth. The righteous are therefore rich. By inference, to be rich is the outward sign of righteousness. The pursuit of wealth is a pious enterprise. Whatever.

When Croats — or any other Slavic nation — have command over something that Jong Blong[3] in Kuala Lumpur wants as desperately as he wants money, the whole world will speak Croatian, or that other Slavic language, bless its little vowels and consonants.

It has nothing to do with Shakespeare, Marlowe, Shelley, Keats, Wordsworth or Dickens.

---

3 Joe Bloggs. Geddit? Geddit?

Sean Feeney Trapped

I did slim down. I lost two stone. Mme Kollosa had to take inches off all my skirts and trousers. I felt fit to probe the depths of Life in order to become like Alexandra and Eagerwill and Sean Feeney. My new svelte self would not look ridiculous as I rooted in the mud of the world in search of Experience.

Had I not wasted so much energy in trying not to look ridiculous, I would not have looked ridiculous, ever. Read this sentence again. *Meditate* upon it.

The change in my appearance had come too late to earn me the respect of my classmates. I was Fatso. I was Miss Hairylegs. I was Teachers' Pet. I knew all the answers, yet I refused to prompt other students (we called it 'whispering'). I wouldn't pass around correct answers if I'd completed my written test before the others did. It wasn't moral indignation or meanness that made me behave like that: I was simply afraid of being caught. I was perpetually afraid of being caught at something or other by the grownups.

I am now forty five (like, *duh*! I'm about to be *sixty*, now, as I proofread 'Agram' one last time before publication) and still

109

afraid the grownups will catch me out. I'm not boasting. It's nothing to boast about. Look what happened to Mama because of a similar attitude. She never learned how to *be*: how to dress, how to run a home, how to visit, how to small-talk, how to change with the times. Friends and colleagues around her grew up while she didn't. Papa grew up and she didn't (he was fairly mature to start with). She dug her feet in and remained fifteen. Thus she lost touch and became what my husband used to call a funny.

She never put on pretence of adulthood, though, because she was never afraid of being caught out. She was proudly defiant.

I don't have her self-confidence. I'm a wuss. I'm afraid of my own shadow.

I'm terrified of being caught reading 'Asterix' when I should be ironing or doing some useful thing or other. I still have the habit of hiding my 'Asterix' book under a pile of newspapers when I hear my husband's steps on the stairs. (I'll never hear *those* again. And don't read 'Asterix' any more either. I wonder why.)

I know how a woman of my age ought to behave and I can do it if I absolutely must, but it is never a good show.

I'm going to age gracelessly, you can bet on that.

Although rejected by my fashionable mainstream classmates, I became a member of an inner circle of 'wits'. There was a tall, awkward, blond boy whose name was Struckford Pinter, which in itself was extraordinary enough. Struckford's eyelids drooped heavily over his pale eyes and he moved and spoke in a slow, sleepy way which made an interesting contrast with his fast and wicked wit. There was also his friend, small, frog-faced, bespectacled, with a passion for dressing à l'anglais, and a good student to boot. His name was Donnie Horvath. Everyone called him Homo. The third Exclusive Wit was a newcomer from the town of Pola, Charlie Constantine, a dark, gangling youth who amused us by walking like the Pink Panther. And there was Alexandra. I was admitted once I'd learned how to smoke.

When I was a little girl, I used to write all over Mama's packet of cigarettes, "Mama please stop smoking". Nan, who was so bad she used to smoke while kneading dough for pastry, quit in a single day when I was seven years old. Grandfather Ludwig ordered her to stop. He said she was killing herself. He was right: Nan later found out she was a diabetic, and a diabetic smoker is bound to end up with gangrene, as Nan unfortunately did.

Grandfather Ludwig stopped smoking when I was born. "I now have a granddaughter," he said, "and she needs me. I must stay healthy for her sake." (It would not have done, I suppose, to have stayed healthy for *his own* sake.)

Papa never smoked. His father did, and his brother Christian did, but Papa didn't. He didn't drink coffee, either. He was in favour of sport and healthy lifestyle.

Yet he died of a stroke at the age of sixty-five.

I was totally committed to non-smoking. I had become addicted to black coffee, though, while visiting Forest and Alexandra. I had also tasted alcohol in their company. Sometimes we'd all go for a day out in the fresh air and climb Bear Mountain which protected Agram from the north. Agram's most expensive suburbs sprawled over its southern slopes. No bear had roamed its forests for three centuries. After the War the mountain was declared a nature park. One is not supposed to smoke, pick flowers or litter there, but that is nonsense. Thousands of people climb it every week or ride up in a cable car.

Bear Mountain is taller than Ben Nevis. It would take us all morning to reach the summit which was called the Roofbeam Peak.

Desiré told us we shouldn't drink any water on the way up. His theory was that the more we drank the thirstier we'd be. He said we couldn't carry the amount of water we'd require once we started drinking. We had to wet our mouths with something, though. For that purpose we carried a bottle of vermouth. Every now and then we'd have a sip each.

Since then I've tasted whisky and gin and everything.

I liked the way Alexandra held her cigarette: between the index-finger and the middle finger of her right hand. She kept the two fingers absolutely straight. Only the top joint of her index finger would be slightly crooked. Sean Feeney held his cigarette holder differently. I would have liked to have tried holding a cigarette holder like that myself, but I was not a smoker.

The summer I slimmed down my parents let me spend a fortnight out of their sight for the first time in my life. I was to go with Alexandra and Forest to a place called Cone, on Pushman Island. They had been holidaying there for years. My parents wanted to know everything about the place and the people we were staying with. They pointed out that I was only seventeen and a minor. Alexandra was the same age as I. Forest was nineteen, however. She was to be officially responsible for Alexandra and me.

In reality, Alexandra was in charge, as ever. We took a night coach to the coast. It traversed a formidable mountain range cloaked in midnight mists and then rolled for hours along the Trans-Dalmatian Highway with the calm, moonlit sea to its right. We crossed to Pushman Island at dawn by a small ferry and lay sprawling on the beach by lunchtime. It's weird, but I don't remember swimming with Alexandra and Forest or playing in the shallows although we must have done it.

I do remember our nights out, understandably, because they were my first nights out ever. They all seem to have telescoped into one single memorable Night.

There was only one cafe in Cone and the evening started on its patio, a concrete platform surrounded on three sides by the sea. One could step down from the patio and wade in.

Alexandra had borrowed a sleeveless top from me that evening. It was printed with flowers and had frilly hems. I detested it because of its Flower Power look and was surprised that Alexandra wanted to wear it. Once she put it on, though, the ghastly top underwent a sea change and became a desirable piece of clothing.

I wore something severe and sporty that didn't match my skirt, and a pair of cork platforms. Forest was in her usual long flares which hid her deformed leg and showed off her fine waist and her gorgeous bust.

We were immediately surrounded by a bunch of young men, most of whom were from Cone. Alexandra was instantly bagsied by Delano, a handsome youth whose grandparents were from Cone while he himself came from Agram like we did. He had been named after President Roosevelt. He knew what was what in rock-'n-roll. He had his grandfather's boat at his disposal. We were all to go sailing with him the following morning.

I cannot for the life of me remember what Forest did that night, although we were all seated at the same table.

I became the object of the attentions of an utterly hideous creature. I don't remember how old he was or how young, or what his name was, or anything. His hair was cut very short and he wore a chequered, short-sleeved shirt. He was unfashionably, nauseatingly chubby. As a child he must have had long green stalactites of snot hanging from his nose.

The conversation followed the usual course of a chat-up: music, movies, love. What I thought about love. What he thought about love. Love was something infinitely more profound than mere sex. Sex was meaningless without love. And so on.

I was not a bit interested in what the man was saying. I would have liked to have gone wading in the shallows. I was getting sleepy after a hard day's swimming. It became increasingly difficult to maintain conversation with Snotty.

Why did I do it? Why didn't I go wading?

Because I was worried Alexandra and Forest would say that I was a child who didn't even try to experience Life. If they thought that flirting with boys they hardly knew and staying up late made sense, it probably did. It was my duty to give it a go. After all, Sean Feeney didn't spend his nights catching crabs on the beach and sleeping. To sleep was to be dead when one should strive to be alive, that much was clear.

What else do I remember about that night? I remember that Delano, Alexandra and Forest played "The House of the Rising Sun" more than twenty times on the record player. How did they get to be in charge of the music? I don't know.

Around one o'clock in the morning I was given a cigarette by Alexandra. I managed to light it in the first attempt. I smoked it whole without inhaling. It was my first cigarette. It wasn't too bad. Delano could inhale the smoke, swallow a mouthful of Coke and then exhale. Alexandra could do it, too. A year later I could do it as well as they did.

Around three o'clock in the morning Snotty took me away from the cafe. I followed him to the pier, clenching my teeth and thinking "This, too, will pass". I was vaguely aware that I would probably be made love to. I thought I might as well go ahead and do it, only I couldn't understand why I should make do with Snotty, a man much older than myself and somehow... I don't know... soiled, when the other girls attracted handsome young lads. Yet I didn't dare say "no" to Snotty: if I kept saying "no" to people, where would it end? Also, I thought so poorly of myself that I half-believed Snotty was as good a bird as I was likely to bag.

We climbed on board a sand carrier boat tied to the pier. It was exciting to be on a boat but not in a way Snotty was hoping it would. I put up with his presence only in order to be able to lie on the coiled ropes and look at the stars, imagining myself on board the schooner 'Arangi' sailing along the shores of Malaita under the command of Captain Van Hoorn with Jerry, his Irish terrier puppy, at his heels. I'm referring here to Jack London's novel 'Jerry of the Islands'. Has anyone read it? Captain Van Hoorn ends up as *kai-kai* — a meal — for the Malaitians. Jerry finds a home with a rich couple on their magnificent estate in Sonoma Valley, California.

Sonoma Valley is, apparently, some sort of heaven where one ends up if one's lucky. I wonder if I'll end up there one day, when I've paid all my debts to Life and when everyone else has become *kai-kai*.

Would that be good or bad? I don't know.

Snotty tried to make me sit in his lap. I demurred. He was terribly excited. A kind of pulsing heat emanated from his whole body. I knew what had happened — he was aroused. He would be in agony if not relieved soon. Somebody sometime had told me that. Perhaps it had been Papa. I don't remember. Information, however, is one thing and full understanding another. Snotty's heat felt alien to me. All I wanted was to slip out of its nauseating sphere.

Looking back, I can reconstruct what had passed through Snotty's head, now that I've lived a bit and learned a thing or two about men. He thought of going ahead and raping me, or maybe not quite raping me, but it would have amounted to much the same thing. I wouldn't have yelled for help, I would have felt it had been my fault to have aroused a man to the point where he lost control over himself. I would've succumbed and, perhaps, cooperated. Then he thought again. He remembered what a small place Cone was. He knew I'd tell my friends what had happened and they, he knew, would not be as forgiving as I. They'd tell the Cone boys and the Cone boys would soon deal with Snotty, even if he left the island that very morning. Everybody in Cone knew who Snotty was.

So he did nothing untoward.

I felt sorry for him. Can you credit it? I felt guilty for inflicting such pain on him. I should've been more mature, I felt. I should've liked his lovemaking. Life was supposed to be all about that. It was in all the films and the novels, or in most of them (there was very little of it in 'Jerry of the Islands').

I don't remember at what stage I got off the boat. Snotty followed me to a quiet street corner. We lingered there. I still didn't feel I had the right to say "Don't follow me." He mumbled something about tomorrow evening. Then he kissed me on the mouth.

It was my first kiss. It was very bad. It was worse than bad, it was disgusting. I didn't know I was supposed to open my mouth and, when I finally did, I retched. Still I didn't run. Still I waited until he finally said "Good night". I waited until I was *dismissed*. I couldn't take the responsibility for walking away first. I felt I owed Snotty something.

It was dawning when I crawled into bed. Alexandra and Forest were asleep, but they woke up and looked me over. They smiled. I told them nothing had happened. I felt guilty again. I must have disappointed them as well. I was not ready to join their club. I had spent half the night alone with a man who wanted me, I felt his desire, I knew what it meant, and yet was no wiser that before. Even if I had let Snotty go all the way, I'd still have been no wiser. I had the Apple in my hands, but didn't Eat It.

I continued to smoke from that nigh on, but hated kissing for years to come. Even Fred Quail's kisses made my stomach flip. I carried on like that until I met my husband. His kisses are not to be discussed in this book or indeed anywhere.

A few days after or before my first kiss, Alexandra received a letter from Desiré and blew her top. The day was rainy. We couldn't go to the beach and she had hours at her disposal to rage her fill. This set of circumstances provided me with a rare insight into Alexandra's private life, the one she shared only with Forest, largely, I believe, because I didn't know how to knock on that particular door.

What was it about the letter that made Alexandra blow her top? She read it aloud to Forest and me. It contained confirmation that money would be available for Alexandra to have an abortion when she returns to Agram. The letter went on in a cheerful epistolary manner to inform Alexandra about the latest in Agram's cultural life and Desiré's participation in the same.

Alexandra was to have an abortion!

It wasn't shocking in itself, not for us. We had been brought up almost without religion — in my case, completely without it. (I'll return to that later.) We all knew that Alexandra was far too young to become a mother. It was simply out of the question. She had yet to finish secondary school, and then study something before she would be ready to become an adult and have her own family. She didn't want a baby. She wanted the freedom to decide what her life was going to be like. She didn't want to be pushed onto a course and then whipped into running its full length until she dropped with exhaustion like so many people — particularly women — did. Responsibilities were not to be thrown at her. She was going to take them of her own free will when ready and then she was going to be the most responsible of women.

But the amazing thing was that there was a baby inside Alexandra! It could have been a boy or a girl. To what extent would it have resembled Alexandra? Would it have been more like Desiré? I felt the gulf between myself and Alexandra change its quality. Whereas I used to think I could one day reach across it and really be with Alexandra — the day she sometimes said she was waiting for — I suddenly realised that day would never come. Women can be either mothers or daughters. Alexandra was a mother. I was a daughter.

Alexandra and Forest discussed the ethical and the emotional aspects of abortion. Alexandra was worried. She was afraid of the pain and possibly the remorse that might follow. She sensed the impending death of her relationship with Desiré. It could linger on for a while but it was doomed just the same. Desiré had been tested and found wanting. It hurt Alexandra that it should be so, especially when she needed to muster courage to kill a baby.

Their relationship survived for three more years. I hoped it would, at the time. I hated changes. I knew we'd lose Desiré if he and Alexandra split up, although we all believed in individuality. We believed that our relationships with each other were independent. They had to be, we felt, or else a lot of things we said and did to one another had no meaning and were entirely unjustified. For example, what right did Desiré have to straighten me out each time I did something he didn't approve of? Every right, if he was a friend of mine, since our concept of friendship demanded constant work by each upon the other until such time as Man becomes God. (Dr Scott Peck promotes the same concept.) No right at all if he had simply taken me as part of the package that came with Alexandra but would otherwise not be interested in me at all. We had even discussed the subject. Our discussions invariably ended with yet another avowal of our individuality.

But when the time had come, Desiré disappeared from our lives. I believe he and Forest met up a few times, possibly by accident, and had coffee together. He continued to meet Vicky and Romano — she was with Romano then. Desiré was interested in Romano more than in Vicky. Romano must have dropped him later. I don't think he had time for Desiré.

He couldn't have been bad or worthless — Alexandra wouldn't have spent so many years with him. He simply wasn't the sort of person Romano had time for. Desiré's character lacked the ironic bone. Perhaps he simply lacked bone of any kind.

Lord, how simple it all looks to me now!

Then, I was a daughter. My surface was unscarred, with a high gloss upon it repelling kisses and anything else Life tried to besmirch it with. The glossy surface would not let anything through. Only once did it open: for Sean Feeney. It opened, my Self, sucked him in and closed again. I tried to match the Sean Feeney inside with the world outside, but the glossy surface wouldn't let me.

Alexandra's worries and dilemmas bounced off the glossy surface. Shall I confess how I thought about them? I was terrified my holiday would be spoiled, my precious first parent-free holiday with Alexandra. I thought, now we'll have doom on the beach and gloom in the room, and I'll be full of the sun and the sea and my surface will glow and I won't be able to share Alexandra's whatever and it'll show, so I'll feel guilty and I'll be miserable, and for the wrong reason too, all me, me, me, not you, you, you.

But Alexandra went to the beach with good cheer and all was well again.

Later, in Agram, she had her abortion. I visited her the very same afternoon. Her parents knew nothing about it and

Alexandra had to sit at the table in the drawing room and pretend she was well. Shall I tell you how it affected me? I had come mainly because I wanted to smoke, something I couldn't do at home. I also wanted to see Alexandra's face. A day without seeing Alexandra's face was a day wasted.

I wandered why she hadn't confided in her parents. She said it would've been impossible, but, although I had the highest possible opinion of her judgement, I thought that in this case she simply had to be wrong. I would've told my mother. We'd have had an unpleasant talk and then I'd have been put to bed and made a fuss of. In fact, I would've told Mama in advance. She'd have known what to do. She'd have told Papa and saved me the pain of doing it myself.

I hoped Alexandra would recover very, very soon so that I could visit and be cheerful and talk about myself without feeling guilty. That is how it was.

I am still a daughter, at the receptive end of the Universe. Things happen to me. I sit and wait for Fortune's smiles or blows. Whatever happens to me, I always expect things to get better. There is, I feel, a golden future for this good, well-behaved girl. When I was twenty, I expected that future to have begun by the time I reached thirty. At thirty, I postponed it till I was thirty-five. At thirty-five I was certain the future would begin any moment. I was surprised and, yes, outraged when it didn't. I still believe it'll begin one day. I believe I'm entitled to it. How shall I know it has started when it does? Easily. I shall have no more financial problems. I shall have passed my driving test. (Blooming *done* that since. The driving test, that is.) I'll be recognised as a mainstream writer. I'll have my own flat or a house, all paid for. I'll be able to travel and see places like Venice, Barcelona and the Great Rift Valley before I die. I'll be able to see at least one live volcano. I'll have my teeth repaired and I'll have the hair on my upper lip removed by electrolysis, and I'll have the fat removed from my thighs by liposuction. (And I'll have a facelift. I need one, now.)

And my husband will have a small sailing-boat because he

loves sailing more than anything else in the world. He'll be able to have an ex-rental piano. (Too late for that now.)

Maybe I'll even meet Sean Fèeney one day.

And I'll sit and write. And I don't want any distractions as I do so, like money problems, or world crises. Distractions bore me to death, because I'm a Singer.

I have nothing to support my belief in the golden future. Up to this moment I've had nothing but distractions.

I nursed my grandmother until she died. I lost my dog Michael. I fell in love with a man more than twice my age. I left my country (which has, in the meantime, disappeared and whatever was left has metamorphosed into many little countries). I have not been able to make any headway in earning my living as intellectual. I lost Papa. I had to cope for years with a psychotic mother, and then lost her as well. My closest friend — my cousin Melissa of whom I haven't spoken yet — abandoned me because my lifestyle depressed her (she's come back since – so that's *something* to be cheerful about). My husband and I made an attempt to earn some money which backfired on us and resulted in our having to take unpaid care of an evil invalid, tyrannical, incontinent and unrepentant. I had to live away from my home for long stretches of time completely against my will. When I finally made it back, I only had a few brief years with my husband left. I can't seem to be able to settle down in a decently paid job, intellectual or not.

For a good many years I did not own a vacuum cleaner. I swept my flat with a broom. Back there in Agram, I associated brooms with the nineteenth century.

Sometimes I just sit and weep, thinking how I must be the unluckiest woman in the Western World. I feel cheated. I used to take it out on my husband. He couldn't bear to see me so unhappy and took his own frustration out on me. Neither he nor I could afford to take it out on the people who oppressed us because we had no money and were defenceless. (*Did* anyone oppress us? Perhaps this oppression thing is all in the mind? Perhaps we shouldn't have been taking anything out but putting something in?)

I used to get anxiety attacks. Sometimes I'd stay depressed for a fortnight, swilling vodka just to get through the day. I used to be a Diazepam addict for years.

Yet I didn't suffer! I still don't. No matter what happens to me, my emotional response to it cannot be called suffering! Alexandra must have suffered, although probably not much. Eagerwill, too. And Forest.

How do I know? Quite simply, because Alexandra, Eagerwill and Forest inspire art. One wants to draw pictures of them. One wants to write about them, poems or stories or even a novel, while no one would ever want to write a novel about me. I have found them in other writers' novels and in other painters' paintings.

And Sean Feeney, what an excellent, pure, deep well of inspiration he is!

Listen: my aesthetic theory says that victors are beautiful and losers are ugly. The strong ones, the healthy ones, the powerful ones are beautiful. The active ones are beautiful. Those who are weak and sick, the meek ones, those who get acted upon, they are ugly.

The funny thing — the paradox — is, if the victors, the healthy, strong, powerful ones never ever suffer, they are not interesting. They have no substance and if you cast light on them, they have no shadow. Their colour scheme is devoid of black. They resemble Nazi art. They must suffer, and suffer rather more than the meek ones, if they are to amount to anything at all.

The secret is in the attitude. They must suffer on their feet rather than on their knees, or they are in danger of becoming meek.

What looked like meekness in Jesus Christ was in fact something else. It was supreme understanding. He was able to empathise fully with whomever and whatever hurt him. He was not self-absorbed. He did not indulge in his suffering. He did not indulge in anything. He was *too busy* empathising and understanding. Because of that, Jesus was boss. Had he been a bitter underdog, he wouldn't have made the beautiful sacrifice for the flagellants to get aroused by. He'd have been just another victim of Roman oppression and of Jewish collaborators, destined for the mass grave. He'd have been an ugly, bloody mess.

They — Jesus and other beings of significance and beauty — must be of cheerful disposition. They must be on top of their suffering at all times. They may weep when the pain becomes too bad but they mustn't get depressed. They must be able to dry their tears and smile or, better still, laugh — not play-act at laughing but find something to really laugh at. They mustn't be bitter for any length of time. And if for some reason they become unable to laugh, they must keep their dignity. If not, they become like Hamlet whom everyone detests but no one dares say so because he was written by Shakespeare. The only one who loves Hamlet is Ophelia, also written by Shakespeare, but she goes mad pretty soon. It is impossible to love Hamlet.

Until I first beheld Sean Feeney, I was going to be a glaciologist — a scientist who studies ice. This is not a metaphor. Glaciologists study ice. I was also going to be a volcanologist like Haroun Tazieff and a marine biologist like Jacques Cousteau. Tazieff and Cousteau had written a book together. It is called 'L' eau et le feu'[1]. It is still one of my favourite books. It is a talisman.

When I saw Conrad's Jim (wearing Sean Feeney's face and body) receive a bullet into his heart in order to save his honour and fulfil his destiny, I forgot Science and embraced the Humanities. They were difficult because of my pagan background. The whole complex of guilt, atonement, redemption, sacrifice and so on was alien to me. And all the Humanities are based upon those concepts in one way or another.

This is how I defined good and bad: good was what made

1 "Water and Fire" in French

me happy. Bad was what hurt me. This is how I defined right and wrong: right was what pleased Mama and, with luck, Papa as well, and all the other grownups. Wrong was what Mama said was wrong. Also, wrong was what Alexandra said was wrong. That was a bitch because Mama and Alexandra seldom approved of the same thing.

It had nothing to do with the struggle of the soul. I fought to attract pleasure and avoid pain.

The word 'soul' meant little to me. It was a term of endearment most women used with children, their own and other people's. "Come here, soul" they'd say, and, "Would you run down the shops for me, little soul?" Religion was something I associated with the Middle Ages.

I imagined the Middle Ages as depicted in that glorious comic, one of the best ever: Hal Foster's 'Prince Valiant'. Later, I began to connect the Middle Ages with Walt Disney's 'Sword in the Stone', and a book about Robin Hood I had read. It was printed, I think, in Cyrillic.

In the Middle Ages, I thought, people fought with swords and spears and arrows. Women wore long dresses. Men wore tights. Everybody lived in castles and rode horses. There were also men called Priests who wore long dresses instead of tights and had shaved pates. They were fat. They drank a lot. They wore crucifixes around their necks and often clasped their hands together. That meant they were praying to God. It was their job. Nuns did the same, only they were women. Just as ordinary men and women could be found in castles, priests and nuns hung out in cathedrals, which was another word for churches. I found all that far less interesting than volcanoes or the lemurs of Madagascar.

One day I went to the Army Home cinema to see a film with Sean Feeney in it. It was called 'Becket'. I had been associating the name with the playwright until then (one of Sean Feeney's favourites and an Irishman to boot), but the poster clearly indicated that the story took place in the Middle Ages, and the Becket of the title was written with a single 't.'

Richard Burton was in the film, too. He had been Mr Elizabeth Taylor to me until I discovered that he was Sean Feeney's friend. That made me remember his face as well as his name. And his voice.

Quite a few names had acquired faces and voices since I first saw Sean Feeney. I was grateful for that.

The title and the credits rolled to plainsong, the first I'd ever heard. I have read many books about the Middle Ages since and seen a lot of medieval art. I can whistle medieval tunes like other people whistle pop-songs. Yet all the books and all the art and the music have added little to the profound understanding of the Middle Ages which descended upon me through the sound of that plainsong. I still remember its simple little theme. I hope to remember it beyond the grave, if there is a beyond.

The film opened with King Henry Plantagenet —

(King!!)

— riding to the Canterbury cathedral where he was to do –

(Penance!!)

— penance for failing to prevent if not for actually instigating the murder of Thomas Becket, the Archbishop of Canterbury, who used to be his closest friend.

Embodied in Sean Feeney, the King descended into the crypt of the cathedral —

(Crypt!!)

— shrouded in a huge crimson cloak trailing behind him. In the icy blue semi-darkness of the crypt he let the cloak drop, revealing a bare torso. He knelt down —

(Knelt!!)

— pale and skeletal, and clasped his hands together in semblance of a prayer —

(Prayer!!)

— but he didn't pray. He smiled.

Sean Feeney has a peculiar smile. It looks as if a crescent wound has opened in his face, exposing the bloody inside of him, things which are not meant to be seen and are therefore camouflaged with skin, hidden away from the light of day, forbidden.

The King smiled at the freshly carved sarcophagus of Becket and spoke to the stone effigy on the lid. He said, "Thomas Becket... are you satisfied at last? Here I am, with those treacherous monks of yours —"

(Treacherous!!)

(Monks!!)

"— getting ready to thrash me — me, with my delicate skin!"

I didn't like this last bit. It was somehow flippant and it didn't go well with the bleeding crescent smile.

Then the King said something like, "You never loved me, Thomas. Did you learn to love the honour of God?"

(Honour!!)

(Of God!!)

Or maybe that was at the end of the film.

After the crypt, the film went into flashback. It told the story of the King and his friend Thomas: how they caroused together, how the King decided to make Becket Chancellor, how he later made him Archbishop of Canterbury, how Becket took the appointment rather more seriously than intended, how the King and the Archbishop fell out over the question of Crown jurisdiction over criminal members of the Clergy, how Becket handed in his resignation as Chancellor and went into exile, how he and the King attempted reconciliation and failed, how the King got drunk with his barons and uttered those infamous words which have echoed through nine centuries: "Will no one rid me of that turbulent priest?"; how the barons nudge-nudged and wink-winked and went and killed Becket in his cathedral.

The story is extremely well known. It was new to me. It was about friendship as passion, an absorbing subject for me, Alexandra's passionate friend. Something told me Alexandra's ultimate interest would be the Honour of God or whatever stood in its stead in her agnostic mind.

'Becket' was a mediocre film of a bad play. It was cliché-ridden: royal carousing, brainless barons, pretty French prostitute, Normans versus Saxons — just imagine, nationalism in the twelfth century, when the nations of Europe didn't even exist and people defined themselves by personal loyalties alone — and the inevitable cry of any King in any film: "I am the King!" The characters were not only flat but improbable and inconsistent in what they said and did. The King in particular appeared to have been patched together, vaguely justifying his incongruities by claiming to have been a stupid Norman oaf like his barons until Becket made an intelligent, sensitive man of him. That sort of thing just could not happen.

Becket himself did not manage to convince me of his search for honour which he was supposed to have found in defending the Honour of God. He did not even convince me that he believed in God.

The King, on the other hand, for all his irreverence — although, come to think of it, when and how does he show this irreverence which the playwright, Anouilh, obviously wants him to possess? — anyway, for all his irreverence, is a deeply religious man who fears God, respects God, resents God and is sometimes grateful to God while at other times despairing of Him — in a word, who has a meaningful relationship with God rather than using Him as a vehicle for self-justification.

The King shouts and screams a lot and makes a point of being rough and tough and lustful but he does that mainly to bolster his self-confidence in the face of the gaping, fanged, slavering jaws of Life.

For some reason it is his lot to have to cope with Life while it is Becket's lot to be spared — a funny thing to say, considering all that happened to him: the decisions he had to make, the responsibilities he had to take, the suicide of his girlfriend, the banishment, the bloody death at the hands of the King's men! Yet he is spared, standing outside Life. None of the things that happen to him *touch* him, not even death. He fears death like he would fear going to the dentist. He relates to events and people in his life as to means for achieving self-realisation or self-fulfilment, not as to objects or subjects in their own right.

While Becket strives to find meaning in Life which he fully understands but does not cherish, the King constantly struggles in Life's midst, fearful, trembling and defiant, loves it and is petrified at the thought of death.

Very little of that was meant to be in the play. The characters, as written, were much simpler and the issues the play dealt with quite different. To begin with, Becket was the hero of the play, not the King.

Sean Feeney upset Anouilh's apple-cart, I believe, quite unintentionally. He merely stepped into the King's shoes, fearful, trembling and defiant as he was, Sean Feeney, the lover of Life.

For the first time I began to understand what Alexandra and Forest and Eagerwill were on about. Standing in the King's shoes, Sean Feeney gave me a glimpse of it.

I understood smoking, for example, although the King, a twelfth century character, didn't smoke. I knew that, had cigarettes been available, the King would have smoked like a chimney, because smoking reduced trembling a little and fortified defiance.

I was proud to have learned to smoke. It made me believe I had defiance to fortify. I know now that I have none, because, not being threatened, I don't need any. I've stopped fooling myself. I don't smoke any more. (I *do*, actually. Again.) My smoking was very much like Becket's carousing: he imitated the King's worship of Life and his defiance. When he understood that life bored him and that he didn't need defiance, he stopped making an ass of himself and devoted his energy to more meaningful exploits.

I have this to say in favour of Becket and myself: our respective efforts to be like the King were almost heroic. I would say that we were like Andersen's Little Mermaid, but Thomas Mann has said it before me, about another person who was, like us, neither hot, nor cold, but indifferent. He said it about Adrian Leverkühn, a fictional German composer, the hero of Mann's novel 'Dr Faustus'. Only, I am not as courageous as the Little Mermaid, nor am I a genius like Leverkühn.

Sean Feeney — the King — is essentially like Alexandra: in Life, he is like fish in water. He is a Song.

I understand it all now when it no longer matters, one way or the other. It is not that Sean Feeney or Alexandra or Eagerwill or Forest in the course of their life have undergone more pain than Thomas Becket or I. It is not that life has dealt them harder blows. Quite simply, unlike Becket or myself, they have been and still are interested in the blows they receive. They pay attention. They stand up and confront Life with their whole being, aware that the confrontation is, at the same time, an act of acceptance. They know theirs is the lot of all living creatures and are willing to roll up their sleeves and deal with it. If their powers are adequate, they survive and manage to be happy from time to time. They never complain. They may curse their destiny or cry or silently despair, but they don't complain. One complains of headache and toothache, of inflation and taxes. One doesn't complain of suffering. Sometimes one cries out like Job did, but that is hardly a complaint.

I complain all the time, because I experience all pain like headache and toothache. Suffering is an inconvenience (for Becket and me) and life would be fine without it. Alexandra could never understand my point of view. How can life be without suffering? One is the essence of the other. One *is* the other.

Not for me. I want suffering to cease so that I can get on with my life. For example, when Nan lay on her deathbed, I had to look after her. As her condition worsened, my workload got heavier and more loathsome. I dreamed of an uninterrupted night's sleep. I dreamed of never having to smell urine again. Did I feel compassion? No, and yet I distinctly remember loving my Nan. I thought, "One day soon she'll die and I'll be able to get on with my life." Never mind not feeling compassion, one is not in the mood for it, perhaps, while emptying a bedpan at three o' clock in the morning. The bad thing about this whole affair was that it never occurred to me that I was living there and then. Instead, I complained right, left and centre. I remember how little sympathy I got from my friends. Melissa, my cousin, was the only one to give me moral support. She thought my predicament was appalling. But then again, Melissa is a Singer who has mistaken herself for a Song, an error not as tragic as it would be the other way round.

What did my life, the one I so badly wanted to get on with, consist of? It consisted of getting up late, doing a few chores I had to do, taking my dog walkies, drinking innumerable cups of coffee, smoking innumerable cigarettes — duty-free Rothmans when I could get hold of them — spending a few pleasant hours at the University, taking part in endless discussions with Alexandra, Eagerwill and Forest, watching TV, going to the cinema and, most important of all, reading books and messing about with pen and paper, trying to write books of my own.

I was happy like that but I didn't know it. Instead, I felt the moral obligation to Live a Life. I felt I had to have a boyfriend and desire independence from my parents

I know better now. No one has the moral obligation to live. One cannot live to order.

And here is another paradox: having arrived at this realisation, one breathes a sigh of relief and realises that one is, miraculously, alive at last! Isn't that amazing?

Had I known that summer in Cone what I know now, I would've paid more attention to Alexandra's pregnancy. Instead, I just writhed with frustration of not understanding Life like Alexandra did. If an abortion was the price of that precious knowledge, if that was the kind of pain that would cloud the glossy surface encasing my Self and allow me the glimpse of the real world, I believed I was ready to pay it. The trouble was, the Pain began by getting pregnant. One got pregnant by making love. For that, one needed to find a man. And all the men who were interested in me seemed to resemble Snotty. In order to be made love to, one had to endure an overture of mindless conversation, halfway through which one would yawn and that would be it. Anyway, I was too busy thinking about Sean Feeney. I would yawn as soon as the prospective lover opened his mouth. That, as I said, would be it.

Alexandra spoke openly about her knowledge. She told Forest and me about a dream she had: that she was brought before a strange man in black who must have been a Sage or a Mage and the Mage placed a tiny heart of gold on her palm. She had been a good student of Life so far, he said, and that was her reward. She must carry on and learn as much as she can and, when the time is right, she'll dream of the Mage again and he'll give her a diamond heart and it will mean that she has learned everything there is to know about Life.

I wonder if she has dreamt of the Mage again.

The night Alexandra dreamt of the Mage, or perhaps some other night like that one, I slept and I dreamt and here is my dream:

Sean Feeney stands with his back against the outside wall of the apse of a Norman cathedral. He is breathing heavily. His eyes are darting around in panic: he is surrounded by armed men who are holding him at gunpoint. They are all British and belong to a secret service of sorts: MI5, perhaps. They act for the Government or some other powerful authority. Sean Feeney's knowledge of Life and his freedom and creativity constitute a threat to that authority.

The Agents have obviously been instructed not to harm him. They try to coax him into obedience, to lure him into their custody, to make him see the advantage of fetters over freedom. If he gives himself up, they tell him, he'll remain almost completely free. He'll be permitted to be creative up to a certain point. Ah, but which point? Well, not really up to a point. He can be as creative as he likes, within reason. His freedom will be organised for him. He will really find it much easier to live than before. The most important thing is to be reasonable —

Sean Feeney sees right through their strategy: he is being called to move to the House of the Outcasts. He creeps along the apse wall, performing a strange kind of monodrama in proud, albeit hopeless refutation of the Agents' arguments. He speaks, I think, in blank verse, a clear case of *margaritas ante porcos*[2]. With his right hand, without looking, he draws a picture on the wall. It represents a window hung with net curtains, with geranium pots along the sill. The window overlooks a bleak vista of houses on the other side of the street: Ladbroke Grove on a rainy day springs to mind, or Potter's Bar. The image represents the life the MI5 have prepared for Sean Feeney. He knows that kind of life very well, Sean Feeney tells them in blank verse, he has tried to live like that, with geraniums and everything they represent, but couldn't keep it up because it is a lie and it is not in his nature to live a lie: he'd get all perverted and then he'd die.

Sean Feeney's defence is poetic and beautiful but sad because it is all in vain. He'll never agree to life in Potter's Bar with geraniums. The MI5 will have to seize him and make him, and he still won't be able to, and they'll make him and make him and sooner or later something will crack, most probably inside Sean Feeney.

Why geraniums? I don't know, but I understood, in my dream, all the fear and the loathing. I knew what the score was for Sean Feeney, his back against the wall.

To conclude the story of my holidays in Cone: I never saw Snotty again. After a fortnight of mixed anxiety and bliss, I left Alexandra and Forest and set out on my own to Vallegrande where I was to spend another fortnight, with Papa and Mama. I first had to take the coach to Split, the main ferry-port for the islands. If the coach got there on time, I would be able to catch the midday ferry to Vallegrande.

I left Cone by ferry at four in the morning for the tiny port of Whitton where I boarded the coach for Split. Just before departure, a young, bashful Coneman slid into the seat next to

---

2 Pearls before swine

mine. He was very tall, suntanned to perfection and extremely blond. His eyebrows and eyelashes were white. His eyes were picture postcard blue. He was dressed in a white sailor's uniform. He was a Navy National Serviceman returning to his ship. His name was Paul. He was nineteen.

I know I keep on about 'Lord Jim', but has anyone actually read that book? Remember how Conrad describes Jim? His Jim looked like Paul, not like Sean Feeney. Jim blushed. It had to be important or Conrad wouldn't have mentioned it. And Sean Feeney doesn't blush, he blenches.

Paul blushed all the time.

On the coach, he told me all about himself. I don't remember a single thing. I told him all about myself. We shared sandwiches. He had one of mine. I had one of his. We had coffee from my thermos.

Halfway to Split, the coach had a puncture. All the passengers got off and walked about while the driver and the conductor changed the wheel. It was hot. The sky was white, the road was white, the stony ground was white. The olive trees were grey. Their leaves were grey.

Paul and I walked around hand in hand and he kissed me. He kissed me on the mouth. It wasn't too bad. He didn't want to part my lips, not much. His tongue didn't probe.

Paul blushed crimson. He walked on, quite fast. He kept his eyes on me and smiled. Thus, passing under an olive tree, he hit his forehead on a low branch. A bump sprouted over his right eyebrow. It grew very large and red. I found a cool stone in the shadow and held it against the bump to make it better.

Paul gave me his photograph and wrote his name on the back. I still have it.

I caught the ferry in Split. The coach was not very late. The timetable, it would appear, allowed for a puncture per journey.

Paul changed coaches and went to the southern port of Flats to join his ship. He wrote to me once. I wrote back. Then we wrote no more.

Second Meditation: Life on the Sun

Does anyone know a film by Ingmar Bergman, called 'Scenes From a Marriage'? It is about a couple approaching mid-life crisis. Their marriage is on the rocks, not because of infidelity (although there is a bit of that, too, more as a symptom than as the root cause of the problem) but because both the husband and the wife have lost confidence in themselves and the life choices they'd made.

There is a particularly interesting moment in the film when Marianne, the wife, who is a lawyer specialising in divorce, interviews a client, a middle-aged woman determined to divorce her husband for no particular reason. She no longer loves him, she says, and there is no reason for her to go on living with him. Moreover, she realises she never loved him. Does she believe she's likely to find love somewhere else? No. In a loveless marriage, however, she feels she is somehow being slowly, painlessly extinguished as a person and, even more seriously, as a being.

Marianne, who at first regards the woman with I'm-better-off-than-you sort of pity, suddenly begins to pay attention. And then the woman says, "Have you noticed that the world around one does not seem as colourful as it used to be? That the sights and the sounds of it are perceived through a kind of a semi-transparent grey film?"

Close-up on Marianne's face. Bonnng! (There is no actual "Bonnng!" sound in the film, but for years I imagined that there was.)The blow has struck home. It is obvious that she knows what her client is talking about. Somewhat shakily, she asks the woman if she believes the grey film will go away once she is free of her husband. No, the woman replies, but at least she'll be able to respect herself again. She owes that much to herself now that her children have grown up and she does not owe anyone else anything any more. It is entirely possible that she is heading for disaster, but if she settles for the status quo, she is as good as dead.

Bonnnng! At a certain moment in your life, you discover that you're viewing the world through a grey film. And when you do, you realise it has been so for quite some time, only it took you a while to notice.

It is absolutely true. It's happened to me.

It could be partly explained by the deterioration that age brings to one's eyesight and hearing. Partly. Because contact lenses and hearing aids do not cure it.

It is, and I firmly believe that to be true, a matter of redistributing one's attention. When you're young, and I do not mean young in years alone, you have most of your attention at your disposal to use as you please. You use it to look at the world around you and to listen to it. And the world is full of colour and sound. Even the gloomiest street in the gloomiest town in the world on a rainy day is full of colour and sound. The colour is grey, not associated with drabness if drabness doesn't bother you, and the sound is pitter-patter.

Some years later, when you've acquired a shop, a gloomy rainy day will mean that you'll have few customers. Or, if you merely work in the shop, that the boss will have few customers and will begin to contemplate getting rid of you because he can handle the work himself. Or maybe you'll be unemployed, but will have acquired other responsibilities, like a family, in which case rain will mean dragging heavy shopping with one wet slippery hand while trying to hold the umbrella straight with the other wet slippery hand, maybe with children and a dog in tow. If you can afford any shopping to drag, that is. If you can't, you'll worry about your poverty.

Whichever of those be the case, your attention will not be on the grey or on the pitter-patter. It will be on the details of your job or on the carrier-bag in your hand and the rain and the gloom will have become concepts, not sensations. A grey film will have covered the world and would have done so even if the day were sunny, with roses blooming in every garden.

That film is not sadness. It is not boredom. It is not the symptom of being fed up. It is merely a grey film, no more, no less. You cannot spare attention for perceiving the world and it goes out of focus. It does so even for very happy people enjoying their life.

There is only so much attention in any one of us.

How and when does our attention begin to shift from the colour and the sound of the world to other matters? When we have to do the Necessary. Remember how you hated to do whatever was Necessary when you were little? To brush your teeth? To eat at regular times? To go to bed at nine? To go to bed at all? It was Necessary and that was enough for you to hate it. To say please and thank you. To put away your toys. To flush the loo.

It was not so much that you resented being told. It was the fact that it was Necessary and there was a lifetime of it ahead.

How one loves to postpone the Necessary, even when grown up! One lingers on after midnight, half-asleep, but does not go to bed, even though going to bed would fulfil a genuine need of one's own, not merely please a parent who is probably dead anyway. One puts Necessary things off even when they're pleasant.

Only the Necessary demands a purposeful focussing of attention. The rest is the energy flow of the Universe. Our attention is naturally focussed on it.

The only real holiday is the holiday from the Necessary. We simulate it by taking ersatz holidays which also consist of the never-ending Necessary. We simulate it a bit more effectively by taking drugs. There are other means, too.

One of the reasons so many young people take to drugs these days is the fact that we, the parents, have failed to teach them to do the Necessary. We were too afraid of their anger and hatred. Perhaps we ourselves were not as convinced of the necessity of the Necessary as our parents used to be.

Most of our parents were intrepid doers of the Necessary. We are somewhat less so. God knows how our children's children will cope.

As long as we do the Necessary only under duress, the grey film does not exist. The moment we begin doing it willingly is the moment of its first appearance. That is also the moment we become grownups. It can happen at six and it can happen at sixty. In many cases it never happens. I know it from experience. It happened to me at forty. It happened in a nanosecond.

All real grownups are good at doing the Necessary. (There is such a thing as a fake grownup — millions of them.). Not all of them enjoy being grown up. Those who don't are unhappy people. Those who do — and there are those who do — are happy people who make other people happy. That doesn't mean they jump around with joy all the time. They can even suffer. But they are happy people.

Of course, they see everything through a grey film. They often don't notice because they don't have time, and if they do, they blame it on myopia or astigmatism. Who cares?

The grey film is the price.

What happens to those who don't learn how to handle the Necessary, and don't become drug addicts or schizophrenics? They never suffer because of what other people do to them, and are never happy because of what other people do to them. Or because of what they do to other people. They suffer: toothache if their teeth ache, deprivation if they're deprived, fear if they're afraid, and so on. Colours and sounds and dogs and sunshine and so on make them happy. My mother Patricia was like that. She never lost sight of the energy flow of the Universe, even when she'd become almost blind.

The question is, is it possible to focus on the Necessary and not lose sight of the energy flow of the Universe?

In the ordinary course of events, no. I don't think it is. It sounds grim, but, as Robert Heinlein would say, TANSTAAFL: There Ain't No Such Thing As A Free Lunch.

However.

There appear to be people who, after years of following a certain discipline, become able to integrate the Necessary into the energy flow of the Universe. The Necessary *becomes* the energy flow of the Universe. That is radical, if it can be done. Mind you, the Necessary must not cease being Necessary, otherwise there is no merit and nothing has been achieved. Such people are called the Realised Masters, perhaps, but also go under other names, depending on the particular tradition they represent. Their discipline, likewise, goes under various names. Information about them can be found in books and on the internet. If one is bothered by the grey film, it would pay to investigate.

The Necessary was a large part of what Alexandra meant when she went on about Life, because without it there can be no serious engagement with other people. I did not know about it then, although I wrestled with it day and night.

When did I learn about it? When I turned forty. I have already mentioned that. I began doing the Necessary much earlier, but not of my own free will. I did it for any number of reasons, mainly because I wanted Mama to carry on being nice to me. Because I wanted the status quo to go on forever. If I did some Necessary stuff, I was guaranteed time to indulge in the energy flow of the Universe in comfort.

As years went on, the proportion of the Necessary in the total of my disposable time grew and I began to sense a future taken up entirely by the Necessary. I began to feel trapped and depressed. I felt I was not getting value for my input. Nothing significant was ever going to happen to me. I was going to live through a succession of days and nights, and then die. (That is what actually happens to everyone: we live through a succession of days and nights and then we die.)

One night, depressed as I was, I slept and I dreamt and here is my dream:

Terminal overpopulation and unbearable living conditions have forced mankind to abandon Earth and move to the Sun. How come? In my dream, it has been discovered that under the Sun's deadly photosphere there exists an atmosphere and a hard surface able to support organic life. A way has been found to penetrate the photosphere and settle on the surface of the Sun.

Only sheer despair could have driven mankind to such a decision because the surface of the Sun is a ghastly place, veiled in perpetual night with an orangey glow in the sky similar to that over the Earth's major cities at night, and oppressed by uncomfortable heat and stifling humidity. The settlers adhere to a twenty-four hour cycle which bears no relationship to the Sun's rotation.

Cities which are exact copies of existing cities on Earth are being built, with people moving in all the time. The overcrowding, the poverty and the squalor are unbearable, and so is the realisation that there can be no return to Earth if something goes wrong with the colony.

My parents, my grandparents and I have been allocated a flat, jointly with another family, in the exact replica of the Proletarian Brigades Avenue, in the exact replica of Agram. Alexandra and Forest have also arrived, with their families. We all try our hardest not to change our habits and live as if nothing has happened. I visit my friends as before and generally try to make myself busy, but I am in fact cracking under the burden of sadness and misery brought about by the realisation that Life on the Sun will never cease, meaningless as it is. It will only end in death, which may come any moment, since the colonisation of the Sun has been made in a rush, with insufficient preliminary research, and no one can really say whether the very next moment we might not all be wiped out by some unforeseen natural catastrophe.

I feel, and I am probably right, that, having laboured so hard to create an illusion of Earthly normalcy, we suffer more by living within the confines of our lie than if we had recognised the fact that we are no longer Earthlings and tried to live like Sunlings instead.

So there I am, with my family, crowded into a small, damp, smelly bedroom with another family of complete strangers, trying to sleep on a bunk bed. We all have to endure another charming feature of Life on the Sun: every night, everywhere, in the streets and inside the houses, underground water rises and floods everything up to the level of about four feet.

I seem to have forgotten about the water and have chosen a very low bunk. Surely enough, just as I'm ready to drift off to blessed sleep, the water rises and my bed is submerged. I must get up, dry my clothes (I only have one set), and find another, higher bunk. By the time I'd done all that, the "morning" will have probably come and I will have had no sleep. Again. Because it has all happened before. And will happen again. And again. It will never stop. And it hasn't stopped to this very day.

3. Socket

Vampire

What happened after Cone? Alexandra, Vicky and I matriculated[1]. We were all to go to the University. That was taken for granted. We *owed* it to ourselves. Our parents wanted good careers for us. My father did not want me to be a worker like he had been. Alexandra's father did not want her to be a restaurant manager.

Here and now, it sounds weird. Compositors are not considered to be working class: printing is a *trade*. Restaurant managers earn good money. They are respectable people. Back there in Agram, a restaurant manager was regarded as a sort of clown. He had to say 'please' and 'thank you' and smile at customers even when he did not feel like smiling. He was in the service industry. He was a servant. People would put their money on the table and because of that he had to jump when they said "hop". In Croatian, you say "Hop!" when you jump.

Vicky's father wanted his daughter to be a professor like he. That was all right. Vicky *wanted* to study philosophy.

---

1 Completed our A-levels.

Philosophy was held in awe. It took discipline to sit and think abstract thoughts. It was supposed to give one insight into the ultimate truths about Life.

Alexandra was going to study medicine. She wanted to do something real for mankind, not something airy-fairy. She wanted to grapple with Life.

Forest was already studying Indology.

I decided to study English, the language of Sean Feeney, in order to get closer to him that way. What else did I expect to gain from my studies? I don't remember; probably nothing at all. I hoped to go and live in the United Kingdom one day. Perhaps that was all there was to it.

Before matriculation, the entire secondary school went on a trip, or trips, as each form chose its own destination. My form, the Fourth C, went to Austria. It was no fun to travel around one's own country. One did that at the end of primary school.

In view of what took place in Yugoslavia later, that primary school trip looms large in my memory. We went to Bosnia.

Bosnia was the arena where the most gruesome, the bloodiest, the most heroic, the most sung-about events of the Partisan campaign in the Second World War had taken place. It bored us kids to death even to think about it. For us, born after the war, Bosnia was the place where casual labourers came from, builders, navvies, waiters, that kind of people. We made jokes about Bosnia similar to jokes about the Irish made here, in Britain, or American jokes about Poles.

I didn't know Alexandra then, and had yet to discover Sean Feeney. I was fat, with huge thighs. Men kept making passes at me. I had no clue of what they were after. As far as I knew, I was not a woman. Women looked like Lauren Bacall and came in black and white. They were courted by men like Humphrey Bogart. Women who did not look like that and men who did not look like that were not women and men. They were girls and boys, or mothers and fathers, or teachers, or workers, or aunts and uncles. They worked or shopped or cooked for their children.

I was a girl, not a woman. I could not understand what a

lorry driver, not a man, wanted from me when he shouted and make lewd gestures, but it scared me.

Most of my schoolmates were different. They flirted and went to disco clubs. I only danced at school parties, and each time my dress would split.

My best friends were boys who had problems with dating girls because they couldn't muster enough interest for silly mating games while serious matters like science, exploration and adventure demanded their attention. They also happened to be fringe characters: a grotesquely fat blond boy with a fine nose, pale eyes, sensitive mouth and devastating wit, nicknamed Parrot; an unruly, antisocial, delinquent genius called Darius, who could not read and write properly but was, for his own pleasure, learning Classical Greek; a spoiled rich brat who knew everything and was the only one to have better marks than I, but was uncontrollable and a wonderful liar and actor — we called him Broff. He was skinny and squirrel-like.

I had two girlfriends, Wisteria and Georgina. Wisteria was tall, dark, quiet, hard-working and desperately poor. Georgina was very, very small, wiry, muscular, jovial, smart, unfazed by anything and, like Wisteria, poor. She had a younger sister and an older brother who had learning difficulties. Her mother was a factory canteen cook. I do not remember her father. Georgina was extremely loyal to me, because I told her stories on our way home from school. I had read those stories in children's books. Georgina had no time to read. She had to cook and shop and look after her baby sister.

I didn't like the others, not much. They made fun of me. They made me face myself as I really was, when I imagined myself as Hayley Mills. (Does anyone remember Hayley Mills? Sir John Mills' daughter? 'The Parent Trap'? Ring any bells? No? Oh.)

Once –during that trip to Bosnia, perhaps – one of the posh boys, one of the teasers who used to hang out with teaser girls, suddenly came up to me and dropped on his knees in front of me. His knees actually touched my feet. He clasped his hands together in supplication. "Darling," he said, "I love you. I adore you. I cannot live without you. Be mine. Please say yes." And on. And on.

I stood there paralysed, in shock. He moved forward on his knees. They were warm. That, too, shocked me. He had a clean-cut, small, foxy face and glossy, golden hair. His name was Goldie. Something had to be wrong. I knew in my bones, my stomach, my lungs that he would sooner kiss a toad than touch me. Yet he clasped my hands, on the verge of tears!

But I could not face the knowledge in my bones! My head swam. I looked down on him and thought, "Now I'm just like everyone else. I can finally be friends with Olga and Mary and Beata and go to their parties." I did not like Goldie. And then I did! His face was suddenly beautiful! In defiance of my wise bones, a strange, sick, mellow feeling rose inside me. My eyes began to water.

Goldie moved closer, squashing me against the wall. Or against the bus? Where the hell did that scene take place?

"Goldie... no... please," I mumbled, tore myself away and fled. When I stopped and looked back, Goldie had already got up and joined the teasers. Where had they been during the scene? I don't know.

They did not laugh. They whispered among themselves and looked at me. Smiled.

Incredibly, I held on to the dream for a few seconds more. "Laugh, damn you!" I thought, "Then I'll know where I am." They did not laugh.

But I did know where I was. And they did laugh, later. For days. They acted the scene out to one another. Goldie had, apparently, done it for a bet. Or maybe from pure malice. He had cold eyes.

In Bosnia, I stayed close to Parrot, Darius and Broff. I missed out on clandestine drinking, smoking and groping, but I did see the subterranean temple of Mithra. I did crawl into the cave behind the monster waterfall of Eggy and stood there while the wind drove my hair vertically upwards. The teasers did not do that. They were too busy playing power games with each other. They were rehearsing their future lives.

I bore them no grudge. On the contrary, I envied them. I blamed myself for being unattractive and inadequate. And I was right! They were the brave ones. They were eager to grow up and live among their own kind, according to rules, because they were *interested* in their own kind. They were prepared to undergo the rigours of training. They were able to forego the thrills of waterfalls and ancient temples for the sake of that training. (Of course, because they were children, they thought that temples bored them to death.)

As a trainee human being, I was lazy and cowardly. I wanted the instant gratification of waterfalls.

But without training there can be no prowess. And lazy and cowardly beings are never attractive.

I'm not moaning. I'm glad I understand these things now. I keep going on about them because I think it may be useful for other people to understand them, too. Those who already do may be pleased to find out that they have company.

Back to Bosnia: we were taken to see the hidden bowels of a hydroelectric plant. We walked over the concrete dam. We could see huge trout swirling in the clear water at the base of the dam. It was cloudy and wet. It was mysterious, deep in the Bosnian mountains. On the other side of the dam, we approached the sheer face of the cliff and the rock opened for us. It swallowed us and closed after us.

Inside there were corridors, offices and a control-room with lights, maps, dials and screens, all straight out of science-fiction movies. Further on, in an enormous cave, there was a steel gallery overlooking huge generators underneath. The walls were bare rock. It was Wagnerian, but at that time I knew nothing about Wagner.

We were taken down another long corridor, to a vast, dark space full of wires, transformers and other objects I could not quite identify. We were told to keep our arms tight to our sides, walk in a single file and not touch anything. They told us we were surrounded by billions of volts of power. We could hear the power hiss. Or maybe it was just the tension in the murk. Still, I swear I heard the power hiss.

The hydroelectric plant was even better than the waterfall.

The rest of the Bosnian trip is a blur.

I remember standing by a wooden fence in the middle of the night. Broff is beside me, leaning on the fence. Over our heads, a streetlight shimmers through the leaves of a plum-tree heavy with half-ripe plums. Broff is smoking a cigarette. We are not talking about anything. We are listening. For what?

Afterwards, I go to bed. It is a kind of dormitory with no washing facilities. The bed-linen is grey. I lift my pillow and find two large spiders sitting there.

The rest, like I said, is a blur.

Years later, Parrot visited me out of the blue. He was as fat and as blond as ever. We looked at old snaps, had coffee and smoked a cigarette together. He told me he was working in Germany and had come home on a short visit. Then he said, "I've always loved you. Did you know?"

My jaw dropped. "You never!"

Surely people like Parrot never fell in love with anyone! (Surely I deserved better than to be anyone, someone that Parrot could fall in love with for lack of choice.) (To be sure, Parrot was a very nice person, but still.)

"That's not all," Parrot said in his calm, quiet manner. "I still love you."

He must have been an adult even back then in Bosnia, because he never let on. True, he slept on my shoulder on the bus, but that was because he had got drunk and had been sick into a plastic bag.

"Are we going to do something about it?" Parrot asked and lit another cigarette.

"Look," I said, "you were my best friend, but — "

"I see," said Parrot and got up. "In that case, I'll go back to Germany." He kissed me on the cheek. "Bye," he said and left.

Parrot, if you can hear me, you're a Big Bwana man. Big Bwana men, however, often don't get the girl, like Tom Doniphon in 'The Man Who Shot Liberty Valance' didn't.

Incredibly, only a few months later, Darius turned up, likewise fresh from Germany. He was married and running his own business. He wore an ill-fitting suit and would have looked an absolute prat but for his smouldering madness. One could catch glimpses of it like red-hot cracks in a cooling flow of lava on the slopes of a live volcano.

He bragged and boasted of his successes and then he said, "You know what? I've been in love with you all this time."

"I never knew," I said sheepishly and truthfully.

"Even now," he said.

"But you are married," I said, like a whole flock of sheep being sheepish. "What about your wife?"

"What about her?" He grinned his lunatic grin. I shrugged and said, "Nothing, I suppose. But I'm not in love with you."

"That's all right," grinned Darius. "I'll be off then. If you need money or anything else, let me know. Here's my business card." He gave me his card and departed.

In a daze, I searched my notes for Broff's phone number. I had to know. He was the only one of the three whom I'd found remotely attractive. I did get through to him, but he could never find time to meet me. He had a good job and was busy making money. He came from that sort of family.

Later I saw Georgina, once, and Wisteria, once. And, years later, I managed to see Olga, one of the teaser girls. She had become an actress, got married, had two children and got divorced. She lived in Whiteburg. She was profoundly unhappy. Meeting her depressed me because I wanted her to be happy. I used to idolise her and imitate her handwriting. I never saw anyone else, afterwards. I never shall. I'm pretty certain of that. It has nothing to do with moving out of Agram.

Mama had also left her home town, a few years before I was born, and yet, look what happened to her one fine summer when I was just about to turn seventeen!

That June, Mama had taken a couple of days off work to visit Eszeg, the town where she was born and educated. The occasion was the twenty-fifth anniversary of her matriculation.

In Yugoslavia, we make much of such anniversaries.

(There is no more Yugoslavia, but I intend to finish this story the way I started it. It makes more sense that way. Trees, after all, grow there still. And mountains mountain. And the sea seas. This, at least, I know for a fact, although I'll have a word or two to say on the subject somewhere towards the end of the book.)

So Mama put her dentures in and off she went. She was only forty two, but she went around without her dentures. And she had a full set! She had all her teeth pulled out when she was thirty. The dentures hurt her mouth. They could have been adjusted but she had never made the Necessary Steps to have it done.

She is at the moment going blind with glaucoma. An operation could save her sight, but she does not want to take the Necessary Steps. (At the moment of *writing* this chapter, that is. As you *read* this, she is dust.)

I know where she's coming from. The Necessary Steps are my bane, too. They injure one's spirit. Life consists mainly of taking Necessary Steps. That is why we tend to find life hard and full of pain. There is, however, a neat trick by means of which one can take the Necessary Steps without injuring the spirit. Some people know that trick. Such people are popular and everyone seeks their company, to bask in their sunshine. I've said that before, but it will not hurt to repeat it.

No, I don't know the trick. But I ought to know it. Everyone ought to. There should be a law about it — in fact, there is a law about it. It is not part of any canon, and yet it exists. How do I know? Very simply: whoever does not know the trick gets severely punished sooner or later.

In Eszeg, Mama found her old schoolmates. I have recently seen snaps of that reunion. They show middle-aged men and women in a classroom, seated at battered desks covered all over in names and comments carved by generations of students. The men are wearing suits. The women are wearing frilly blouses, dark skirts and tiny feminine wristwatches. Their hair is permed and sprayed with hair-spray. Most of them smoke cigarettes. Their faces are ravaged when compared with average forty-something faces of today. Their bodies are podgy and self-conscious. Their meat is meek. They look like a bunch of very nice people who all have problems with taking Necessary Steps.

Mama is definitely the most interesting person in the pictures. Why? Because everybody else, in spite of finding it hard and painful, had been taking all the Necessary Steps that needed to be taken. Mama had not. Consequently, her spirit was not injured. Her everyday life, though, was an unholy mess.

On all the photos she is standing or sitting close to a fat, tall, fair-haired, mellow-eyed man.

She came back and said she'd had a lovely time. I was busy slimming and worrying about Sean Feeney and Alexandra, so I accepted her statement at face value and immediately forgot all about it. In fact, I was sorry she had returned so soon. Never before had I spent two whole days at home without her being about. The experience was very agreeable. Papa was less permissive but, by the same token, less demanding than Mama. His wrath was usually no more than storm in a teacup. He found it difficult to keep on being angry. He was not relentless in taking offence. He gave one a break.

Some two weeks later, one Sunday afternoon while Papa was playing tennis in the sunshine at his sports club, Mama suddenly chose to make a confession. She flung herself on the double bed where Michael the dog and I lay wrestling and growling at each other and told me that she had fallen in love.

Magic words. You utter them and whoever is within earshot becomes your ally and accomplice. You are encouraged, supported, given tea and biscuits, champagne. It's happened to you: that means it can happen to any person... Life is possible.

If you don't offer enthusiastic support to a person In Love, you reject the value that lies at the core of the Western Civilisation. Who would be crazy enough to do that? Worse, you might be implying that you are not In Love (or have never been In Love) and who dares not to be In Love?

I fell for it, of course. It meant that Mama did not love Papa. Had stopped loving Papa. Maybe never had loved Papa. Amazingly, I failed to make this obvious deduction. Why? "Who with," I said, "and when did it happen?"

"In Eszeg," said Mama. "He's one of my old schoolmates."

"What is he like?" I was curious. What sort of bloke could win my mother's heart? (Meaning that I must have known all the time that Papa didn't win it, was not that sort of bloke.)

Mama opened her mouth to answer, but I put my finger on her lips. For a moment I felt all-knowing and all-powerful. "Don't say anything," I said and smiled. "I'll tell you what he's like. He's a Pierre Bezoukhov."

Pierre Bezoukhov is the good, sweet, bumbling, overweight hero of 'War and Peace' by Leo Tolstoy. He wins the heroine, Natasha Rostova. Tolstoy had to work very hard to make it happen. He had to kill off Prince Andrei Bolkonsky, or Pierre would not have stood a chance. He gave a lot of space to Pierre's inner life and his soul's torments. He made Pierre's soul survive all the torments because Pierre was, above all, *good.*

Goodness was Mama's religion. It turned her on. How sincere her regard for goodness was and whether or not she would know goodness when she met it, I was not qualified to answer at the time.

"How did you guess?" Mother said, impressed. "Yes, that's exactly what he's like."

I have completely forgotten that man's name. Mother and I called him Pierre between us from that day on. That made us a kind of members-only club.

Apparently, Pierre had loved her in secondary school, without hope of ever being loved back. So devoid of hope was he that he never spoke out. He passed by the beautiful, haughty, long-haired Patricia Prochazka like a shadow in the night. He went on to live his small, ordinary life full of goodness and empty of romance. He held a good job, was married and had a daughter of seventeen; exactly my age.

My next question to Mother was, "Did you sleep with him?"

"Yes," she replied, "once."

"And?"

"He said it was like Holy Mass."

Mama was not religious, and neither was Pierre, I was told later. Yet he must have said what he had said in all earnestness, without a trace of irony.

"I rely on you not to share this with anyone," Mama said. "Absolutely no one must know".

"I promise," I said at once, without pausing to remember that 'no one' meant Papa, too. Thus I found myself in a covenant with Mama against Papa. *Why?* If I was to be honest, I knew he was a more deserving human being than she. But Mama was In Love and Love was the override switch.

"I must ask you to look after these letters for me," Mama said and handed me a bundle of them. There were more than four as far as I could see without counting, and scarcely a month had passed since the inception of the Pierre affair. "He writes to a colleague of ours here in Agram," Mama explained, "and I collect the letters from her. We arranged that in Eszeg. Hide them in your wardrobe; Papa never rummages through it."

Indeed, Papa had too much respect for my privacy to rummage through my wardrobe. Mama, on the other hand, had no qualms about rummaging through it. Yet I made a covenant with her, against Papa. Such is the corrupting power of Love.

I'd managed to keep my smoking secret for four years because Papa did not rummage through my wardrobe. I kept my fags there.

"You'll meet Pierre one of these days," Mama warbled. "That is, if you want to."

How could I not want to? I wanted to.

In the autumn Pierre came to Agram on business for a day and stayed overnight in a hotel. Mama was to meet him in a restaurant. I picked her up after work and she and I traipsed the hot streets of Agram for two hours looking for a place called 'The Three Doves' or 'The Three Turkeys' or 'The Three Sparrows', Mama was not sure which. She found the place on her own, later.

In November, I accompanied her to Eszeg for a short holiday.

We checked into a hotel called 'The Royal'. It was an old place, pleasant and seedy. Mama had booked two bedrooms. I was to sleep in one, while Pierre and she were to celebrate Holy Mass in the other.

Mama went upstairs to make herself presentable after the trip. I was to remain on watch downstairs in the bar and hold Pierre up when he comes. I did not know what he looked like. Mama gave me a brief description and said I'd recognise him at once.

I had a miserable time waiting for Pierre in the bar. I was not used to sitting alone in cafés — without Alexandra or Forest, that is. I felt abandoned by Mama. I felt she had no business involving me in such a direct way in what was her own intimate affair.

At the same time I felt proud and excited because this, surely, had to be Life at long last! Dim lights in the bar, I alone with an espresso and a cigarette, like a real person (like Sean Feeney, perhaps), waiting for my mother's lover! (No, I thought, despairing for a moment, neither Sean Feeney nor Alexandra would be waiting for their mother's lover.) It was life all right, but it was Mama's life, not mine.

She took her time up there in her room, Mama did. Meanwhile, down in the bar, I wrote a poem. Into a notebook. Into which I wrote poems regularly. I had the notebook on me in the bar. Conveniently. Got that?

This is what I wrote:

> As I sit here, as here I languish
> Under men's stares, I shrink in anguish.
> Their eyes infest my body like lice;
> They fancy me, they assess my price.
> What would she charge, they wonder, I bet,
> As at my table I fidget and fret.

All dogs are asleep: the hour is late.
Vampire rises from his crate.
Coffin, it should have been coffin, but coffin didn't rhyme.
To continue:

Tucked up in bed lie young maidens all
As I drain slowly my cupful of gall.
The clock on the wall coughs up a chime.
Come to a stop, o endless time!

Before me a glass, faintly glowing.
An ashtray full to overflowing.
Sod this life, sod all! Sod! Sod! Sod!
If only I could pray to God...

Did I really feel that way? No. Did I wish to pray to God?
No. But then, poets often don't what they say they do.

On cue, in answer to my unprayed prayer, Pierre walked in.
Mama was right; I recognised him at once. He looked around, I
half got up. He saw me, reached me in two large steps and took
my hand. "Hello," he said, "I'm X."

I cannot remember his name, damn the man!

"Hello," I said. "Patricia will be down in a minute." I said
Patricia, not Mama. That was how I felt.

She did come down almost immediately. I think they kissed,
or maybe not. Eszeg is a small town and Pierre was probably
known to more than one person in the bar. Then they both
looked at me, beaming. "She's the image of you," said Pierre to
Patricia.

Mama told me to go to bed. She and Pierre would go for a
walk and return later. When I wake up in the morning, I was to
come down for breakfast. Pierre would be gone by then: he d'
have to go to work.

To bed I went and tried to wait up for Mama and Pierre.
After all, they were to sleep in the adjoining room. The murky
light and the muffled sounds of Eszeg came in through the
window when I switched off the light. I felt sick to my stomach,
but the sickness was not really in the stomach.

To call a spade a spade, I was outraged at the thought of someone other than Papa fucking the pussy I came out of.

I cried a bit, then fell asleep, because I was healthy and well fed.

Some time later, Mama and I talked about prospects and possibilities. After the Eszeg experience, I felt entitled to discuss anything with her. All her business was my business, because I had slept in the other room.

"What are your plans?" I wanted to know.

"I don't know," said Mama.

"Why don't you divorce Papa and go and live with Pierre? Have you discussed it with him?"

"I have," said Mama.

"Well?"

"It doesn't depend entirely on me. He has a family."

"His daughter is quite grown up," I said, "and so am I. You two should be thinking of yourselves."

"You and Papa need me," said Mama. "And Nan and Grandpa! I have my obligations."

"We don't need your sacrifice," I said magnanimously, not aware of the wound I'd inflicted upon Mama's conceit. This kind of conceit is often all some people have to live on. I didn't know that then. "Papa and I can manage perfectly well by ourselves. And we can look after Nan and Grandpa. You cannot remain in thrall to your parents all your life."

Meaning that I intended staying with Papa, not with Mama. She gave me a sharp predatory look. I think she made up her mind there and then to give up the love of her life.

"I don't think Pierre and I are ready to destroy two families," she said, looking away, her eyes filling with tears. "Maybe it will become possible one day, but not now."

"Oh, do go away and be happy," I went on. By then, my wise blood, stomach and bones had sensed what was going on. Who, however, can resist the licence to hurt one's nearest and dearest?

I certainly couldn't. I had to twist the knife in the wound. "Papa and I will be all right. I don't mind, honestly I don't.

You're simply afraid of taking the decisive step. Afraid of change."

I was right, of course. There was no need to check that with Alexandra or Dostoevsky. I knew. Because, yea verily, I was like Mama myself.

Mama did not leave us. She and Pierre met from time to time. They wrote. Papa eventually found out (or had perhaps known from day one) but never spoke to me about it. And I never admitted I knew.

Later, I went to live in the UK. Before leaving, at Mama's request, I burned in the kitchen stove all the letters she'd entrusted to my keeping.

We had a lovely coal-fired stove in the kitchen. In the winter, Papa used to light it at five AM sharp. He would then sit for half an hour and listen to the "wooh-wooh-wooh" of the young fire.

There were to be no more letters. The affair had ended: Pierre and Patricia had decided there was no future in it nor would there ever be any.

I seldom saw Papa once I got married, and when I did, the moment was never right for me to confess my treachery. Then he died. And he must have known! He must have waited for me to broach the subject. He had a lot of patience. He had probably been waiting to see whether I had guts enough. Whether I had what it took.

I did not. I never had guts enough to string a racket.

That night at The Royal, I slept indecently soundly for the circumstances, and as I slept I dreamt the following dream:

I am somewhere abroad, in a hotel, old and not very large, but respectable. The hotel was full when I arrived. The only option for me was to book into a room with two other new arrivals, both men. One of them turns out to be a surly European who never takes his hat off, and the other one is a young Japanese man, pleasant and good-looking in an ethereal sort of way. Our room is not very comfortable; it is dark and full of creaking wood: creaking floor-boards, creaking wardrobes, heavy creaking doors. We hardly bother to undress before hastily repairing to our respective beds.

In the dead of night, a vampire comes and attacks us. Glowing with a bluish light, he appears to be in an advanced state of decomposition, and is absolutely terrifying. We fight it off and escape, managing somehow to survive the night. In the morning, the surly gentleman with the hat and I persuade the management to find us another room. The hotel is buzzing with talk about the vampire. The room we'd spent the previous night in is his habitual haunt, but his last visit was years ago and people have all but forgotten him.

While sorting my luggage out in the new room, I notice that I have left something behind. I return to the old room to fetch it and, as I open the wardrobe, I see that the young Japanese man has not checked out. He is there, lost in thought, arranging some objects on his bed. Collecting my things, I turn to him and ask him, "Aren't you afraid of the vampire?" "No," he replies with a melancholy smile.

At that moment I remember being told that the vampire was, in fact, a Japanese Prince who'd committed suicide or had been murdered in that very room. I also remember the fact that the Japanese youth in the room is also a Prince or royalty of some kind. Of course! That is why he is not afraid of the vampire. He *is* the vampire.

I look into his eyes and see that he knows I know. I suddenly feel sorry for him, and at the same time wish to show off my compassion and fearlessness. I reach out to him to give him a brotherly kiss. He seems to accept my offer of friendship and our faces drift closer. His face is white and painted like an actor's in a Noh play. His lips part slowly, revealing huge, sharp canines dripping with saliva, and bleeding, rotting gums which exude an unspeakable stench. A low growl rumbles in his throat as the long-dead Japanese Prince sinks his teeth into my jugular and begins to suck.

I screamed myself awake, but I must have screamed only in my head, because no one had heard me, so I went back to sleep.

In the morning, Mama and I had soft-boiled eggs and went for a walk. I liked Eszeg. It reminded me of how Agram used to look when I was a baby.

Years after Papa's death, Mama's love story repeated itself, however unlikely it may sound. The second time round, it had a much darker mood. That is the general way of things in this world. The fair maiden turns into a hag the second time round. I learned that from mythology. And from Jung, Karl Gustav. He was Freud's disciple. Freud and Jung are like Marx and Engels or Laurel and Hardy: their names are paired forever. But Marx was cleverer than Engels, more profound. And Jung was cleverer than Freud, more profound. Or maybe not. Slavoj Žižek thinks he wasn't.

I learned about mythology and Jung because of Sean Feeney. I read Irish myths and folktales and they pointed me towards general mythology. And comparative religion, and so on. (Remember the Honour of God?) By and by, I discovered that myths happened to everybody. Did that make me feel better? A bit, maybe.

Following general mythological patterns, Mama turned into a hag. She suffered from depression for years. She hated herself because she was made of flesh and not of pure love and goodness. Unlike pure love and goodness which shine eternal, flesh needs to be looked after, cherished and maintained. That is done by taking a number of Necessary Steps every day. As I said before, Mama was not good at that. Despised and abused for not being able to be what it wasn't, Mama's flesh rebelled and transformed her into a monster.

As soon as she was allowed to, she took early retirement and sat around smoking, always too unwell to do anything. She became fat, dirty and dishevelled. Her eyesight got poorer and poorer, but she refused to take the Necessary Steps. And she never went out. She languished in the murk.

When I left home, her condition worsened. By the time Papa died (and yes, he should have done something about it), she had not set foot outside the flat for full seven years.

Semi-blind and deprived of human contact, she did not use the mirror or seek her reflection on other people's faces. Her expressions and gestures became strange. She spoke weirdly, without the usual restrictions of civilisation. People were scared of her or, at best, embarrassed.

And then — out of the blue — Steve!

Steve used to go to school with Patricia, like Pierre did. He was somewhat older. She adored him from afar, unable to imagine that this handsome, mature fourteen-year old who smoked and discussed politics at Young Communists' meetings, could take interest in her silly young self.

At that time, before the Second World War, Communism was sexy and cool among bright young things. It was an excuse for clandestine gatherings in dark places. Sexes were supposed to be equal among Young Communists.

Steve was dark and saturnine, with a broad chest and well-developed muscles. His chin was firm, his neck short and powerful. He thought Patricia was gorgeous but unattainable: so clever and beautiful, and a manager's daughter, with a carriage and horses at her disposal, and servants in the house.

They passed each other like ships in the night.

Many years later, in Agram, Mama found Steve's number in the telephone directory by accident. She phoned him. He returned the call. They talked and talked together. They developed code words. They made love on the phone. Steve did not know that Patricia had become a hag.

What had Steve been up to all those years in between?

He had a wife and a daughter. (A pattern? What makes those patterns? The Force which is with us? Or isn't?) After the war, he had pursued a career in the Police. Eventually he ended up with the Special Branch, the Yugoslav equivalent of the KGB.

As a Special Branch officer, he had to be cool and calculating and sometimes put his life on the line. Other than that, he led a very ordinary Agramian life. I visited him once on Mama's business and can tell anyone who cares to know that the Special Branch, at that time and in that place, watched football on TV, jogged, had a conventional taste in home decoration, grew houseplants, owned pet canaries, were DIY freaks and were not overpaid. Their wives made jam and had to go out to work to supplement the family budget. When they wanted a bigger flat, they didn't simply ask their bosses for one; they had to get it by means of flat exchange just like all the other common mortals of Agram did.

Having become a hag, Mama was very open with Steve. It is a privilege hags can, if they so wish, avail themselves of. She told him she was in love with him and that she lusted after his body. She told him she had lusted after his body already as a schoolgirl.

"If I'd only known that," Steve said into the telephone.

Mama would not have married Ladislas. She would not have married Papa. I would never have been born.

Some months into the affair, in one of our transcontinental telephone chats, Mama told me about her new passion.

Steve had been to see her. She had told him in advance what to expect. She did not wash before his visit or tidy up the place. There was something orgiastic in her decision to fully reveal her monstrous self to him. It must have been excruciatingly painful for her. She must have had boundless trust in the Dark Side of the Force, regardless of her perpetual enthusing about love and altruism.

The Force seemed to have been with her then because Steve sat down on her bed which was covered in dust and hair and flakes of dry skin and talked to her, trying to persuade her to do something about her condition. He was still dark and saturnine and very fit, and Patricia listened to what he had to say.

He came again and again, and, between visits, talked to her on the phone. She met his wife Lelia and his daughter Vera. She knew what any one of them did at any time of day. Lelia sometimes came around with a cake for her and tidied up a bit. It gave me the creeps to hear about all that. It was a dark, dark affair. It was a half-past-midnight affair of indecencies, impossibilities and improprieties.

I visited her in the summer of eighty-nine. My job was, on

that occasion, to persuade Mama to check into a hospital. She would not hear of it, because it was a Necessary Step. I had a lot of my own reasons to be depressed, and staying in that gloomy cavern of filth and stale air that used to be the warm nest of my adolescence made me ill. I couldn't sleep for a fortnight and had to be given sleeping pills in the end.

Steve came to my aid in a very unexpected way. He visited, sat on Mama's bed and said, "Patricia, if I made love to you, as you are now, would you agree to go to the hospital?" She agreed at once and did not demand the actual reward. How exceedingly dark it all was!

And off she went, in an ambulance, screaming and hyperventilating because the world had to her become an alien place and her perception could not handle it any more. She was to stay in hospital for a whole month. Steve would take her home when she was discharged. I was free to leave.

Was I in the midst of Life during that visit to Agram, was I alive? You bet. Was I aware of being alive? No. It was, for me, just another toothache.

Two months later, Mama asked for and got my consent to exchange flats. She wanted a first floor flat, or at least one with a lift, so that she could go out.

Our old flat was on the fourth floor, without a lift. She could not manage the stairs. The flat was too large for her and difficult to heat.

It had been Steve's idea. He wanted a large flat. He knew a lady customs officer who lived in a small, warm flat with a lift but was getting married and wanted a larger one: Steve's, to be precise. It was all agreed at once, of course. The customs officer took Steve's flat. Mama took hers. Steve took Mama's.

And she started going out! For walks! She was better! She went to the nearby park and sat on a bench. One day she even walked the few blocks to the old flat and visited Steve and Lelia. She had coffee with them, and then Steve drove her back. But a few months later, she stayed in with a stubborn cold that wouldn't go away, and never went out again.

Yes, but listen: when you exchanged a large flat for a smaller one, you were given compensation for the difference in the square footage. That was how it was done in Agram. The transaction was not legal but it was nevertheless accepted practice. The customs officer was to compensate Steve and he was to add to the money and pass it on to Mama.

It did not happen. No one mentioned any money, Mama least of all. She was infatuated with Steve and profoundly grateful to him and to Lelia and Vera. Lelia came to see her almost every day.

Mama's new flat was too small for all our furniture accumulated over decades of sedate living. She left an expensive lounge suite in the old place. Left it to Steve. He did not have to pay for it. It was a present for everything he had done for his old flame.

After some six months or so, his visits became few and far between. Lelia, too, had less and less time for Mama.

On my next visit to Agram I visited Steve to see how he had renovated the old flat. It was decorated in chocolate brown and beige. Steve received me alone. We had coffee and chatted. Some fifteen minutes into the session, he asked me, point blank, to sleep with him.

"I beg your pardon?" I said.

"You turn me on so much," he said. "You're absolutely like Patricia when she was young. Come on, kiss me."

"Right," I said, rising, "that's it. Don't ever let me hear from you again, Steve. But before I go, tell me one thing: how long have you felt that way about me?"

"Since I first saw you," he replied calmly. "No, that's not true. Since Patricia first showed me your picture."

Patricia had to bring *soul* into it, then. She could not do without this soul business, not even as a hag.

From day one Steve had wanted the flat and access to my pussy. He got the flat. One cannot have everything.

Mama and Steve are not on speaking terms any more.

Had Pierre not been kept at distance, would he, too, have eventually seen me as Patricia's Second Coming?

It is ever so dark, this dark business, but my eyes have grown accustomed to seeing in the dark. And they have seen that Patricia had wanted it so.

She wanted me to live instead of her. I went to family funerals instead of her. She was too ill to attend. I voted for her in the elections. And listen to this: the year I went down to Agram to help her move to a residential home, I had a very open conversation with Mama. The subject of Pierre came up for discussion, so I said: "What on earth possessed you to involve me in that whole affair to the point of taking me to Eszeg to meet your lover?"

"I wanted to show you off," she said, rising her chin proudly.

"Whaaat?"

"I brought you along as a sort of offering," she went on, "as a gift to Pierre."

"Woman," I roared, "can you hear yourself? Can you hear your own words?"

Almost blind, her eyes could not smile. They had a permanent expression of panic in them. But she smiled with her mouth. "I brought you to him like one would bring flowers," she said.

Barbarossa

Alexandra could not make herself dissect corpses in her anatomy class. It was more than she could stand. Thus, after the first term of medicine, she joined me at the Faculty of Philosophy to study 'Anglistics' and 'Comparative Literature' (Forest's second subject). By that time, Eagerwill had moved in with her.

Alexandra's parents were brilliant! They let their daughter live in a common law marriage with Eagerwill under their own roof! They never said a word. They treated Eagerwill as their own son.

His parents were not a bad lot either. They paid him an allowance to live there and study whatever he pleased. It did not matter, in those days, whether you were from Whiteburg or Leibach, or wherever. You could study in Agram if you wanted to. And if you were from Agram, you could, if it made you happy, study in Whiteburg: no questions asked, no strings attached. All you had to do was pass the entrance exam.

Why am I making this point? Here in Britain, too, you can study wherever you like provided your grades get you in, and *provided you pay the tuition fees.* In that silly old Yugoslavia that was so prone to disintegration, there were no tuition fees. If you made it through the entrance exam, you were in. No other criteria mattered, officially at least.

Eagerwill wanted to study geology, but changed his mind and opted for philosophy. After one term, however, he decided that his first duty was to earn a living for himself and for Alexandra. He knew a bit about computers, and in those days to know a bit was enough, as IT experts were thin on the ground. He got a job with the local ICL dealer and became, after a short period of training, a computer engineer.

Agram was full of ICL hardware. ICL was big in Yugoslavia.

Apropos of corpses: I wanted to see what the big deal was. Charlie Constantine was studying to be a dentist, which meant that he had to do a year of general medical studies first. He had to do dissection in his anatomy class. I got him to take me along, to see what there was to see.

That sort of adventure was strictly forbidden, so I had to pretend I was a medical student. Charlie gave me a white coat and in I went with the others.

The anatomy class was taught in a huge room full of gruesome exhibits. There were wall-to-wall shelves with hundreds of glass jars containing human parts in formaldehyde: eyes, ears, livers, kidneys, brains, whole heads cut in half and worse. The centre of the room was taken up by a number of stainless steel tables with corpses in various stages of dismemberment lying on them. There was a rather fresh looking brain and a chopped-off finger in the sink.

Smoking was allowed. On entering the room, all the students lit up like one man.

I had never seen a dead person before, yet I did not faint. I was doing fine.

The Professor invited us to approach the dissection table with a corpse of a middle-aged man on it. It must have had floated in formaldehyde for a long time: the texture of the flesh did not look remotely like that of a living person. The skin had a dirty ochre hue to it and rubbery texture. The chest and the abdomen were open. One half of the skull had been removed.

The corpse's lungs had turned into dark-brown dust. The Professor pointed that out, explaining that it was typical of dead smokers.

The students were asked questions and told to dissect bits and pieces of the corpse with their scalpels. I did not have one and had begun worrying about what would happen when my turn came, but the Force was with me. The Professor gave me a pair of tweezers and told me to identify the *nervus vagus*.

The nervus vagus, or the wandering nerve, is the largest and thickest nerve in the human body: purely by chance, I happened to know that. I took the tweezers and looked at the body. There it was, a brown rope running through the middle. I pinched it with the tweezers and pulled it out a bit. "There it is, sir," I said, "the nervus vagus, sir." "Very good," said the Professor. "Thank you. Now, Mr Constantine, be good enough to tell us —"

I stepped aside and lit a cigarette, then sauntered to the sink and looked at the chopped-off finger as I smoked. Then I slipped out, left the white coat in Charlie's locker and went home, proud of myself.

That evening, however, I could not eat, something that had never happened to me before. Worst of all, I found it difficult to talk to anybody, because I would immediately visualise their skin peeling away, their cheeks opening up and flaps of meat dropping off the bones. Eventually, a skeleton would remain, standing there talking to me.

I could have brought this under control, but I indulged in it instead.

It was an experience which did not generate any thoughts or emotions. It did not make me write a poem. I could have, for example, written "O Death, you are but a lump of meat breeding flies in the heat," but I didn't. I had no opinion on the subject. I simply could not eat, at least till the next morning, when I had scrambled eggs.

167

Anglistics – the English Language and Literature – turned out to be an agreeable experience. The Faculty of Philosophy was housed in a large modern building in an undeveloped part of the city. It was surrounded by cottages and meadows, with a tram stop conveniently near. There was a reference library in the building, long, cool corridors with large windows and a canteen in the basement, selling snacks and affordable espresso coffee. One could smoke everywhere. Alexandra, Forest, Vicky and I met there several times a day, between lectures and had intellectual discussions.

I have recently gone through my old study notes. It is amazing, but I still don't know why the Augustan age is called Augustan. There certainly never was a King Augustus on the throne of England. Maybe there was a Queen Augusta? I was never really good at history beyond the twelfth century when Henry the Second was King. At school, we did not learn history as a rota of Kings and Queens, or even as a succession of events. We were taught about the succession of social systems and the development of the means of production which brought about the well-known historical events as their consequence. This kind of approach is called historical materialism. In all socialist countries history was interpreted by means of historical materialism. It did make some sort of sense, but so did Kings and Queens.

Wait: in the notes, it says, "The name of the Augustan age derives from the prestige of Latin literature at the age of Augustus, and it may be applied to any national literature at its highest stage of refinement." This sounds contrived, somehow. English literary historians would not name a period in the English literature in such a way that its name could be applied to the literature of *any* nation. They would stick to English labels and let other nations name their own periods. I've checked my notes since against Wikipedia, and they are right, but I still feel there ought to have been a Queen Augusta.

Another quote from my notes: "The sin of Faustus is presumption, the rebellion against God's creation. It happens in his study. In the last scene, again in his study, his final sin is the opposite of the initial one: it is despair. These are sins against the Holy Ghost. Presumption takes away the fear of the Holy Ghost and desperation the love of Him. They are two faces of the Sin of Pride." The words of Dame Helen Gardner on Marlowe's 'Faustus'.

Since 'Becket', my head had been slowly but surely filling with such stuff. There was precious little chance that I would ever be so lucky as to sin against the Holy Ghost: ambition to be Sean Feeney's woman could hardly merit the lofty name of Presumption and being overweight, in awe of one's friends and inadequate in human relationships while still able to enjoy a sunny day and a tasty wiener-schnitzel definitely didn't amount to Despair. Yet I had to have that experience! I had to make it my own or else stop reading and studying and get myself a job in a factory or in a launderette or something, because without it I would not have *substance*.

By the way, since the time I wrote the above, I had worked as a part-time helper in a launderette, among other things. And right now, making the last corrections in the manuscript, I work as an agency supply teaching assistant when a placement can be found for me. The rest of the time, I abuse my credit cards. Things are this way because after nearly thirty years in the United Kingdom I still don't know the ropes.

And let me add that it is really preposterous to say one needs substance in order to read and study, while factory workers and launderette attendants don't require any. You need your substance in a launderette; you can have that from the horse's mouth. In an intellectual worker, however, lack of substance can easily remain unnoticed.

Contrary to reason, contrary to all one's instincts and according to overwhelming evidence, substance was generated by means of suffering and despair and how one dealt with it. I had to concede that; all the writers and philosophers, all the poets, Ingmar Bergman, John Ford, Sean Feeney, Alexandra and Eagerwill could not be wrong and I alone right.

Anyway, on with the story: the Quest for Substance.

I had to acquire substance or die. The experience which would generate it had to come from within myself, not from books.

As I sat through lectures on Elizabethan poetry, I doodled faces. Faces and bodies. People in situations and conversations of great significance, full of tension. Their huge eyes and cheekbones under tautly stretched skin spoke of weariness and suffering.

They were characters from a number of inane stories I attempted writing at that time, in imitation of great literature. One of the first things I did, even before the University, was a series of monologues, supposed to represent Henry the Second's stream of consciousness. They were full of agony and despair and revolved around the subject of Becket and the unloved wife, all derived from Anouilh's feeble play. Alexandra didn't know what to make of it. "Where does all this stuff come from?" she asked on reading it. "Where do you get it? Here's a forty-year old man wondering about God... and trying to fuck a wife whose flesh makes him creep... and he's drunk. What do you know about such things?"

"What do *you*?" I asked, audaciously.

"Nothing," said Alexandra, "but then I'm not trying to write about them."

I had no answer to that, except that Alexandra did not *have* to write, whilst I did.

To be absolutely honest, a few years before that conversation, Alexandra had felt an urge to start writing a story. She had written half a page, and then, as far as I knew, abandoned the project. I think the opening went like this: "It was half past six in the evening. Dusk was gathering outside and the room was almost completely dark. In spite of the late hour, he was still asleep on the ancient rickety sofa, covered by his old overcoat."

'He' was, probably, Desiré. The dark room was Forest's kitchen-cum-sitting-room. Alexandra was very familiar with both. I would have liked to have read that novel, had it ever been written, in spite of the first sentence's haunting echoes of

"Crime and Punishment" by Fyodor Dostoevsky.

Still, in my innermost self, I felt I *knew* what I was writing about; namely, Sean Feeney. He was, under many guises, the hero of whatever I tried to write. The other characters came from books and movies. They didn't matter, they were the backdrop. That, of course, was what was wrong with my work: if the others were the backdrop, what was Sean Feeney fretting about? What or who was it that made him suffer? That was what was wrong with me, too: if the others were a mere backdrop, I myself did not amount to much. Alexandra, Eagerwill and Forest knew that. I didn't. I know now.

I started with something utterly daft: a space story which, after the initial chapter, turned into a Conradian romance of the high seas. Remember Lord Jim? I had to make Jim move and speak again, say things I wanted him to say. So there was this space cop who had to deliver three criminals, absolute human monsters, to a penal colony somewhere on another planet, from which, needless to say, there could be no return. His ship developed problems, and our hero — Jack — had to make an emergency landing and repair it. One of the criminals was a very beautiful girl, with long, red hair, presumably Irish. (Yes, Jack was Irish too, what else could he be?) Jack fell under her spell and, if I remember correctly, let her and the other two stay on the lonely planet. What happened next? Can't remember, but he somehow found himself on Earth, in the nineteenth century, haunted by guilt. He became a seaman, all the time haunted and haunted by this guilt business — and I honestly cannot remember anything else except that he fell in love with an Irish lass, short, healthy, pretty, with a proud chin and a flashing eye, whose name was, I believe, Peggy.

The whole affair ended after some twenty pages. I could not construct a plot to save my life. (I still find it a chore.)

Next, there was an interesting young Irishman with evidence of dissolute living all over him, standing in the middle of the swaying crowd on board an Agram tram. How did he get there? Not a clue did I have, but I obviously felt the need to stage the action in Agram: a step in the right direction. The style was no longer Conradesque; it was more in the vein of 'A Portrait of the Artist as a Young Man' by James Joyce. He — the nameless Irishman — finds himself standing near a seated girl with a bagful of groceries on her lap. They become aware of each other, in a sort of semi-conscious way. He wears a brown corduroy jacket and whiffs of tobacco and booze. She is very blonde and young. She gets off at the next stop; he follows without actually knowing why. One A4 page and a half. It progressed no further. No plot.

One of the reasons for no plot was because I could not put my finger on the cause of Sean Feeney's torment. (The torment itself I did not question: there was all this smoking, drinking, bitterness and so on for everyone to see, and also those eyes, behind glasses — *glasses*! For the first time I focused on glasses as a poetic image. Why hadn't I noticed them before?) I read Thomas Mann's 'Dr Faustus' — it had to be the same subject as in Marlowe, and that one was all about torment and Hell being not *locus* but *status* — and found out that Mann's book was about the predicament of artists. By inference, it had to be about Sean Feeney, praise be!

I devoured it. It was not about acting. It was about composing music with the help of the Devil. Music schmoosic — it was about *art*, therefore about acting as well, had to be. I underlined stuff and made notes and felt that I had understood it.

As a bonus, I discovered I could listen to Beethoven for hours and not get bored, because Mann's extensive explanation of how music worked had clicked somewhere deep where clicks like that happen. By the same token, I began to find Tchaikovsky boring, likewise all other pop.

These days I'm more into Britten, Tippet, Messiaen and early music, but I don't think that all of Tchaikovsky is pop any longer. I don't think that all of pop is pop any longer.

The next story, with Thomas Mann and Sean Feeney's glasses taken notice of, was about a scientist, a genius, Irish (natch), interestingly pale and lean. His name was Ceartach O'Murchadha (that would be O'Murphy were he a New York policeman and not a scientist). Ceartach had at a tender age acquired a number of PhDs: in maths and in nuclear physics, and in psychology, of all things. He had published a number of highly popular books and also some pure maths. He was an unapproachable celebrity. Haunted by his knowledge, he was nervous and ironic. He drank. He had a predilection for low digs and played the Spanish guitar rather well. (Why Spanish? Because I'd seen Sean Feeney in 'Man of La Mancha' in the role of Cervantes, whom he'd portrayed as a tormented intellectual.) Ceartach had a solemn, serious sidekick who was in fact writing his biography, just like Serenus Zeitblom had written the biography of Adrian Leverkühn, the composer in Mann's 'Dr Faustus'. Or like Dr Watson had written the biography of Sherlock Holmes, but at that time, not having had read any of them yet, I considered Sherlock Holmes stories to be pulp.

Ceartach's personal life was a mess. He had a girlfriend; a tiny wisp of a girl, raven-haired, huge-eyed and not very beautiful. She was half-mad, very inarticulate and utterly useless in the world of everyday life. She was a superb painter. When Ceartach came across her, she was living on her friends' charity and painting in taverns. She became pregnant with Ceartach's baby and lost it through his fault. How? What fault? I don't remember.

Where would one find such *taverns* today? One thing is sure: it would not be in an English-speaking country.

Everyone in the story suffered a great deal and everyone was bitter. But as there was no plot, because I had no knowledge either of the background or of what made all those people tick (what generally made people tick), the story petered out after fifteen pages or so.

I read some of it to Forest one evening. She was not my audience of choice but no one else was available at that particular moment when I had to read or explode. Forest had a lot of problems of her own just then and was not particularly

173

keen on listening to my drivel, because that was what it was: necessary drivel but drivel just the same.

Why *necessary* drivel? Because every writer, when learning her craft, has to write the drivel out before she becomes able to handle the right stuff.

Forest liked the scene where Ceartach spends the night in an armchair overcome by nervous fever, with his faithful sidekick watching over him. She liked the way light reflected in his glasses, rendering his eyes invisible. But, "What exactly is nervous fever?" she asked. "Do you know?"

I didn't know. Characters in Dostoevsky's novels seemed to be extremely prone to it. I wondered how strongly one had to feel about anything — anything at all — in order to actually experience such a fever. Apparently, I didn't feel that strongly about anything, but perhaps Forest did. She was in love with a man who reminded her of Mitya Karamazov.

Soon after that reading, Forest politely let me know that she would prefer to dispense with my company. This had to do with something entirely unconnected with the reading.

What had happened? I doubt that I'm qualified to give an accurate account, because the guilt I felt at the time most likely made me twist the facts and remember only the twisted version of the event.

I had coffee one day with Vicky and remarked that Alexandra was turning into a regular housewife who could discuss only knitting and shopping because that appeared to be her only occupation at the time. What I had probably meant was that I would have liked Alexandra to be engaged in some kind of creative activity like philosophy or poetry, so that I could see her work and pass judgement on it instead of constantly submitting mine and being judged. Vicky told Alexandra and Forest about it and very likely embellished it a little (Vicky could sometimes be a bit of a gossip).

I ran to Alexandra's to explain that I didn't mean it quite like that. Alexandra almost believed me, but Forest remained adamant.

Over the years, however, I came somehow to connect

Forest's withdrawal of friendship with my reading the story of Ceartach O'Murchadha to her at an ill-chosen moment. That, too, was possibly true.

My relationship with Vicky remained cool afterwards. With Forest there was no relationship at all from then on, although we sometimes met, unavoidably, at Alexandra's. I think that Alexandra cooled off just a whisker towards Vicky, because of the *schadenfreude* element in her report of our conversation. Alexandra hated *schadenfreude*. So did Eagerwill. (I didn't, nor was I entirely free of it.) In spite of that, she and Vicky remained firm friends. What else could they do? They went back to primary school, those two. That is good and exactly as it should be. Friendship is not all instant gratification.

Does this sound like a platitude? It is one. Once one turns forty, one finds out that all the best-known platitudes are true. Why are they called platitudes? Because they are flat, I suppose. Simple truths are flat. They can be found in popular proverbs. The people are wise. And that is another platitude.

Anyway.

Anyway, it was obvious I wouldn't get very far by forcing Slavic dialogue and Spanish passion upon an Irish scientist living in London. It didn't ring true. Unfortunately, at that particular moment in time, Slavic dialogue (as in Dostoevsky and Tolstoy) and Spanish music and London excited me wildly, indicating that therein the Truth of Life had to reside. But I did not know how to separate the liquid from the vessel (Perhaps one *can't*, ever? I'm still not sure about that.) and pour it into a glass I could hold in my hand — or, in plain terms, how to get wildly excited about whatever surrounded me and see the Truth of Life in that.

It still had to be done. It still has to be done.

I had another go. I wouldn't give up Sean Feeney as the Incarnation. Wouldn't give up Ireland, England, Spain. Would not, in fact, give up anything at all. Instead, I set about placing a Sean-Feeneyan character in Agram and making him speak Croatian, to make the Slavic dialogue more plausible.

I invented yet another Irishman, Donncha O'Lochlainn, an

extraordinary linguist who spoke all European languages including some obscure ones, like, for example, Croatian. He couldn't forget a word once he had heard it and could tune into the spirit of any language after a mere lesson or two.

He hailed from the darkest Connemara, the son of a beautiful but aloof young woman whom he believed to be his sister. She had run away from home at the age of fourteen and gone to live in Dublin. Some time later, she returned home with a baby and never again set foot outside her village. Like mother like son: once fourteen, Donncha set off for Dublin and learned, after much hardship, to fend for himself. He was proud and independent. Eventually, he went to sea and became a fisherman.

Why fisherman? Because I wanted to have the reason to sit at my desk and imagine Donncha with a wide-brimmed Aran hat on the deck of a fishing boat in a gale. That image was somehow epiphanic to me.

On his travels with the fishing boat Donncha learned many languages and had many Experiences of Life. I only mentioned the fact but did not elaborate on those: I did not know how to, not having had any myself. Finally, in Spain (!!), he left the boat and, together with a sidekick, hiked in the Pyrenees. There, in a remote village, he won the hand of a strange and wealthy woman, the eldest of three orphaned sisters. Her hand had been the stake in a game of poker, and Donncha had played just for the hell of it. Be that as it may, honour demanded that he marry the unlovely, intense, taciturn girl whose name was Montserrat (as in Caballé).

He spent the rest of the story dashing all over Europe with Montserrat in hot pursuit. Eventually, he found himself in Agram (why not? Agram is, after all, not the Moon) which was convenient as he spoke Croatian perfectly. (Why not? There are people who *do*. Not many, but *some*.) Fresh off the train, Donncha accidentally struck friendship with Joseph, a student of theology and, I think, philosophy or something of that sort. He moved in with him, to share the rent and for company.

I needed Joseph in the story to create an excuse for lofty

discussions. Joseph was the tormented, serious, *bona fide* man. Donncha was the self-contained, proudly suffering (*why?*) ironic man.

A schoolgirl of seventeen visits Joseph almost daily. She is rebellious, unconventional, childish, with an inquisitive mind. She falls in love with Donncha and, inevitably, he responds, against his own better judgement (she is a child and he has seen the world). Joseph is also strongly against the affair.

And here the story comes to a sudden and final stop. There was absolutely nothing I could do with all those people. They would neither speak nor move. They had neither reality nor substance, which was only natural, as I had neither the worldly knowledge nor innocence and, consequently, no substance of my own.

This time I knew better than to read my concoction to anyone.

In the meantime, I had finally managed to set my foot on the British soil where Sean Feeney walked and to breathe the air he breathed.

It happened thus:

Not being a member of the Warsaw Pact, Yugoslavia was not under an obligation to restrict the foreign travel of her citizens. In the seventies, when suddenly there seemed to be a lot of money around (the dinar was convertible, three to a pound), travel agencies mushroomed and people began to gad about big time.

It was possible to travel abroad in previous decades too, but you had to have a reason for the trip. I, for example, went to Germany in 1960, aged eight, with Mama and Nan. We had a legitimate reason: we wanted to visit Nan's sister Gabrielle, who lived near Munich.

Her husband, a Ukrainian Cossack, had served in the German army in the Second World War and was killed. When the war ended, Gabrielle was expelled to Germany. She was transported there in a cattle wagon. The journey nearly killed her. But the German government gave her citizenship and a pension. She was a soldier's widow.

She would have preferred to have had stayed at home, but she didn't have a choice.

That does not mean that she blamed the Partisans who expelled her. When one fumigates a liberated country to get rid of vermin, one inevitably makes mistakes. Aunt Gabrielle understood that because she was an angel. She understood everyone, and if she didn't, she loved them just the same. And pitied them.

Kind people in Germany gave her a home. They felt that she was doing them a favour by living with them. Gabrielle had that sort of effect on people, and on everything. Had she ever asked the Red Sea to part for her, it would have parted.

And those Germans were really nice! I met them, so I know. They owned a bicycle shop in Gauting, Bavaria. They took me to see the theatre in Oberammergau where the famous Passion Play is staged every ten years. I got to touch the gorgeous costumes. Oberammergau is full of shops with religious figurines and crucifixes and rosaries. They bought me an ice-cream there, my first ever. They took me to see the Starnberg Lake, and mad King Ludwig's castle Linderhof, and everything.

Their garden was crawling with huge brown slugs. I had a lot of fun with the slugs. I collected them and kept them in a shoe-box. In the back of the garden one could find blackcurrants and wild strawberries.

And Walter, their son-in-law, played badminton with me.

They bought me Lego cubes. They asked Mama if they could adopt me. They said I'd be better off with them. They could afford to give me a really good education.

Was that a nice thing to say? I don't know. I got a really good education anyway, for nothing.

I still feel there must be a small locked door somewhere there around Munich. It leads into this incredible enchanted Wonderland. Today, though, I'd first have to eat a biscuit labelled "Eat Me" to get through the door. At that time, I was just the right size.

In the seventies people went to Germany in droves. There were a million Yugoslavs working there, as I have already mentioned. They also went to Austria and to Italy to do their shopping. Mostly they went to Trieste. My cousin Melissa went all the time.

Trieste had quickly caught on and had become one vast flea market. It was full of Yugoslav Gypsies buying Giovanni jeans to smuggle home. Melissa and other respectable people like herself and her parents shopped in Benetton, Coin and Upim. Coin and Upim are department stores like Debenhams or Peter Jones.

One left at midnight from Agram by coach and arrived in Trieste before the shops opened. Trieste looked bright, prosperous and posh, yet sufficiently homely for one to feel at home. Most shop assistants understood Croatian, not because they wanted to but because they needed our business.

Trieste once used to be a major port. In the seventies, it had nothing else left to do but sell jeans to despised Yugoslavs. I don't know what Trieste is up to these days when a Donna Karan store has opened in Agram. Probably not much. Pity, because I'm very fond of Trieste.

It has a very superior eleventh century Byzantine basilica. Unlike most shoppers, I went to see it once. Ya-boo-sucks to you, most shoppers!

And so, because one could go everywhere, one fine day in 1971 I said to myself, why not go and see London? Papa and Mama had nothing against it. There was enough money. And I went! I took a five day all-in trip with Atlas Tours.

And before I knew it, I was on the plane! To London! Two hours was all. I was there! At Stansted. At the time, flights from Yugoslavia went to Stansted.

And then I was on the coach, hurtling towards London through the British night. Somewhere in the darkness around me there was everything that mattered: Oxford and Cambridge where Ceartach O'Murchadha may have studied, the coaching inns where Mr Pickwick and his friends stayed, the Jodrell Bank radio telescope, Canterbury Cathedral where the Honour of

God had been washed clean by blood, and, above all, somewhere out there was a street, and in it a house, and in the house there was Sean Feeney, doing whatever he would be doing at that time of day. I was in the midst of it all, driven by a driver who spoke English. It was his mother tongue, because I was in England.

Never before or after had I felt so nourished. No ill could befall me here. That was how I felt.

We, the package tour, were lodged in a small but pleasant hotel in Lexham Gardens off Cromwell Road. It was situated near the Yugoslav Embassy, but I didn't know that.

The first thing I did was to find the nearest tube station and take a ride to Piccadilly Circus. It was my first ever ride on the Underground. The sounds and the smells of it were completely alien. Nothing in Europe sounded or smelled like that. I am still addicted to the tube because of its sounds and smells.

What did I do on Piccadilly Circus? Not much. It was, after all, nearly nine PM. Once I had taken in the fact that I was there — on Piccadilly Circus, that is — I had a cup of coffee somewhere there, can't remember where. After that, I went back to Lexham Gardens and had some rolls and salami in my room. I had brought those from Agram.

Then I slept with London roaring around me. I slept like a log. I sleep well in the UK even now, unless I'm jobless and with bills to pay.

The following day we went on a sightseeing tour: the Tower, Mme Tussaud's, the works. In the middle of the tour I set off on my own. I bought a street map and off I went.

I saw Holborn, the one from Dickens' novels. It was there. I don't remember what else I saw, but I remember how it all felt: the air smelled British, and the shadows were very black in contrast with the bright sunshine. The contrast between sun and shadow is never that sharp on the Continent. In London, it is a bit like on the Moon.

And the houses were small. The windows were small. They were made of small panes of funny looking glass, very shiny and uneven. There was a lot of red brick everywhere. The place was incredibly colourful. In comparison, the Continent was drab.

I loved the red busses and the red telephone booths. And the red mailboxes. And regulation style lettering on everything. It made me feel good all over.

I ended up in Soho. Everybody does. I was hungry.

I found an Italian place in Moor Street, called 'Barocco', took a seat by the window, ordered spaghetti Bolognese (my first ever spag bog) and tucked in, reading a book I had just bought: the complete screenplay of Kubrick's 'The Clockwork Orange'. After the meal, I had a cappuccino and lit a Rothmans. At that moment a man walked in and, seeing no free tables, asked if he could join me at mine. "Of course," I said and smiled.

This is going to be a very long chapter. It is already long, but it will be longer.

The man was short and chubby, with a fluffy beard. His full lips moved inside it as he ordered his spaghetti. He wore glasses and had a very strong French accent. The spaghetti arrived. He ate and I read on.

Having finished, he called for a cappuccino. "Would you like another one?" he asked. Me.

"I was just going to order another one," I said.

"Well, there you are."

The cappuccinos arrived. "What are you reading?" he wanted to know. I showed him the book. "Aha," he said. "Well, well. I'm a bit of a film-buff myself, or used to be."

"Really?" I was pleased to have met a like-minded person, because at that time I counted myself among film-buffs, of which later.

"Yes. I even published a book of essays on film, years ago." He offered a hand and we shook. "Georges Lacroix. I'm Belgian, and you?"

I told him who I was and where I came from.

Mr Lacroix then proceeded to tell me about himself. He was

from Liege. He taught French at a language school in Camden. He liked cooking. He cultivated his French accent because the English found it interesting. He was divorced. He was the grand-nephew of a famous Belgian writer, Charles de Coster, whose books I loved.

I gobbled it all up. I had never spent so much time talking to someone who was not Yugoslav. It was my longest English conversation ever.

He took me to see a Yugoslav film. It was called 'WR — Mysteries of the Organism', directed by Dušan Makavejev. It was banned in Yugoslavia, the only Yugoslav film ever to be banned in Yugoslavia until then. I thus became one of the few Yugoslavs who had seen it. It was not particularly good.

The film was about Wilhelm Reich and had to do with sex and the revolution. It contained scenes of people fucking in a meadow to the soundtrack of Communist songs from the Second World War. It also contained scenes of an American sculptress taking casts of men's penises and making sculptures from the casts. She would smother an erect penis in hand-cream before pouring plaster over. She had to make the penis stand up first, of course. I couldn't see any reason why the film should have been banned. Given time, it would have banned itself, I'd have thought: it was boring.

Georges seemed to like it.

Later, he took me home, his. He lived off Marylebone Road, in a flat consisting of a tiny antechamber with a wine-rack and a coat-hanger, a kitchenette so small I had to stand in the doorway while he made coffee (with *cardamom*, yuk), and two rooms heated by one small electric bar heater. One room was completely full of books. It was Georges' study. The other room was furnished for socialising, with a pull-out bed which stayed hidden in a wall unit during the day, pretending to be a wardrobe. Another door led into a bathroom-cum-toilet. The windows in both rooms were too high up on the wall to provide a view.

I asked if I could smoke. Georges said yes. He said he had quit, but when I lit up, he took a drag on my cigarette. He did it in a way which was meant to be sensuous.

How did I know that? I simply knew. It struck me as a bit ridiculous but then, who was I to judge? What did I know about sensuality? Perhaps that was what sensuality *was*. Perhaps I was just a dumb immature dumb dumbo.

Georges was very proper. We talked some more, about Life, books, love, film and so on. Later, he saw me back to my hotel, because "London at night was dangereux". That was news to me.

We met again the following day, in the 'Barocco'. We had coffee and exchanged addresses and telephone numbers. I was very excited. I finally knew the address of someone living in London.

We parted with a kiss, just a touch of the tongue. I wondered why he wanted that. Surely he didn't think I could be interested in his *body*? He was, I thought, too fat to be erotic. And too bearded. In spite of that, I was ill at ease. Somewhere inside me, something independent of my aesthetic principles woke up and wriggled about a bit before going to sleep again. It made me want to cry with no reason I could identify.

In my hotel, the night before the departure, I wrote my first poem in English:

> *Happy we'd met*
> *We sat,*
> *Smoking the same cigarette.*
> *When we were parting*
> *The World wasn't a farthing*
> *Worth to me:*
> *I wasn't free.*
> *A part of me*
> *Was left to rest*
> *In your nest.*

This was way over the top and I wasn't sure whether farthings were still.in use as currency, but it made whatever was flopping about inside me go quiet and lie down.

That night I slept and I dreamt and here is my dream:

I am staying somewhere in some kind of a boarding house, or a cheap hotel. I have no idea where Somewhere is; it is not a particularly nice place and yet many people seem to be staying there. The room next to mine, for example, is occupied by a Polish family: a man, his wife and their two teenage daughters. They appear to be in Somewhere on holiday.

In the middle of the night, the Polish family enter my room. They suddenly look very different, as if they had previously worn masks and then taken them off. Even their daughters don't look like schoolgirls any more: in fact, they are grown women.

The four take no notice of me. As if I wasn't there, they rummage through the wardrobe and the desk drawers, looking for something that has been left for them there. And they find what they're looking for: a set of small glass ampoules containing red dye.

Oh God, *I know who they are!* I've read about them in the papers: they are the notorious international gang of robbers who call themselves the Barbarossa[1]. They fear nothing, they have never been caught and no one is safe from them anywhere, ever. The Barbarossa break their little ampoules and smear their chins with the red dye: without the dye, they cannot operate. It gives them magical powers which make them invincible.

My first impulse is to run for dear life, but after a mad dash through the rooms and the corridors of the boarding house, I remember that it is useless running away from the Barbarossa: they never fail to get their victim. They are probably busy murdering other guests of the house and its owners at that very moment, and when they've finished everyone off, they'll find me, too.

I can do one of the two things: sit down and await my doom or turn around and fight.

And I turn back! Everything is possible in a dream. I find

---

1 'Redbeard' in Italian

the Barbarossa in the act of slaughtering the owners of the boarding house. Their red beards are dripping with blood. What to do? What to do? Ah: I spot a bottle of wine on a cabinet, grab it and thump one of the bandits on the head. Once, twice, thrice — and his skull breaks, oozing a mixture of brains and mashed bone. Now for the next one, thump!

For some unknown but fortuitous reason, I am able to kill one bandit at a time – at my leisure, so to speak. And the bottle does not break. And no one wakes up. Why hasn't anyone tried to do this before?

Because, as I realise while finishing off the last bandit, the Barbarossa will be back. They will re-constitute, regenerate, re-emerge, be re-born and ride again. One *cannot*, I repeat, *cannot* defeat the Barbarossa.

I woke up with a scream — who wouldn't? I feared going back to sleep, but it was just as well because I had a plane to catch that morning.

What became of Georges Lacroix? It is quite interesting. Listen:

A few months later, a parcel from London arrived. From Georges. There was a postcard in it, from Crete, and a pair of corduroys. He had been to Crete, Georges wrote, and the hols had been fab. He remembered our sojourn in London with pleasure, thought I was a lovely and interesting little girl, and there was a pair of corduroys in token of his affection. He hoped they would fit.

I unwrapped the corduroys. They were brick red. Ugh. Georges ought to have known I wore only black.

At that time in Agram black had not yet become a fashion colour. It was the colour of mourning, actresses and tarts. Old ladies wore it because they had buried their entire families and were always in mourning for someone. It was considered improper for young women to wear black except to school, but Alexandra had had a black phase, and it followed that I had to have one.

I wallowed in it for years. I wore only black. Georges ought to have noticed. But he hadn't.

Furthermore, the cords were made in Albania. I had received a pair of cords from *London* and they were *Albanian!* I wondered if Georges had been trying to insult me. Perhaps he thought that Albanian cords were just the thing for a miserable East European waif like me.

I thought about it and decided he could not have known how East Europeans felt about East European goods and about other East Europeans, Albanians in particular. The truth was, I wanted to continue our relationship if a relationship it was. Nowadays I'm inclined to think that my original hunch came closer to the truth, insofar as Georges must have thought that a cheap present would be good enough for me. He hadn't bothered to notice that I wore Levis and Wranglers.

What became of the Albanian cords? They languished at the bottom of the wardrobe for years, and then I had the brilliant idea to dye them black. They fitted me perfectly and were extremely durable and I wore them and wore them and wore them until I had worn them to shreds. By that time I had lost all contact with Georges.

In 1973 I made another trip to London, this time without the safety net of a package tour. Allbright told me where to stay: at a place in Shepherd's Bush Road called 'Hotel 75', after its house number. It was owned by Yugoslav emigrants. It was a cheap B&B, but it was clean.

I was alone in London, at last!

The first thing I did was to phone Georges. We met a few days later. He invited me home for dinner. He cooked me a Chinese meal: cabbage and chestnuts in some sort of a greasy, spicy stew. I had to learn how to use chopsticks. It was fun. After the meal we talked, and our talk got serious.

Georges wanted to know if I could ever love him. The fun went out of the situation at once and I sank into a mire of guilt, like I had done with Snotty that summer in Cone. There was yet another real man wanting something real from me, but that real man was yet again unlovely, ungraceful (likewise fat), and did not appear to suffer.

On that one issue I was wrong. Everyone suffers, at least some of the time. I learned that, as I said earlier, by proxy. And yes, how that can be done is still a secret I shall not reveal. There's no point leafing through the pages in search of it.

Because I felt so guilty, I sat on Georges' lap, partly to comfort him and partly to be comforted myself. (He was, after all, so much older than me.) I confessed my love for Sean Feeney and cried. I don't remember Georges' reaction. He did not have much time to talk it over with me because he had to go to work that afternoon. I begged him not to leave me alone when I felt so aaaawfully sad. (When one is aaaawfully sad, even a fat, unsuffering companion is better than none. And at that moment, great big roaring London outside Georges' flat was full of *none*. I didn't know or comprehend at all the vastness that stretched in all directions around me. It was *none*.)

Georges suggested that I stay in his flat and wait for him. "Read some books," he said. "Amuse yourself somehow. When I get back, we'll go out."

"Okay."

He gave me a peck on the cheek and left, locking the door. For my safety, he said. London was "dangereux".

Hardly had Georges stepped into the street when I found a bottle of Bacardi in the fridge. I poured myself a tumblerful, opened a book — an anthology of French poetry Georges had been editing — began to read and downed the drink.

I was completely unused to spirits, but in spite of that, the Bacardi could just as well have been water. By the time Georges' key clicked in the lock again, I had all but drunk the bottle dry without getting even mildly drunk. The only noticeable effect of the booze was that the time had passed without my having had been in it. I had barely finished reading one poem. I did not know what the poem was about. But I was stone cold sober.

Georges nearly had a fit but calmed down when he realised that I was none the worse for my feat. "Well, well, well," he said, "can Russians drink or what?"

"I'm not Russian," I said.

"Whatever you say, girl. Let's hop into bed."

In 1973 I was still a virgin. I felt, though, that it was time I stopped being one. In spite of that, I turned to ice, first inside, then outside as well as I watched Georges coax the double bed out of its hiding place. It came out complete with pillows and sheets. A moment later we were in it.

We wriggled in the same for about an hour. Every time Georges got near his goal I would cry out in pain. I don't remember ever having felt such pain before. Finally he patted me on the head, said that it was all over and went to the bathroom.

I looked under the blanket. "There's no blood," I said. "There ought to be blood."

"Of course there's blood," said Georges, poking his head out of the bathroom and showing me a bloody finger.

Had he used his finger? Anything was possible. The pain had been so dreadful that I would not have noticed the difference. Ah, well, brilliant, I wouldn't have to go through *that* again. But even as I sighed with relief, part of me knew perfectly well that Georges had cut his finger on purpose in the bathroom, lest I should think he wasn't man enough to deflower me. The part of me that knew this grew very angry with Georges and decided that there was no future there to pursue.

But the conscious part of me was pleased and felt all warm and cuddly and ready to plan an imminent London future.

Over dinner in a Greek restaurant called 'Hellenic', I told Georges that I wanted to come and live in London, and could he please find a job for me? He said he'd try, but he did not sound very enthusiastic.

Back in Agram, I had a letter from him. It was all about the advantages of experience over innocence and how I resembled the harsh taste of new wine while an older, more experienced woman resembled a bottle of spicy, mature claret.

I didn't know what claret was but thought it had to be wine as well. Georges was always going on about wine.

It was clear that Georges did not want to have a relationship with me, at least not that kind of relationship. That turned out to be a relief. I could go back to dreaming about Sean Feeney and Georges proposed to stay in touch anyway, thus enabling me to still "have someone in London".

A few years later, in 1977, I spent a whole month in the UK. Yes. We East Europeans could do that without breaking the bank. I didn't stay in a nice hotel, though, nor did I stay in London. I stayed in Hitchin, in an appalling hovel called 'Digrado', where a room cost a pound a night, to be paid up front for a week. Alexandra and Eagerwill were also there. Eagerwill had been sent on a year's course with ICL in Letchworth. By staying at the 'Digrado', he was able to save most of his expenses allowance. Alexandra, by then Mrs. Eagerwill, stayed with him. There were other Yugoslav ICL trainees there.

I had a wonderful time, but on my way back to Agram, I missed my train from Victoria.

I missed it by seconds. In fact, I nearly managed to hop on as it was leaving, but I had a lot of luggage. My new LPs of medieval music spilled out of a torn HMV bag. I went down on my knees to pick them up, swearing.

There was no other train to Dover which would arrive in time for me to make my connection in Paris and catch the Simplon Express.

The Simplon Express as a regular railway service no longer exists. It was named after the Simplon tunnel, Department of Useless Information. Today, it is a private service known as the Venice Simplon Orient Express, and its objective is to provide a luxury retro travel experience.

The booking office at Victoria made another reservation for me, for the following day. That was the best they could do, and very kind they were to do it free of charge, too.

Not expecting to miss the train, I had spent all my money. I was penniless. Well, not quite. I had a few pennies. Not pounds. Pennies.

I could have phoned Alexandra and Eagerwill to come and fetch me, but I couldn't make myself face the music. (They told me later there would not have been any music.) How stupid could one get? How incapable of handling real life?

I phoned Georges instead. He said he had to go to work. I was to put my luggage into Left Luggage and spend my day in London. If I return to the Victoria Station at seven PM, he would collect me.

"But I have no money!" I wailed. "Could you not collect me now so that I can stay in your place?"

No, he could not. He would be late.

"What am I to do, then?"

"Sit where you are, I'm afraid," Georges said. "Read a book. Have a coffee. See you later. Bye."

I had no money for a coffee.

I sat there till seven o'clock, reading a book and drinking water from the fountain in the Ladies. When Georges came to fetch me, I was half dead with hunger and poisoned by nicotine (I had a carton of Rothmans in my luggage). Georges helped me drag my suitcases to the tube and paid for my ticket to Baker Street station.

"You're probably hungry," he said casually when we finally squeezed my belongings into his flat.

"Oooooohyes," I said, "yes, I am. Very hungry."

"I don't think I have anything at home, really," he said, rummaging through the shelves, and produced a can of Baxter's soup. I didn't know what it was. I didn't know soup came in cans. I thought it only came in Knorr paper sachets.

I had a bowl of soup and some bread. The soup tasted strange. It was glutinous and very salty. "Well?" said Georges.

"It's not very nice, I'm afraid," I said.

"That's a can of soup wasted on you, then," said Georges. "I thought you were hungry."

And I thought I was dreaming. Was that the same Georges? What the hell had happened? What had I done?

Perhaps he had been like that all the time and I never noticed?

I finished my soup. After that, I was permitted a cigarette in the corridor.

"Thank you for putting me up," I said. "I'll sleep on the sofa."

"You'll sleep in bed," said Georges.

"On the sofa will be fine."

"In bed," said Georges, "with me."

"You mean — "

"Yes."

"Georges, I'd rather we didn't," I said. "We've tried that once before and it didn't work out." I was no longer a virgin but I really didn't feel like sleeping with Georges.

"It's a cold, rainy night," said Georges. "There have been street protests in London all day and the place is crawling with police. It's dangereux outside."

There had indeed been a lot of disorder in the streets that day. I had heard the noise in the railway station. I could hear groups of angry men roaming outside even as Georges spoke.

"So the choice is yours," he went on calmly, moving his full, moist lips inside his beard. "You can share my bed tonight or take your chances outside."

I cried. I found the situation unbelievable. "What pleasure can you possibly get out of this? Why make me do this?"

If I had stopped to think I would have understood how terrified Georges was of rejection and failure. But I couldn't stop to think.

"Because I can," came the answer.

"But — but — don't you care at all about my feelings?"

"You should have thought of your feelings before you spent the money and missed the train," said Georges bluntly. "This is a hard world."

Was this Georges? Did I once write that a part of me was left to rest in his nest?

I made my decision. It was not a brave one, nor a proud one. It was a prudent one. And I said something very mature, although the reason for saying it was mainly to make my decision look less prudent, less cowardly. Nevertheless, what I said was mature. I said, "Let's stop this filthy ugly conversation and go to bed. I feel dirty talking like this to you. Making love to you won't be dirty. Bodies aren't dirty. Only minds are."

"Whatever," said Georges.

"I'll have a bath, if you don't mind."

"Go ahead. I'll make the bed."

So we made love. It was not unpleasant, nor was it pleasant either. I did not just lie back and think of Agram. In for a penny, in for a pound. I tried to please Georges. (Pleasing myself as well would have been somewhat overambitious under the circumstances.) When he'd had his pleasure, he said, "You can have a glass of wine now. One."

I felt a pang of sorrow for Georges: not pity, for I was not a better person than he, but plain, stark sorrow. There was no humour in him, no joy. He was in earnest. "It's Jerez," he said, pouring. "I got it on a trip to Spain. I bought a case. I want it to last."

He was sincerely concerned for his wine. He didn't want to use it all up, see? When and how would he able to re-stock? It was one hell of a worry to have on one's mind while enjoying one's one-night stand.

I began to feel quite comfortable in bed, with a glass of Jerez to keep me warm.

"You know," Georges said, post-fuck confidentially, "I'll have myself sterilised."

"What?" I said, not quite able to suppress a giggle.

"Sterilised. Don't want to worry about babies every time I have sex."

"Are you being serious?"

"Absolutely."

"Ah well." What could one say but 'ah well'? Congratulations? How good for you? How clever of you? How responsible? "Anyway," I added, "you needn't worry about tonight. I've just finished a period."

"Let's go to sleep," said Georges.

"Oh yes, let's."

I slept like a log. In the morning I got up long before

Georges. I had a glass of milk and some biscuits. Then I searched his wallet. There was about £1.50 in it. I took that. I wrote a note about the milk and the money. I felt perfectly sanguine about the whole affair.

The £1.50 bought me, in 1977, a tube ride to Victoria and a couple of British Rail sandwiches. This time I didn't miss the train. And I caught the Simplon Express in Paris.

The following morning, as the Simplon thundered down the slopes of the Italian Alps, I discovered that my handbag had gone missing. Moreover, the corridor of the carriage was full of ladies complaining of the same mishap.

The Swiss conductor expressed his regrets and said that our handbags could probably be found in the toilet.

And there they were! I checked mine: everything was in place. The documents, the keys, everything. The other ladies also found all their belongings, less any money. It had been stolen. I was the only one not to have lost any money, because I had no money to lose.

Apparently this was a regular occurrence. The thieves would get on the train in Switzerland, quickly work their way through the carriages and get off in Italy.

They must have been good. I had my handbag under my pillow and the compartment was locked. From inside. How did they do it, short of telekinesis, I don't know. What I do know is that the conductor must have been in on the deal. He must have had his cut.

I never saw Georges again. A few years later I wrote to him, asking him if he had gone ahead and got himself sterilised. My letter came back undelivered. Georges had moved.

Georges.

Americans have a wonderful word for persons like Georges: dipshit. It is not very polite, but in George's case it is made to measure.

Georges, you dipshit.

Children, don't grow up to be like Georges. You must never worry about your wine, whether it will last. Firstly, it never does, and secondly, if you worry too much, you may happen to have your wallet full when the thieves come.

The Masterful Dancer

Long before the thieves came and found my wallet empty, long before I knew Alexandra, I met Melissa, my cousin, whom I like to think of as my sister. Except for the different — but not vastly different — parental influence, and different — but not vastly different — economic circumstances under which we grew up, we *could* have been sisters. Our relationship would have been, I believe, almost exactly the same.

My first memory of Melissa is unclear: I remember her parents and the flat they lived in at the time much better than I remember her. I must have been seven and Melissa two when Mama and Papa took me to visit them. There was another little girl there, Melissa's cousin Gigi. Gigi and I were not related. She was Melissa's father's niece. I found her utterly fascinating. She looked like a living doll: her eyes were black, her hair black and curly, her face very white with bright red cheeks and a rosebud mouth. She spoke in a low, rich voice which seemed to belong to a much older person. I was in awe of Gigi. I had been told that she was extremely clever and immaculately brought up.

No, my parents did not tell me that. Can you imagine Mama disseminating such information? It was Papa's sister Olivia, Melissa's mother, who thought it necessary to prepare me for Gigi. Olivia was that sort of person. It is important for one to know that if one is to understand Melissa.

Where is Gigi now and what has become of her? I don't know. All in all I saw her some two or three times. She was Melissa's best friend for a while. I was jealous, although I hardly knew Melissa then and had not a clue of how to be her friend — or anybody's friend. All I knew was how to be a daughter and a grand-daughter.

Melissa's flat left a profound impression on me. It was less cluttered than ours but much gloomier; perhaps because the building, in the very heart of Agram, dated from the twenties, while our flat at the time was brand-new. Previous to our visit the bathroom had been damaged by a minor fire which had started in a faulty electrical socket. I stared and stared at that socket, realising with mounting terror that our own flat was full of sockets. But they were new. Melissa's socket was *old*. It oozed ancient evil.

It was Melissa's father, Armand, who told me about the socket and by that act became, in my eyes, immediately soaked in ancient evil himself. He was much older than my parents and very tall, with a leathery complexion, piercing eyes and enormous bushy black eyebrows which moved like two live caterpillars, causing his forehead to wrinkle in a most alarming manner. I was terrified of Uncle Armand. Yet, I was told, he loved children.

Uncle Armand was nearing fifty when he and Aunt Olivia, no spring chicken herself, had Melissa. Ancient evil?

Melissa doesn't resemble either of them, outwardly at least. She has been rebelling against them for as long as I've known her. She has just turned forty. She is still living with her mother and a black Poodle bitch. Ancient evil? Socket?

Shit! Bollocks! And other, ruder aspersions! Aunt Olivia has been dead for years, actually! I want this book to bloody *leave* my PC *for good*, or else I'll have to mention my own death in it!

Aunt Olivia was Papa's older sister. They were both born in Krakow, Poland. Their mother, my other Nan, Stanisława, was from Krakow. She came from a very poor family. She worked in the mines as a child, and later as a housemaid. My other grandfather, by a strange coincidence called Armand like Melissa's father (ancient socket?), was an itinerant metal-worker from Bridgeton[1], Herzegovina. He used to travel all over Europe in search of work and, while in Krakow, he courted and married the tiny, hard, sharp Stanisława. He stayed in Krakow for four whole years, during which time Olivia and Emanuel — Papa, that is — were born.

I know there are no dialogues in this particular part of the story, but it is worthwhile learning about Armand and Stanisława. In my memory — for I have known them both — they stand like two grey menhirs, alien and incomprehensible. Nan Stanisława, however, was dear and close and familiar to Melissa in much the same way as Nan Josephine was to me. She did the chores in Olivia and Armand's home.

When Olivia was four and Emanuel two, grandfather Armand and Nan Stanisława moved to Bridgeton. There wasn't much work available there and Armand didn't find any, perhaps because he didn't search very hard. Not searching very hard became, by-and-by, his full-time occupation. He pursued it mainly enthroned on a settee, with a tiny cup of Turkish coffee at hand, and a ciggie. He had very strong opinions on everything. Because of his very strong opinions, he thought very poorly about everyone, and very well about himself. In the meantime, Nan Stanisława went out to work as a charwoman, washerwoman, ironing-woman. She also did all the housework. Grandfather Armand had never in his life made a cup of coffee for himself, never mind for anyone else. My Uncle Christian

---

1 No, it's not on the map under that name. Neither are Agram, Leibach, Whiteburg, Eszeg, Cone, Zara or Vallegrande... Split is there, though.

was born in Bridgeton, their third child. Stanisława never uttered a word of complaint. Outwardly, she had turned to stone. I have a photograph of the family made just before the outbreak of the Second World War, with Olivia and Emanuel quite grown up. On that photograph Nan Stanisława looks like a stone sculpture. The dress she wears is the same dress I saw her wear when she used to visit us, many years after the war. The shoes, too, are the same. And so is her hairstyle: hair pulled tightly back, braided and tied into a small, hard bun.

Grandfather Armand, in the photograph, looks as if he's bitterly complaining about something petty. Olivia and Christian must have had inherited that attitude in their genes, because they often complained bitterly about petty things. Emanuel did not. He took after his mother.

After the war, all the children of the family somehow found themselves in Agram, likewise Armand and Stanisława, by then on state pension. They rented a small bungalow, low-roofed, rickety and damp, on the outskirts of the city. It consisted of two rooms, one of which was the kitchen. The toilet was outside, and water had to be drawn from a pump in the garden. They had no gas. Nan cooked on a coal-fired cooker which also heated the house. The coal and the firewood were kept in the shed. She had to chop kindling and shovel the coal herself.

I don't think she had either love or respect left for Grandfather Armand at that stage. But she stood by him, a stone by a stone, because, for her, that was the thing to do.

She used to bake wonderful pastry and bring it along when visiting my parents and me. She loved me, but I never loved her. I never felt any tenderness for her. She was hard to touch and she smelled of smoke from the stove and of mould from the damp walls of her bungalow. I was afraid of her bun: it looked alive, like a small, coiled, grey snake. She had no imagination and talked to Mama about dreary things. Papa was seldom present during those visits. When he did happen to be about, he would treat his mother with utmost courtesy. He addressed her in second person plural.

Here, we address everyone in second person plural. That

leaves little room for nuances.

He addressed his father in second person plural, too.

I was already at the University when Nan Stanisława began to complain. She had a thin, high-pitched voice which came into its own when, from time to time, she sang old Polish folk-songs. Now she complained to Mama in that thin voice, sounding like a fourteen-year old girl. Life was hard, she said. It had always been hard. She was used to it, she had never known anything else. Yet, suddenly, that hardness had somehow become really, really too hard for her to bear. She could not go on. That was what she said.

In the autumn of the year she began to complain, my parents bought her a winter-coat, because she did not have one and grandfather Armand would not buy her one, pleading poverty. (When he died, he left enough money under the mattress to build a sizeable house. That money was snatched by Uncle Christian. He built a house with it.)

In spite of her new coat, Nan Stanisława was feeling poorly. She was diagnosed with several things, from thrombosis to cancer, but no diagnosis was firm. In the meantime, the coal for the winter arrived and had to be shovelled into the shed. Nan Stanisława did that, like she did everything else. The following morning she died.

Uncle Christian thought her shoes were too good to be buried with her. My father disabused him of that notion. He told him what was what.

Grandfather Armand died some years later.

Aunt Olivia was devastated by her mother's death. "My poor little martyr," she'd say over and over again. "In thrall to that selfish, unfeeling bastard." Saying that, she really meant, "I am a poor little martyr, married to a selfish, unfeeling bastard." Because Armand, her husband, reminded her of Armand, her father, although, objectively, he wasn't like him at all. For one thing, he was successful. Through his wartime Partisan connections, Uncle Armand held the job of Postmaster General of Agram. He always knew exactly what or whom to use, how and when. He had a car at his disposal at the time when horse-drawn carts made the bulk of traffic in the streets of Agram.

Cars were so rare then that I was afraid of them. I knew which streets were likely to have a car living in them and begged my parents not to take me there lest the resident car should suddenly start while I was around. I knew where a motorbike lived. It used to scare me out of my wits.

That was how I met Melissa for the second time: her father, Uncle Armand, took us both for a ride in his official black Tatra somewhere outside Agram. I hardly noticed Melissa for fear of the car. It was so very black, inside as well as outside. (Charred? Socket?)

We stopped somewhere in the countryside, by a wire fence, to look at some chickens. I remember the chickens. Melissa stayed in the car. She was not interested in chickens.

Uncle Armand was a keen naturalist. Years later, when he acquired a holiday home by the sea, he would get up at dawn, to watch the wildlife frolic. There was plenty to see there, from vipers dozing in the morning sun to swordfish leaping out of the shallow water. Swordfish can be found in the Adriatic. I have seen one myself.

Melissa had a very urban childhood. Both Armand and Olivia worked. They could afford domestic help, recruited mainly from the ranks of very young, often extremely uneducated peasant girls flocking to the bright lights of the city. As a baby, Melissa was looked after by a whole series of such young, clueless girls. One of them put her in a lukewarm bath and then proceeded to heat the water on the hob with Melissa in it. While doing so, she left the flat for a moment, locking herself out with the baby still on top of the cooker.

Baths for babies were not made of plastic in those days. They were made of metal.

I don't know how the situation got resolved, but Melissa is alive and well today.

When she got a bit older, Melissa attended a playschool. She holidayed in children's holiday camps. She was always with other children. She was taught manners and social graces. She could eat with knife and fork when she was four. I couldn't, even at the age of fourteen. No one in my family used knife and fork together. We would cut up our food first, and then eat it with a fork. One's left hand would thus be free to hold a book or a newspaper. I read a lot of books that way.

Aunt Olivia found my upbringing objectionable. She laid great store on social graces. I didn't understand it at the time, but it had to do with her humble origins, which did not bother my father, her brother, in the least. As a worker in a workers' country, he felt equal to anyone. He became disillusioned in his later years, profoundly so. But even then he still felt equal to anyone. He had integrity, in spite of having had stolen cutlery once.

Aunt Olivia did not have his self-assurance. She needed props, like money and manners. She was disturbed by people able to live reasonably normally without either.

In the times before the secondary school and Alexandra, Aunt Olivia used to visit once a month and bring little Melissa along to play with me. I did not know how to play with smaller children and she did not like to draw or write stories. Instead, she played with my Lego cubes. I would leave her to it and go listen to Aunt Olivia and Mama talk in the kitchen. Aunt Olivia thought I did not love Melissa. But I did.

Then she was nine and I was fourteen. We went for a day out on Bear Mountain with Mama, Uncle Armand and Aunt Olivia. I talked to Melissa all day long, about Pat Boone and his family and all the movies I had seen him in. That was our first conversation. On the way up to the top, I developed monstrous blisters on my big toes. Uncle Armand cut the toe ends of my shoes off so I could walk. At the end of the day, Melissa's eyes were glazed with boredom and confusion, because she was too polite to tell me to shut up.

We even went to Vallegrande together, minus Uncle Armand, because he was busy at the time supervising the building of his holiday home on the coast just north of Zara. Melissa ate a lot of ice-cream, hated fruit and was fatter than I, which was gratifying. She was squeamish about marine wildlife. She wore glasses and spent most of the time reading 'Asterix', 'Prince Valiant' and 'Flash Gordon' in the shade, while I swam and swam. Aunt Olivia called her "my delicate little mimosa". I thought Aunt Olivia was being ridiculous because Melissa was no mimosa. But I didn't blow her cover, because I loved her

Today, with Melissa past forty (past *fifty*!), I have come round full circle and believe that Aunt Olivia knew her daughter better than I. Melissa, it seems, used to have two masks: a delicate mimosa one, hiding a tough, ruthless, healthy, intelligent person, which in turn hid the real Melissa, who, believe it or not, was a delicate mimosa after all.

By and by, the Mimosa Number One vanished and a tough, worldly, canny, intelligent, capable, self-confident, athletic, lean Melissa emerged. She grew tall, cast off her specs, had her teeth drilled without anaesthetic, dived like a seal, went clubbing every Saturday and knew all there was to know about fashion. Her cover was impenetrable. I bought it, lock, stock and barrel.

How we dived! We founded an unofficial Jacques Cousteau Fan Club, together with a pack of teenage boys whose parents had holiday homes near uncle Armand's. We brought glittering trophies up from the bottom of the sea. In the evenings we hiked for two miles along the busy Trans-Adriatic Coastal Motorway to Hotel Alan and its all-night disco. Uncle Christian's daughter, Daisy, was with us most of the time. She was only a kid. I, I was twenty and a smoker (not that Aunt Olivia, Uncle Armand or Papa knew; the only parent-type person who knew was Mama, because secret sharing went two ways. She never holidayed at Uncle Armand's though, being unable to cope with Aunt Olivia's regime).

I coped with Aunt Olivia's regime, oh yes. It demanded strict apportioning of household chores, regular hours for everything, decent appearance and language, innocence of thought and deed, immaculate cleanliness and leaving one's shoes outside. Whenever one raised one's voice above the polite level, Aunt Olivia would say, "Ssssh."

On one of my visits to Agram, more than ten years ago,

Aunt Olivia treated Melissa and me to a Chinese meal. We got quite merry, the three of us, and then she went, "Ssssh." Only, on that occasion I was almost fifty and did not mind, while then I was twenty and didn't but should have done. I should have minded, and then indulged Aunt Olivia because I recognised that it was too late for her to change her ways. Instead, I did not mind her regime much, and when I did, I did not *indulge* her. I *obeyed* her. I was afraid of her anger. If she became angry with me, I could not watch the Energy Flow of the Universe in peace, and that was what I was there for. It used to be a holiday from Alexandra and Forest and their demands.

Melissa was not interested in the Energy Flow of the Universe. Listen to this

One afternoon Daisy and I went out shopping, mainly so that I could smoke a fag in peace. After we'd bought whatever was on our list, we turned back and saw the mother of all storms advancing at us from the west. In Hellhole — yes, that was the name of the place — storms come like that. You walk for a while, then look over your shoulder and there it is, the storm, already upon you. It makes no sound, it breathes no breeze, it is simply there, out of nowhere at all.

One glance at the rapidly swelling black cloud told us we would never make the twenty-minute walk home dry, possibly even alive. We made for the nearby cafe instead, which doubled as the Tourist Information Office, Hellhole being a very small and scattered village. I ordered an espresso for myself and, as there was no parent in sight, one for Daisy, and lit my second ciggie. Then the storm descended. Within seconds nothing could be heard except the roar of the downpour, an almost solid body of water mixed with chunks of ice, rendering everything outside the cafe door invisible. One could discern occasional louder noise of roofs being blown away. Then the thunder came, bolt after bolt, with no gap between the flashes of lightning and the sound. Giggling with sheer excitement, Daisy and I pulled our feet up onto the seats of our chairs because water was streaming in from the street. Next, the espresso machine blew up as lightning struck the building. Daisy got worried; even I, who worshipped the Energy Flow of the Universe in whatever form, thought it would be best if the storm stopped there and then. In a little while it did stop, as such storms do, leaving a drizzle in its aftermath. Daisy and I took off our sandals and waded out of the cafe.

Outside, we saw something amazing. There, it is called the fire of St. Elias and it is probably what we here refer to as St. Elmo's fire. In the wake of the storm, the whole horizon was on fire. Sheets of silent, shimmering electrical discharge stretched all the way between the low, purple clouds and the sea. We wowed and gasped and then ran barefoot through the thin drizzle and the nauseatingly powerful smell of vegetation rising from the drenched countryside.

Back at the ranch, Melissa was warm and dry and reading her comics while Daisy and I tiptoed to the bathroom to clean up our muddy, sodden selves. "Have you seen it, have you seen it," I babbled, drunk with excitement, "the fire of St. Elias! Fire, fire, cold fire all over the sea!" "No," said Melissa. She was not silly, to get wet and muddy. She did not come with us because she knew the weather patterns in Hellhole and was pretty sure there would be a storm that afternoon. She was proved right. That made her feel good. She knew what she was doing, then and always. But she did not get to see the fire, and I was sorry for her because I loved her.

And again, that same summer, a most wonderful thing happened while Melissa watched television. The evening had just begun to turn from blue to black when a meteorite came hurtling down from the sky. It was a fireball, the colour of white-hot steel, with chunks of molten rock tearing off it all the time. It roared and hissed and disappeared behind the jagged peaks of Mt Majestic which rose like a bone-white wall to the north of Hellhole. I waited to hear the impact, but no sound came, and the ground did not shake. That meant that the meteorite had burned down to nothing seconds before reaching the ground.

As the fireball passed above Hellhole, a cry rose out of the village. Hundreds of people screamed at the same time, expecting instant annihilation. I might have had screamed too; I don't remember.

Breathless, I ran to look for Melissa. She had seen nothing. She had been watching the telly; an old episode of 'Bonanza', I believe. I was quite angry with her this time. What right did she have not to witness such an event? How dare she not be devastated for not having seen it?

She was not devastated because, in order to hide Mimosa Number Two, the *real* Mimosa, Melissa had turned herself into a doer, a Song. (Does anyone remember at this stage what I said earlier about Singers and Songs? If not, please look it up and remind yourselves.) As there was nothing one could *do* with the meteorite except see it as the Energy Flow of the Universe and scream, she did not miss out on anything.

On another occasion, Papa, Uncle Christian, Daisy and I went on an expedition up Mt Majestic, following the mountain trail which led through Hellhole Gorge. We merely wanted to have a look and get back to the ranch for lunch. After half an hour's uphill trek, Uncle Christian and Daisy decided to return to the foot of the mountain and wait for Papa and me, as Papa pressed on and would not be persuaded to stop.

It took Papa and me two and a half hours to complete the trail, have a coke at the mountain top where there was a small shelter-cum-cafe for mountaineers, and get back down. It was my only adventure with Papa ever. We hardly spoke; the climb and the subsequent descent were too arduous. One also had to keep one's eyes open for vipers and carefully assess each step because the path was full of sharp, unsteady pieces of rock.

After two and a half hours of unflagging concentration, Papa and I felt tired but exuberant with achievement. At the bottom, we found Uncle Christian and Daisy sheltering under a protruding rock, half dead with heat, thirst and boredom.

Back at the ranch, Melissa had a lovely time, swimming and diving and reading comics. She was neither hot nor tired because she had worked out the best way of never being uncomfortable. Such a vulgar, unsubtle predicament as being uncomfortable could not befall her. That was for fools, and Melissa was no fool. But she had been comfortable the day before in exactly the same way, and would be so the following day and the day after next. Meaning there only ever was one day for her.

I think I've made my point.

Very perceptively, Daisy soon began treating Melissa as if she were a Parent and even rebelling against her leadership while remaining extremely relaxed with me, even though I was seven years older than she and Melissa only two. I thought it was so because I had no leadership to offer, but now I see that Daisy's reaction to Melissa was a healthy one: after all, Parents seemed to live the same day over and over again, all the time. They had learned how to get comfortably through that particular day and simply kept repeating the exercise ad infinitum. Ancient socket?

These days, I'm waiting anxiously for Melissa's socket to catch fire. I have recently spotted a thin wisp of smoke emerging from it. It is high time.

Everyone thought Melissa would study marine biology, but she went on to study Art History and Archaeology (to be fair, it was not possible to study marine biology in Agram). Art itself would have involved contemplation, self-examination and solitude as well as suffering the company of drunken louts (art students). Art history had ropes which could be learned, offered prospects of foreign travel as part of a job or study, and was popular with well brought up young things from old Agram families. Needless to say, Aunt Olivia and uncle Armand — well, Aunt Olivia, anyway — did their best to pass for an old Agram family. It was not easy with Nan Stanisława and grandfather Armand still living in their two-room hovel with no plumbing and a coal shed out back. It became easier when they died.

This is a boring chapter, because I cannot recall a single conversation with Melissa, in spite of the fact that she used to visit me every day once we moved back together with my grandparents. The flat we moved to was a five minutes' walk from Melissa's.

She used to come because she enjoyed the relaxed, intellectually adventurous atmosphere of my home. She would sit for hours with Mama and me, discussing everything under the sun. She could smoke in our place. By then, I had started smoking in front of Papa. He took no part in our conversations. He thought we were wasting our time in a lazy and self-indulgent manner instead of doing something constructive. On the whole, he may well have been right.

But Mama loved it. She hated the company of stuffy, steady, balanced mature people who had all learned how to Take the Necessary Steps. And she could have me there all to herself, far from Alexandra's disturbing influence. Only, some years later, I began taking Melissa to Alexandra's. By that time Alexandra was already married to Eagerwill.

What did we talk about? If only I could remember! Of Life by and large, the meaning of it, that kind of thing. Melissa was very good at structured discussion. She was good at anything structured.

Aunt Olivia would have wanted Melissa to spend her evenings somewhere else, where uncomplicated, single boys from good families could be found. She thought Alexandra and I had no aim in life. I, in any case, didn't. Alexandra was married and her husband had a job, so she could be said to have reached some kind of a goal. But I puzzled her. Having graduated, instead of looking for a job, I had decided to study painting.

That was due to my being in Alexandra's thrall. When we had both collected our degrees, she said, "Why don't you go on to study painting?"

I said, "Why?"

"Because you draw so well. It would be a shame for your talent to remain undeveloped."

This was how we thought in Yugoslavia in those days. Amateur dabbling was not considered serious. If you wanted to paint, you had to study it formally — for five years – then exhibit your work at least once and become member of a professional association. You were then a painter, good, bad or mediocre, but a painter. The same went for writers who usually studied Comparative Literature and Yugoslav Studies, published a couple of poems or a short story, became members of a professional association and were then writers.

Joe Bloggses did not wield brushes or bang on typewriters in Yugoslavia.

There is something to be said for that system, provided formal artistic education is available free and for anyone who qualifies. What is wrong with acquiring expertise? Nothing. What gives people the right to think that one needs no expertise to write and hardly any to paint, while one must be formally trained to play the violin in an orchestra?

I had always imagined myself *writing* one day, not painting. In spite of that, I said, "Yeah, okay, you have a point, but five more years...?"

"You'd be waiting that long and longer for a job."

Yeah, I would be. (I could never be fired, though, once I got one.) Interestingly, I never questioned Alexandra's opinion of my talent. I took it for granted that she was right. She knew what was what.

"Yeah, I suppose I could try."

And I did try, and was accepted by the Fine Arts Academy. Mama was immensely relieved because she knew I would not feel moved to learn how to Take the Necessary Steps for five more years and would thus remain with her, would be like her. She would be able to continue transferring her neuroses into me, like that thin, long-legged species of wasp which injects her eggs into a caterpillar where they hatch and eat the caterpillar alive.

Papa was fooled for once. He thought it would be a smart move for me to acquire another degree.

Working people in Yugoslavia were able to afford keeping their child during ten years of university study. We didn't have a car or a video, but who cared? Only fools would drive when it was difficult to squeeze cars in among public transport vehicles swarming all over the city, and as for video, there weren't any at the time. I used to go to the cinema every evening. Sometimes I went twice a day, if I liked a film very much ('Star Wars', for example.) Nowadays I think one must be a millionaire to do that, but if one is a millionaire, one owns a home cinema.

And I started buying at least some of my clothes in Trieste, because it was nice, and also lest Melissa should disown me. I never consciously thought she'd do that, but I must have known somewhere in my bloodstream that it was a possibility.

Years later, she did exactly that. Years and years later. In the meantime, she went to the UK with me one winter. We were to stay in Hitchin, at the 'Digrado', with Alexandra and Eagerwill. I mentioned that before. Remember? When Georges revealed his true face.

It was a bursting-out for Melissa, an unfolding. She had been on holiday by herself before, but as a child, with other children. She had gone skiing in Austria. That was what proper Agram children did. Staying in the UK with me was different, not to mention the company of Alexandra and Eagerwill, a married couple, yet not Parents but Mates. Who had sex. The spectre of Sex must have loomed all over the horizon for Melissa at the time, which I failed to perceive, largely because the very same spectre blocked my entire field of vision too.

We started our trip to the UK from two different planets, as it were. I took the Simplon Express, a train which crawled in the wake of a snowplough through the Italian Alps the whole white, frozen night. It arrived in Paris too late for me to catch my connection to Calais which left me with ten free hours — yes, that is how it was then — to wander through the vast alien city whose language I did not speak. Its roar was incomparable to London's homely noise.

I thought London was cuddly in comparison.

I only got to London at seven thirty the next morning, after a second sleepless night. I had yet to find Eagerwill in Letchworth where he did his training, get directions from him on how to find Alexandra in Hitchin where they lived in the 'Digrado', book a room there for Melissa and myself, get a train back to London and meet Melissa at the West London Air Terminal — yes, that was where one met the arrivals from Heathrow in those days — at seven in the evening.

Melissa had taken a plane directly from Agram. She arrived sweetly fragrant, sleekly groomed and well rested. Her eyes, though, were wide in an anxious kind of way and her voice was higher than usual and unsteady. Something had unsettled her. It could have been the sight of Heathrow or the motorway or the sheer quality of Britishness which pervaded the very air she breathed in on disembarking. Whatever it was, it had made a deep crack in Melissa's gloss.

We first collected my luggage from Victoria where it had languished the whole day. That done, we proceeded to St Pancras and on to Hitchin. The train, unlike anything Melissa had ever seen before, had no compartments but boasted an abundance of doors, was panelled in wood all over and its seats were designed for dwarves. As it creaked and rattled, one could see Melissa's crack opening ever wider.

Inside the 'Digrado', she gave up trying to beat off the onslaught of alien impressions. The sight of Alexandra and Eagerwill in that dump must have struck her as utterly surreal. We all had a cup of instant coffee made with lukewarm water from the hot tap. I do not remember the disjointed conversation that must have gone on because by then I was barely conscious. We went to bed without a bath, which completed the dissolution of Melissa's known universe.

That night I slept and I dreamt and here is the dream:

I happen to be in Paris, with Melissa, in a theatre of sorts, watching the world's most celebrated dancer, one Michel St.Clair, perform his famous show. He dances alone for a while, and then together with a female partner, his disciple.

St. Clair is fifty if he is a day, rotund of shape and not particularly tall, but with a charismatic personality. His muscle control is superb, almost superhuman. He moves slowly, exquisitely, bringing together the traditions of several cultures and periods: Indian temple dancing, classical ballet, modern expressionist dance, mime and god knows what else. With his partner he performs a curiously unspectacular, ordinary number, accompanied by drab, sentimental South American tunes. They are both completely naked and only partially lit, the spotlight exposing their bodies, including their intimate parts, in a seemingly random manner.

Next, they do 'The Bed Dance', in an actual bed complete with pillows and a duvet. Their movements are not really dance, nor are they completely sexual. They simply play with each other's naked bodies like two kittens in a basket, emitting happy guttural sounds and giggling. I find it all very weird and somehow less than I expected. Disappointed and excited at the same time, I giggle, too.

The Master looks straight into my eyes from where he sits on the bed and says, "You're laughing? This is the Latin-American dance. Stand up and remain standing, you'll see better that way." Ashamed and even frightened by being singled out like that, I slowly get up, and in doing so begin to feel a strange elation. Melissa watches me, admiring my daring. The whole theatre is silent, expectant.

The Master descends from the stage, naked as he is, approaches me, takes my hand and, holding it, makes a dance step. Mustering all the courage I can, I make a step too, imitating his style. The Master smiles approvingly and dances on. I follow suit as best I can, taking off my coat and my knee-length boots while muttering bashful apologies for being "fat and with my clothes on." The Master's partner sits on the stage in lotus posture, watching us with interest. "Where on earth did you find the nerve?" whispers Melissa. Entranced by my own movements and the whole new world they seem to open for me, I reply busily and breathlessly, "It's far better to dance than to watch!" The Master is smiling; he seems pleased with me. I have a feeling he'll take me with him and teach me his dance.

Why did I dream that I danced with the Master to Melissa's chagrin, while in real life it was always Melissa who could and would dance the minuet of artful gracefulness — or graceful artfulness, I'm not sure which — while I couldn't and wouldn't? I don't know.

Perhaps Master St. Clair's dance was not about artful gracefulness, but something else. What? I still don't know.

But I do know where he lives. He lives in the House of Outcasts. He had been let out for the recital and promptly locked up again afterwards.

After the initial shock, Melissa began taking in 'Digrado', Hitchin, the trains, London, the museums and galleries, and, above all, the shops, in huge, open-mouthed, greedy gulps. Alexandra was free to gad about with us while Eagerwill grafted on in Letchworth. She loved exploring but soon tired of shopping, partly because she did not have any money to spend: she and Eagerwill were saving his expense allowance to buy a flat of their own when they return to Agram. Had it not been for that, they would have been able to stay in a much better hotel or rent a flat. I didn't have much money either, but Melissa was flush. She would meander among the clothes racks in Harrods for ages or spray herself with scents while Alexandra and I smoked outside the main entrance, watching the bustle of Brompton road. We both found that half an hour of Harrods gave us headache.

The fact was, I would have liked to have been able to enjoy myself like Melissa, but I was fat and wore a full length sheepskin. Harrods gave me headache because I felt out of place inside it.

I still have that sheepskin. And wear it.

In the evenings, with Eagerwill back from Letchworth, we'd all stroll down to the other end of Hitchin, to Janice's.

Janice was a single mother, living in a council flat on social security. I didn't know then what that meant. The council estate where she lived looked not all that different from the modern housing blocks in Agram. Moreover, she had under-floor central heating. Coming from the 'Digrado', I could hardly wait to sprawl on her carpet.

Eagerwill's colleague from the training course, Harris, lived at Janice's as her tenant. Harris was from Bosnia — a Muslim (not that it meant anything to me then) — and his name was, really, Haris, meaning 'protector' in Arabic. The English, of course, pronounced it "Harris" and that was who he was for everyone.

Harris had an arrangement with Janice over and above paying the rent. It was glaringly obvious, only I did not see it because it was not in a book but in real life. Melissa did not spot it either, while Alexandra and Eagerwill knew all about it. Only years later did it click in my head: Harris used to order Janice's two little girls to bed, he used to pat Janice's bottom in a proprietary manner, he shopped for her dinner: well, I'll be damned! Good old Harris must have been fucking Janice.

Oh Janice, you good-time girl.

She was moderately corpulent, older than Harris, although not much over thirty, with lovely skin and shiny hair, pleasant and accommodating, with large, eager, hungry eyes. She drank hard and smoked hard and was, all in all, a good sport. She tolerated our almost daily invasions for Harris' sake. She took her pleasure where she could find it, and who could blame her for that? Not I, not now.

There was another chap from Bosnia on the training course with Harris and Eagerwill. His name was Steve but I don't remember anything else about him, in spite of the fact that he went to Janice's with us nearly every evening.

On our way to Janice's, Eagerwill and Steve would pop into an off-licence for a bottle of Bacardi or Bells or whatever was to be the poison that evening. (Eagerwill was rather partial to Drambuie.) How incredibly cheap those things used to be then! Oh, woe! Oh, frabjous days! Callooh! Callay[2]!

See how eagerly the lobsters and the turtles all advance!

And Melissa did, but, just like the whiting in the Lobster-

---

2 Paraphrased from "Alice in Wonderland" by Lewis Carol. The reference to lobsters, turtles and the Quadrille has to do with the same book.

Quadrille, she ended up all over crumbs, with her tail in her mouth.

She became the object of Harris' interest.

We would all sit there on the warm carpeted floor, drink, smoke, talk about things lofty and things common, even sing folk-songs, our own and English-Irish-Scottish, and it turned out that we knew quite a few of those. Janice would admire our cosmopolitan culture, feed us crisps, go and check on her little girls, and drink, and drink, and drink. The only one who did not drink at all was Alexandra. When admonished, she'd say, "I don't need Bacardi to be drunk. I can be drunk whenever I wish without that shit." To prove it, she would roll over on her back, spread her arms and legs, and moan blissfully, "I'm on a Caribbean beach right now. The sun is blazing hot and the waves are lapping at my feet. Oooh, it's so lovely. I wish you'd join me, but you cannot, because you're all so bloody drunk." And Eagerwill would support her. "That's right, you daft blonde," he'd say, stroking her hair, "you just go on sunbathing, never mind us. We'll learn one day."

I was concentrating on Alexandra's perfection and my inadequacy too much to notice Harris hovering around Melissa. (Initially, he'd hovered around me a bit, but decided that I was not interesting and — or — stylish enough. Whereupon I stopped paying attention to what he was doing. He was chubby and had a beard, in any case. Was not my type.) He hovered and hovered and one night, softly and inconspicuously, took Melissa upstairs. I only became aware of the fact when they rejoined the company, and even then I did not fully understand the situation, because Melissa looked quite normal, although she seemed to have suddenly, in the space of an hour, lost a lot of weight. She smoked a ciggie, had another sip of whatever, and then we all made our way home, as it was nearly dawn.

Janice must have noticed the goings on which involved her bedroom and her lover, but she never said a word. She knew Melissa would leave soon and Harris would stay.

At the 'Digrado', Melissa suddenly broke down. Alexandra slipped an arm around her shoulders and took her to her and

Eagerwill's room, while Eagerwill went with me to Melissa's and mine. I protested, wanting to go to bed or else to join Melissa and Alexandra, but Eagerwill quite simply forbade it. "Leave them alone," he said, sat down at the small table in my room and lit a cigarette. "Alexandra knows what to do. Melissa doesn't need either you or me at the moment."

"But what is the big deal?" I said, like the stupidest moron in the world.

"Don't tell me you don't even know," said Eagerwill, a bit impatiently.

"Is it what I think it is?"

"Yes, it is."

"But why can't I be with Melissa now?"

"Because you weren't with her then. Now, you can stay out of the way and let Alexandra deal with it. You can do that much for Melissa."

I was very sad and remorseful. Not because I had failed Melissa in the garden of Gethsemane, no. Because Eagerwill — and probably Alexandra as well — thought I was such a useless little shit.

And Sean Feeney, had he been around, would have thought me a useless little shit, too, and would not have given me a second thought. Boo-hoo-hoo.

Whatever Alexandra said that night to Melissa must have worked. She remained delightfully relaxed for the rest of that month in the UK. The very air around her seemed to have developed a lower pressure. She did not mind having a bath in a cold and dirty bathroom, or sleeping with me in the same bed to keep warm. Everything delighted her. But I cannot remember how the Harris situation resolved itself or whether it went on at all during the rest of our stay. How come I don't remember that? I don't know. All I know with certainty now is that Harris provided a blueprint, a mould which Melissa applied later on, when she fell in love.

That happened some years later. I was already living in the UK, married and incredibly poor. Melissa fell in love with a chubby bearded chap from an old Agramian family. Chubby was a sharp fellow who owned a contract-cleaning firm and rally-raced as a hobby. He took Melissa to expensive restaurants and raced his Lada Niva with Melissa riding shotgun down Bear Mountain in the middle of the night. He practised some kind of dark art or other because he could slow down his metabolism at will until he would be almost dead. That in itself was nothing strange. Most young people (other than the weary factory workers with unhealthy complexions who, like I said before, stayed out of sight) were into something New-Agey or esoteric then. There was, after all, a war pending, although we were not consciously aware of its imminence. Nevertheless, the future war was creating, like they would say in 'Star Wars', a disturbance in the Force.

After a few months of going steady, Chubby had Melissa completely in thrall. They began planning to pool their savings together and open a business abroad. At that stage, my lifestyle began to depress Melissa. I was her poor relation who was happy to be given her old clothes. My talents rotted unused. My husband was ancient and unworldly. My mother was mad and bad, and I was dangerous to know, because misery could be infectious, like TB.

She must have been very deeply affected by my predicament because she was prepared to forego the pleasures of Harrods and walks in Hampton Court and Winchester in order not to see me again.

Things are never quite as they appear to be. Melissa is not that awful, uppity, mercenary, snobby bitch you now imagine her to be. She is a Mimosa curling up under real or imaginary threat. You know? Or maybe you don't. Native to South America, mimosa is a shrub which, when touched, curls up its leaves shyly. The leaves are very delicate. Its flowers, too, are very delicate and smell very, very sweet.

And I am not this poor abandoned betrayed childhood friend. I should not have been miserable because I could not shop at Harrods with Melissa. I could have learned the Necessary Steps a bit sooner and taken charge of my life.

Taking charge of one's life does not guarantee success,

health and wealth, whatever the Fukuyamas of this world may say. But it does get rid of misery, for what it's worth. And if one fails, instead of being miserable, one can despair. That is grander and more elegant.

To experience despair was one of my goals, remember? Like Marlowe's Faustus? I missed my chance then.

In nineteen ninety five, having taken the Necessary Steps, I got hold of some money and informed Melissa that I was no longer dangerous to know.

While I was quarantined, however, an awful thing happened: Melissa ended up all over crumbs, with her tail in her mouth. One day, Chubby went abroad with her savings to start their business and was never heard of again. Just like that.

Why Chubby? Who or what sets up these moulds? (Yes, I've already asked that question before, but the matter keeps coming back.) A wise person once said that the first in a series determines the series. (This is a cryptic statement and I want it to stay cryptic. Just read it aloud to yourself and feel scared.) But how does the first become the first? By choice? By epiphany? Or by recognition? I prefer the second option but I fear it might be the third. In any case, because of the blueprint, Melissa ended up like the whiting when her Determining Moment came.

What is a Determining Moment? A Determining Moment is when we make a radical move all by ourselves.

What else did we do that month in the UK, Melissa and I? I don't remember a thing, except for the Georges episode at the end of it all. Melissa had flown home by then, never to see Harris again. She never asked about him, or he about her as far as I know.

In the latest Bosnian war, Harris had gone missing. Eagerwill told me. He is still making enquiries. He liked Harris, in which case Harris must have essentially been a decent sort of bloke.

I brought a lot of LPs of medieval music home from London, because Sean Feeney had played the role of Henry the Second in 'Becket'. I went completely potty about medieval music. Later, I learned to paint lovely little pictures in imitation of mediaeval miniatures. And Romanesque sculptures and frescoes helped me to understand and embrace cubism in my study of painting.

And I still plan to write a big novel taking place in the twelfth century, with Henry the Second and his grandfather, Henry the First, as its heroes. It will probably derive from Thomas Mann whom I discovered because, in order to understand Sean Feeney, I needed someone to explain art and artists to me. Most likely it will also derive from Dostoevsky, whose work would not have interested me had I not read Conrad's 'Lord Jim' first (played by Sean Feeney), and had I not wanted to please Alexandra. Only, Henry II will no longer be like Sean Feeney. He will resemble Picasso's 'Boy with a Pipe'. In character, he'll be a blend of Alexandra and Eagerwill. He will be surrounded by a number of interesting characters, mainly taken from the novels of Dostoevsky.

Stamp! Stamp! Stamp!

I'll start soon.

Evil

Alexandra and Eagerwill spent a whole year in the UK. That was how long the training course lasted. When they returned to Agram, they bought a small flat with the money they saved by living on lukewarm tins of baked beans in the 'Digrado'. The flat was equipped with only the very barest of necessities. It had a cooker and a double inflatable mattress to sleep on. They bought the rest bit by bit, as money became available.

While they were away, I had to find new soulmates, because it was unimaginable to spend a single day without going to see someone, have coffee there, smoke and discuss matters of importance: Art, Love, Life, Death.

Contrary to what Western readers may imagine, we did not discuss politics, nor did we young Agramians worry about it. We took for granted the Cold War world we were born into. We knew we could all be annihilated by the Bomb one fine day. We knew there was the Soviet Bloc, whose inhabitants did not wear fashionable clothes, did not get to see the latest American movies and could not travel. If they wanted to see the British Museum, for example, that was tough titty. They could only see the Mona Lisa on a photograph. They had zero chance of watching the Royal Shakespeare Company perform. The Rolling Stones would not come to Moscow. They had to be the most miserable several million people on Earth (excluding the Chinese, but the RSC would not have meant much to them anyway, we thought).

Then there was the West where, we thought, people lived exactly like us: normally, that is, only more so. That meant that they did not need to go abroad if they wanted a Benetton jumper, Italian boots or really good cosmetics. They did not suffer inexplicable shortages of essentials like toilet-paper, washing powder or tights. It was easier to be creative, we thought, in the West: Western artists did not have to worry about the unavailability of Levi's jeans and their stationery was superb, as were their painting materials. (All the materials I used were Western, bought in Agram. I used to buy loads. I did not know how expensive they would have been to buy in London or Paris. If I wanted to paint a large oil now, I'd have to apply for a loan.)

Yugoslavia itself was not part of any bloc. It was Non-Aligned. So was India, and Egypt, and a number of other Third World countries. (Perhaps the word should be 'Non-Allied'? If that is so, too bad. I prefer Non-Aligned.)

That was the situation, and we expected it to last forever. We did not question it much because most of us hoped to go and live abroad at some stage or other. Abroad, of course, meant the West. We were intellectuals, and they, we thought, were wanted and cherished everywhere. All the young painters of my generation were going to be the toast of Paris or New York.

That is no laughing matter. It meant that a great number of very creative and talented young people made no plans for any future involving their immediate surroundings. They — we — paid no attention to their daily environment. We left that to our parents and sad mediocrities to worry about.

And look at the place now.

And look at me now.

Alexandra and Eagerwill, back from their year in the UK, told Melissa and me and Vicky and whoever cared to listen, that the West was very unlike Yugoslavia. It was completely different. The *people* were different. They had, Alexandra said, dead, dull eyes and could only talk about money: how to get more of it, how much things cost, and so on. They were not interested in one another. They were alienated.

I did not notice anything of the sort on my travels in Britain and other Western places. The people I met appeared to be lively and interesting. Everything abroad was crisp and better defined. The box-hedge was trimmed. The doors and the windows were painted. The house fronts did not peel and crumble. The cars were washed. The men were cleanly shaven. The women's legs were slimmer. What was Alexandra on about? "When you have lived there for a while," said Alexandra, "you'll know."

"I shall," I said, "and I will."

I have done and I do.

While Alexandra and Eagerwill lived in the UK, Forest, too, went abroad. She went to Germany, Western, of course, to study for a Doctorate in Indology there. She could do that because her father lived and worked in Hamburg.

Forest was a brilliant student. She learned German in no time at all and soon began teaching other foreign students. Eventually, she decided to stay in Germany. She made an arranged marriage to obtain a passport. It was a perfectly ordinary thing to do.

I was not terribly sorry to see Forest go. Her departure meant more space around Alexandra, the space I hoped to fill one day (after all the years we spent together she still would not let me call her Alex: that was a privilege reserved for Forest and Eagerwill). But a departure of any kind was worrying insofar as it was a change. When a number of changes in one's environment reaches critical amount, the quality of the environment itself changes. (That is an example of dialectics which is the basis of the historic materialism, and, indeed,

Marxism.) When the quality of the environment changes, its inhabitants must likewise change or move on.

I moved on, stupid sluggard that I was, rather than change. I'll come to that later.

This is what happened to Forest in Germany: she became a Doctor of Indology but found out that her doctorate did not butter any parsnips. She had to support herself if she did not want to sponge off her father forever. She was already familiar with teaching through giving German lessons; she went a step further, acquired teaching qualifications and became Mother. Not *a mother*, but House Mother in a village for young offenders. It was her job to live in the same house with a group of juveniles of various ages and sexes and be their Mother: look after them, get them to school on time and generally help them socialise. She was convinced she loved children and wanted to do things for and with children.

But listen: among her charges, there was a boy of seventeen, beautiful and rather mature for his years. Some juvenile delinquents can be like that. His name was Arne. He was not unlike Eagerwill when Alexandra, I and she — Forest — first met him on our camping holiday.

Why do I say "not unlike Eagerwill"? I don't know. I never saw Arne, I just feel it had to be that way. Perhaps I'm just a stinker with a filthy mind. Perhaps it is the mould. Stamp. Stamp.

Listen, listen! Forest fell in love with Arne, and Arne with her. This was against the rules, naturally. House Mothers were not allowed to have relationships with inmates. But Forest and Arne began having clandestine meetings and became less and less careful, because they were happy and felt their happiness to be harmless and beautiful.

Inevitably, they were found out. Forest lost her job and was never to get a similar one. She had a nervous breakdown, a burst ulcer and something resembling a heart attack. She nearly died. Alexandra flew over to Hamburg to be with her. Arne somehow managed to fight his way to her bedside. Alexandra was very impressed with Arne. He became of age at that time, was released on probation and for a while set up house with Forest. He wanted to be responsible, to work and look after Forest who was still recovering from her illness.

But Arne was, ultimately, too young. He had the will but not the stamina for the long haul. He loved Forest but had no experience to help him deal with her mature woman's problems and moods. He drifted in and out of jobs, began to stay out till late, then not come home at all for days, until he finally re-offended. And that was the end of the romance.

That was what it had been for Forest, of course: a romance with purity and beauty, in the face of stuffiness and convention and all things dead. Arne had, obviously, seen everything in much simpler terms. The simplest terms, unfortunately, require the greatest strength and the most level head. Arne lacked those.

Soon after Arne, Forest saw her German husband to discuss divorce. They had hardly spoken before, but on that occasion they spent some time together, talking and drinking. Some months later Forest and I happened to be visiting Agram at the same time (I was already living in the UK, and poor Allbright had been dead for a year), so I invited myself over to her place. We had a restrained, polite chat and then I noticed she was wearing her wedding ring. "I didn't know you got married again," I said.

"I didn't," she said, blushing with pleasure. "It's Peter's."

"You mean, you two are actually together now?"

"Well, not quite," she said cautiously, "but it is becoming a possibility."

Remember my having mentioned once that Forest was looking for a Mitya Karamazov? Well, it turned out that Peter, her husband of convenience, fitted the bill at least to a degree if not fully, once she took a closer look at him. She began seeing him on a regular basis and was about to move in with him when he got blindly drunk while sitting on a fourth-floor balcony one hot day, fell down – just like Frau Margarete's leg in that German primer – and died.

For a while I heard nothing of Forest and then strange news

began reaching me in dribs and drabs. Forest had begun shopping a lot. Forest had bought a car, passed the driving test, smashed the car. Forest was sued for debts.

Then Alexandra, obviously deeply distressed, wrote to me that Forest had gone mad.

Come off it, Alexandra, people only go mad in novels and films. I had never met a mad person. Schizophrenics were disturbed from early youth. One cannot be normal one day and mad the next.

But wait. I *did* know a person who was to all intents and purposes normal if a bit wild and then went mad. Weirdly, her name, too, was Forest. She was a very good painter and a reasonably close friend of mine at the Academy of Visual Arts. She used to drink quite a lot, but then, we all used to drink quite a lot at the Academy. She was not terribly fortunate in her choice of boyfriends and had been let down a few times — but one needed the hide of a rhino to endure Forest's sneers and moods for any length of time. Forest was an obsessive person and a devourer of everything. At the same time, she loved all things spiritual. No wonder she and my mother got on so well.

One day, this other Forest bought a book from a Hare Krishna girl. She began chanting and soon wouldn't stop even to eat or drink or sleep. She had to be hospitalised for dehydration and sedated so she could sleep. When she got better, she was released and was able to keep her chanting under control henceforth.

She started a love affair with one of the professors from the Academy next (by no means the only student to do so). After about a year she stabbed her lover in bed. He did not press charges. Forest left him for a moody young lad with whom she shacked up in a remote village where they drank and painted together in medieval circumstances through a cold and gloomy winter. Towards the spring, Forest killed first her lover, then herself.

Still, in her case, one could have at least sensed it coming — sensed *something* coming.

But the other one, *our* Forest, had shown no early signs.

And yet, Alexandra wrote, Forest had gone mad. She insisted she was much younger than her birth certificate claimed, and said that her memories had been implanted into her brain by aliens, who were also poisoning our water. She had found them out and they were after her.

Alexandra thought, probably correctly, that Forest was trying to escape the mess of her life, and that things could still be put right if one could break through her fantasies to the sane core of her person. It was a job for a psychiatrist, if she could only get Forest to see one. The trouble was that Forest acted so normally that no hospital was prepared to keep her inside. Unfortunately, because Alexandra had tried to help her, Forest lost faith in her and began to hide even from her and Eagerwill. She disappeared for a while in Germany, surfaced in Paris, then vanished without trace. No one has any idea where she might be now.

Forest is now out of this story. I shall not mention her again.

While Alexandra and Eagerwill were away in the UK, I did not see much of Vicky either. In any case, I have already said everything there was to say about Vicky, except that she is now a Steiner teacher, mother to two little sons and wife of a man ten years younger than herself. She hates her husband. She seems to have already hated him when she became pregnant with their second child, but she wanted two kids, most likely because Alexandra had two. And she probably started going out with her husband in the first place because he was so much younger than she, like Eagerwill was younger than Alexandra.

Stamp.

Correction: Vicky is no longer with her husband. She is toughing it out on her own as insurance saleswoman and independent publisher, with two little sons. And she had the first one at the age of forty two! That girl is bloody fearless!

While Alexandra and Eagerwill were away in the UK, I learned quite a lot about painting, a subject which never really interested me in the first place.

I learned how to do without a story when painting a picture. I also learned how to get rid of *pretty*. And of symbols. And of desire to express stuff. And of message.

Once you get rid of all that, you're left with form, which is its own content. This form *doesn't have to be* abstract. Once you get into the 'must be' business, you're back to desire to express stuff, and to message. But it *can* be abstract. It can be *anything*. When you work on it, you discover that form which is its own content produces more content, and to some of that content you can eventually relate, just as you can to objects and events from the everyday world.

(That is exactly how the real world is made. Stamp!)

(If that is another cryptic statement, tough.)

Fine, you say, but what's that got to do with the price of hay? Well, here is what it has to do with the price of hay: by making the above discovery, I suddenly understood movies. Not only the ones with a message, but movies like the ones by Ford and Hawks and De Mille and Hitchcock, to name but a few Names.

I used to love movies before that, but only the ones which were blatantly *about,* preferably about something that interested me very much: about Life and Suffering, for example, because I forever hoped that someone would finally explain to me what it was, or about space, provided it was realistically treated, like in '2001'. I did not think that Ford's westerns were about anything. I thought they were pure entertainment, or, in other words, crap.

Having contemplated form for some years at the Academy, I went to see 'Star Wars', merely to keep abreast with the trend. I left the cinema in a daze, completely transformed. It was payoff time. By appreciating the *form* of 'Star Wars', I was able to see its *content* which would have, a year earlier, passed me by completely unnoticed.

First, I went to see 'Star Wars' some twenty — thirty times to wallow in the experience, then threw myself at the Old Masters of Hollywood. And the gates of Paradise opened! Ford was, I discovered, the new Shakespeare, an inexhaustible fountain of wisdom, compassion, and beauty. Hawks insisted that mankind's first duty was to build and maintain civilisation, be it in Hell itself. Hitchcock's merciless, stark-naked view of the world would have been unendurable were it not for the rigorous perfection of form which prevented his blade from actually slitting our throats (and his own, I suspect). And so on. And there were other masters, only marginally lesser, or not lesser at all. This is not the time or the place to discuss them. Suffice it to say that, having had my eyes thus opened, among other new and wonderful things I saw Wilfrid Blake.

Wilfrid Blake was my fellow student of the English Lang & Lit. His second subject was Philosophy, because he was fanatical about thought discipline. We used to spend a lot of time together reading and discussing great Eng Lit and going to the movies together, usually in the afternoon. Evenings, he would go to the Zagreb Cinématheque, on his own or with like-minded friends, to watch Old Hollywood Masters while I went home to moon about Sean Feeney or chat with Melissa.

Wilfrid was an oddball, an eccentric, a black sheep, a white crow. In the times of Flower Power and Jesus beards, he went around clean-shaven, crew-cut, with Rip Kirby specs, in a blue suit and carrying a black briefcase. He was, moreover, a brilliant student and an erudite without being snooty about it. He was fiercely secretive about his private life and discreet about the lives of others. He espoused traditional virtues, those of the Ten Commandments.

I felt a bit of a white crow myself, and was therefore comfortable in Wilfrid's company. Besides, he was happy to talk about Sean Feeney till the cows come home and shared my obsession with all things Irish.

Most importantly, hanging around Wilfrid, I discovered that there was life outside Alexandraville. (I knew that anyway, but, as ever, I needed somebody else's seal of approval before I could trust myself.) The Fromm- Saint-Exupéry syndrome which pervaded the salons and the intellectual climate of the seventies would make Wilfrid come out all over in a rash; self-analysis and desire for self-expression equalled self-indulgence in his book, and prolonged discussions about God, Life, Death and so on were preposterous and sinful (although Wilfrid was not religious). In a word, people like Alexandra and Eagerwill were, in his opinion, Sixty-Eighters and the tide of history had overtaken them. He knew them only from my description and had no desire to meet them.

Still scarred from our respective UK experience, both Melissa and I were delighted at the news that it was all right not to have to analyse them to death. It was in fact all right never to dwell on our failures and even more all right to leave everyone else well alone. One was to concentrate instead on the perfect understanding of art, particularly such art which had power and grandeur and celebrated the greatness of the human spirit, rather than indulging in the self-gratifying, navel-gazing art of — mainly European — auteurs. (Talking about art, Wilfrid had film, drama, literature and poetry in mind. When it came to visual arts, he had very little time for any painter or sculptor who did not express himself mainly in terms of the human figure, represented in its full glory.)

I could put away Dostoevsky whom I could not quite fathom and read Bernard Shaw whom I could, or so I believed.

And one was to live one's life in a similar way. One had to be neat, tidy, disciplined, civilised. That was one of Wilfrid's favourite words: civilised. Polite. Restrained. Pleasant in one's appearance and actions, not dishevelled and dissolute like the hippies. One's mind had to be kept clear and bright, not befogged by drink, drugs, pop-music and any other kind of dissipation and licence.

Melissa and I finally felt justified in spending hours poring over pictures of elegant women surrounded by understated — civilised — opulence in the glossies. We thought that Alexandra and Eagerwill were sad cases for not wanting a TV-set or a telephone in their newly purchased flat.

Best of all was that I could feel I had rebelled against Mama — a fantastically dishevelled and uncivilised creature — without having to tear myself away from her in order to have a Life. It was okay not to worry about Life at all. I could leave that to Ingmar Bergman, Alexandra and Eagerwill with a clean conscience. Mama, too, did not fail to notice the advantages of Wilfrid Blake's influence over her Kitten.

I now like Ingmar Bergman again. And I can tell Wilfrid I do. I did tell him, a while ago. It was all right, because I knew why I liked what I liked. Wilfrid respected that.

That is a wonderful trait of Wilfrid's character: he knows how to respect. I wish I could say I know how to respect, too, now, but I fear I would not be entirely truthful. And that is something I know how to do: to be truthful. Or so I believe.

Wilfrid could also understand compassion and humility (not the quality of behaviour which Uriah Heep called "being 'umble", but humility like the one of St Francis when he talked to birds and bees because he felt they were parts of the flow of the Energy of the Universe, no less – and perhaps more – than he). That part of Wilfrid was a total mystery to me. I could not relate to compassion or humility, because they demanded that one opens the door and steps out into the wide world.

I have done that since, and guess who I found out there waiting for me: Alexandra, who, as soon as she saw me standing outside, in the wide world, encouraged me to call her Alex at last. But I found many other people out there, too, who would have otherwise remained invisible, or, worse, mistaken for myself.

Anyway, in that one mysterious part of his person, in this compassion and humility business, Wilfrid Blake remained distant and aloof from me and because of that I was ready to take orders from him. That is how things work with me. I stand in awe from whatever is distant and aloof, and then I follow orders.

Wilfrid was crazy about America and moved in the circles of those who shared his passion. America, he thought, was full of youthful energy which soared triumphant over the graveyards of Europe. America, he thought, possessed an innocence of mind, a childish but immensely powerful self-confidence, which was worth more than Europe's sophistication. America had integrity and was untroubled by doubt. America's link with the Spirit was clear and strong while Europe's was tarnished if not completely severed. Entangled in her own complications, Europe spun aimlessly around like a squirrel in a cage while America marched steadily on to conquer the world. That did not mean that everything America did was good. It meant that it was powerful.

As far as the Far East was concerned, Wilfrid, along with John Wayne in 'Donovan's Reef', preferred not to probe the depths of the Oriental mind. He bowed to its elegance, its refined balance, its tenacity and so on, but recoiled from what he felt was the gloom of ancient and alien evil and the tendency to slavishly submit to the Spirit rather than attempt to be propelled by it. Most of all he felt that the Far East – with the exception of Confucianism – did not place Man at the centre of its world picture. Wilfrid respected Confucianism for its pragmatism and civilised dignity.

And yet, he swore by I-Ching. He made *me* swear by it. He never let me make an important decision without consulting the Oracle first.

Following Wilfrid's reading of the Oracle, I moved to the UK when I did and recognised my future husband as the one I was meant to marry. At the time, I was totally, desperately in love with Wilfrid.

Is there going to be any sex in this chapter soon? No. How come that I fell in love with Wilfrid? Read all about it later. This chapter is about something else.

The younger generation — students, graduates and the young professionals of Agram and beyond — were in a peculiar mood then, at the advent of the eighties. The Wilting of Socialism had begun. It was no longer merely the done thing to have everything Western and be interested only in Western matters and affairs: it was the rule; it was, in fact taken for granted. Everyone was blasé about it and pettily, mewlingly annoyed by not being an actual, recognised part of the West. Everyone wished English to be their mother tongue. Or

German, German would have done nicely. How do I know that? Because I was like that myself, and it took ages for any new trend to reach me.

When I say everyone, I exclude those early morning risers I mentioned earlier, the sallow-faced, shabbily-clad workers of both sexes, young and not so young, who would be swallowed by factories long before I got up to a coffee and a ciggie and leisurely discussions about esoteric subjects with Mama. No one knew what those workers thought. No one knew who they were, where they lived. No one knew that they existed at all. Even the Communist Party had forgotten all about them. They were there because they could not afford not to be; churning out unwanted goods with unpopular socialist labels, which they bought afterwards in shops because they could not afford to go to Trieste or London or Paris.

I make no apologies for mentioning them so often.

I also exclude Alexandra and Eagerwill. And Vicky. They did not wish that English were their mother tongue.

Those of us who could afford to, said that socialism had no sense of dignity and beauty, that it was drab. We said that without capitalism nothing could be interesting or beautiful, because only the pressure to sell and beat the competition made people design and produce beautiful, quality goods and thus eventually make the whole environment beautiful and interesting.

We evidently had little faith in creativity for its own sake.

And everything *was* drab, somehow. (How could it be otherwise when it was not wanted?)

I was in my late twenties, like most people I knew. One quarter of our lives had flown by. It was time we became America, or, at least, Italy, and we had become neither. It was time our books were published, our paintings exhibited, our films produced and filling world's cinemas, but it had not happened. We had not written or painted any, of course, but we thought that was because of the accursed socialism, the all-engulfing morass in the midst of which one could not create: one could merely croak.

The fact was that none of us young bloods had done a day's honest work in our lives. We did not have to. When we opened our mouths, food, drink and fags popped into them.

Perhaps we were right about man needing to be whipped into creativity.

I prefer to think we weren't. I prefer to think that a situation which allowed a large number of young people to grow and create with no other motivation but their own free will to do so was a new phenomenon. After a couple of bored, disoriented generations, perhaps, we would have been able to witness, for the first time ever, unforced work and creativity.

But the rest of the world was not willing to let us develop at our own pace.

It is also true that we were a bunch of lazy, conceited, gullible sluggards.

Now we'll never know. Heigh-ho, oh woe.

So there we were, I and my new crew, Wilfrid and Melissa, twenty five, then twenty six, twenty seven, twenty eight; not having had done anything, but already too late. And while we waited to grow bolder, our parents and indeed everything around us grew older. Hell, truth to tell, I was growing older as well! Inevitably the day would come when I would simply have to take any available job, shut my intellectual gob and become one of the mob. My life would be one long chore and therefore a bore.

It began to look like I would never get to live in the UK or anywhere abroad. It looked like I might have to wake up in Agram every morning of my life. It also looked like I would remain my mother's companion for the rest of her natural life, even if I did find a job, because getting a place of one's own was not a viable proposition in Agram.

How did Alexandra do it? Why, she married Eagerwill and they did it together. They lived for a year in the 'Digrado', in the UK, in Western Europe, and did not shop. They put the money aside instead and bought a flat. That was how Alexandra did it. She could not have done it without Eagerwill, or he without her. Without each other, they would have remained with their respective parents, a daughter and a son, not a woman and a man.

Vicky had also done it. How did she do it? She married Romano. Romano left soon afterwards, like I already said, and went back to his grandparents and his Bösendorfer. He did not mind living like that. He was his own person.

I have not mentioned Romano much in this story, but I am now prepared to confess that I always envied him.. Envied what? I don't know. He always came and went as he pleased. I think I envied him that. He appeared to know who he was. I envied him that, too. He was not a very nice person and I was scared of him. That was yet another reason for my envy. Eagerwill did not approve of him, so I erased Romano from my universe. But I still envy him a bit. He didn't really give a fuck about Eagerwill's disapproval or, if he did, he did not let on.

Vicky then replaced Romano with Allbright. And that was how she did it.

But I, I did not know how or where to begin.

I suppose I could have really gone out to look for a job, in which case I would have found one, as a waitress, maybe, or a cleaner. I could have rented a bedsit somewhere, or worse, shared one with several other girls.

Amazingly, my much younger cousin Daisy did just that. Her parents lived in the Croatian Downs on the other side of the Bear Mountain, in the sticks, in a marital hell of jealousy and venom utterly unfounded on fact. Daisy studied in Agram and wanted to live there. When she graduated, she took on the job of a cleaner and shared a bedsit with three other girls in order not to have to live with my Uncle Christian and Aunt Caroline.

This is how crazy Uncle Christian and Aunt Caroline really were: when their house, built with the money left by grandfather Armand, was completed, Uncle Christian was requested to give up his council flat That was the official policy and it was only fair: another family could be housed in that flat. But Uncle Christian would not dream of letting go of it, and it turned out that he could actually keep it if he divorced Aunt Caroline as they would then be two families and would not be expected to live under the same roof. So they got divorced, both perfectly aware of why they were doing it; yet they chose to embellish the already unsavoury affair with bitter rows, accusing each other of adultery. Uncle Christian went as far as declaring that Daisy was not his daughter while Aunt Caroline sobbed and swallowed tranquillisers by the handful.

It was all for nothing. Someone must have seen through their game, because they had to give up the flat in the end and move into the new house together. They never re-married.

Daisy lives in Canada now, with a model husband and a lovely daughter, May. Good for her.

"Stolen money brings no happiness," was Papa's comment on uncle Christian misfortunes, meaning that grandfather Armand's money should have been shared equally by his three children. He did not speak to Uncle Christian for years.

"Couldn't you at least give him a ring?" I said to Papa. "He phones from time to time when he's sure you're out."

"He shouldn't have done it," Papa replied.

"Please."

"No."

"Daisy would like you to speak to him," I said. Papa was fond of Daisy and she was welcome in our home at any time of day or night.

"Daisy has nothing to do with it," said Papa and did not relent.

Years later, when I moved to the UK and Papa and Mama were left alone, he *did* relent. And Uncle Christian was so grateful! He became like a child, deferring to Papa in everything. He consulted him about every silly little thing and was finally allowed to visit. He nearly went off his trolley on that occasion for sheer joy and gratitude. It was exactly like Alfredo and Michael in 'Godfather Two.'

But listen to this: when Papa died and was buried, I was chief mourner since Mama was, as ever, too unwell to attend. Uncle Christian came with me to the flat after the funeral.

While Mama sat in her usual place, wrapped up in a tatty black shawl, staring into space and smoking, uncle Christian slithered up to her, writhing, grinning, sighing.

"Patty," he said, "how are you bearing up, Patty?"

"As well as can be expected," Mama replied coldly. She could not stand the man and she hated being called Patty.

"Do you need anything, Patty? Just tell me, and I'll... or Caroline, she'll come over at once and she'll —"

"Thank you, Christian," said Mama, "but that won't be necessary. My daughter—" she squeezed my hand — "is here and she'll do whatever *is* necessary."

Uncle Christian pulled up a chair and sat face-to-face with Mama, bending his back to look in her eyes. "Patty," he said in a low voice which trembled with excitement, "listen... I want to tell you something... I have an idea. Patty... not now, you understand, not now, but when you recover, you know, when everything's... settled... I'd be prepared to marry you, Patty."

Mama looked at him as if he was crazy, which he was. *I* looked at him as if he was crazy. I even said, "Are you crazy, Uncle?"

Uncle Christian looked surprised and indignant. It was obvious he had meant what he said. "Why not?" he said, spreading his arms. "What's crazy about it? I'm a bachelor, I can marry a widow."

"We've just come back from Papa's *funeral*," I said, as if the situation needed explaining.

"I don't mean now, at once," Uncle Christian rattled on, "I mean later, later. Look, Patty, see, now the Council will tell you to move into a smaller flat because Emanuel is dead and your daughter lives in the UK... and this marvellous, enormous flat will be lost! It'll go to some swine who doesn't need it! You and I will not live forever, you want to make sure that your child has somewhere to return to when she comes to her senses... and returns to Agram."

All my family thought I had taken leave of my senses when I went to live in the UK with a man forty years my senior.

"Both she and Daisy would have somewhere to be when

they're in Agram... the place is huge... and, of course, my niece is always welcome in my house... as if it were her own. What the hell — it is her own!" He even grinned. "We don't have to live together; I know you wouldn't want to, I understand that. I'd only stay here when I come to Agram — "

"Show him out," said Mama to me in a terrible, gravelly voice.

"All right, all right, Patty," said Uncle Christian and made for the door without my help. "But think about it, it's reasonable."

Mama did not lose the flat. She reported me as still living with her and paid rates for me, as well as a slightly higher rent than before, because there was so much surplus space on the premises. She did not want to change her habits and the familiar surroundings.

When Daisy got married and became pregnant, Mama let her and her husband come and live in the flat. Daisy's husband worked in the oil-fields some fifty miles east of Agram and only came home weekends. When the baby was born, Daisy could not cope on her own. Aunt Caroline and Uncle Christian came to stay with her in the flat. The three of them quarrelled incessantly and the baby screamed. After a week, Mama lost her patience and threw them all out.

I was in the UK when that happened. Melissa wrote and told me all about it. She was very angry with Mama and thought she was a selfish bitch. I remembered Uncle Christian's mad proposal, but, on the whole, agreed with Melissa. One did not throw nursing mothers and babies out, even if they did have somewhere to go. It would have been much more convenient for Daisy to have stayed in Agram. She, in her turn, could have done Mama's shopping and cleaning. And there was room enough in the flat. But there you are.

Melissa thought I could have done something about the situation, but she was wrong. I was in twenty kinds of trouble myself and could not spare the time or the energy.

Besides, I would not have intervened even if I could. Mama was a person, Daisy was a person, Melissa was a person, they were all adults down there and able to sort out their own lives.

Afterwards, a hate campaign started around Mama and has not stopped to this very day. Somewhere between my writing this chapter and the one about Pierre and Steve and the ambiguities, Mama died in a care home. But the myth of Patricia Prochazka, the inhuman, blood-sucking monster-woman lives on.

I had to resort to lies in order to persuade Aunt Olivia to let Mama's ashes lie beside Papa's. I said that Papa had once told me he would have liked it thus. Why was it a lie? Because Papa never talked about dying and ashes.

After Papa's death, Aunt Olivia and Uncle Christian began idolising his memory. Emanuel had been a saint. He had always been wise, honest and ready to help. He would have lived to be a hundred had it not been his fate to fall into the clutches of that evil hag, that serpent Patricia who slowly strangled him with her relentless coils. And then she treated his family as serfs, expecting them to run her errands while she pretended to be ill.

Uncle Christian made a shrine to Papa in his attic. He would go there on his own and sit feeling his clothes and smelling them. He dared not wear them.

By the same token, Mama used to kiss my old slippers once I was no longer with her. We human beings are all as bad as each other.

I still wear Papa's leather jackets. He had wonderful jackets. He was a fashion victim.

Anyway, with Alexandra and Eagerwill in their own flat and no longer children but married adults, I felt ill at ease in their company. I did not know what to say to them except discuss art, literature and philosophy. But they discussed it in their own home, while I had to skulk back to Mama's afterwards. That made whatever came out of my mouth sound hollow.

I was weary to death of feeling guilty for not living. In addition, I was sickeningly certain that my planned novel about

Henry the Second of England would never find a publisher in Yugoslavia. I was equally certain that I could never become sufficiently interested in my surroundings to write a novel about them. What on earth could happen in such a novel? There could be no dramatic moral choices to be made, and no punishments to suffer for them. Consequently, the characters would have no reason to investigate the meaning of life or wrestle with loss of faith in God.

All that people did was work and have children who in their turn became mothers and fathers and went to work, whereupon they started looking forward to their pension and securing a place in an old people's home.

But it did not look like I would be able to leave Agram any time soon.

I realised I was scared.

Suddenly I feared everything. Cancer in the first place, then earthquakes, insects, and the death of Michael the dog who was getting old. Then I feared the morning of each new day: what decisions I might have to make, what queues I might have to stand in, what rain to walk in, what expressions of Mama's displeasures to endure, what headache, what toothache, what constipation. Then the evening of each day as it went by: what lack of company, what indigestion, what heart palpitations, what insomnia.

One night, having stared at the ceiling and listened to the coughing and tossing and turning and farting of old and ageing people in the two adjoining bedrooms, I finally slept and I dreamt, and here is my dream:

In London, amidst vast, exotic parklands planted with trees whose leaves shine with all the colours of the rainbow, there lies a formidable mansion, almost a palace, white and serene. A mysterious woman lives in it, all by herself. She is not allowed out, and is, in fact, without any rights, being completely outside the law. She is a sort of National Criminal, supported in luxury by the state, because she is an indispensable person: her function is to teach people fear and destroy innocence.

She reads a lot and has a massive library. She is an intellectual of Evil.

People come to her of their own free will and even pay to jump the queue. Their need to be *treated* by her is irresistible, although they are perfectly aware that visiting her can be dangerous or even lethal. Almost everyone alive has been to see her, and those who haven't are planning to go. Visits to her can be won as prizes for outstanding achievement at school or at work.

Eager seekers throng up the stately staircase of the mansion to her secret study, meeting on their way those who have already received instruction and are now descending the same staircase staring at the newcomers with huge, terrified eyes out of which the joy of life has forever vanished. It is clear that those people will never laugh again; they'll merely grin and sneer.

Her séances are short, half an hour or less. During that time, the Teacher of Fear takes her students to the black heart of the world. The means she uses to achieve this are numerous, including speech, song, torture, sex and other things, perhaps, unnameable and indescribable. She rips people open to show them their own nether depths, where they find darkness, evil and, above all, fear — fear as the Governing Principle, fear as essence, fear as God. Then they leave, devastated and speechless, while she remains smiling in her dark, stark study.

I have won a visit to her as prize for being a good student. Unexpectedly, I feel quite comfortable in her presence: she is graceful and serene, with shining black eyes full of wisdom, and a warm smile. For some reason she does not wish to apply her usual procedure in my case, but encourages me to examine her library instead. I lose myself completely among her books and soon begin to understand what they are about.

I feel I could love this woman like I have never loved anyone before. I want to spend all my time near her and become like her.

Asleep, I must have known something I did not know awake. Awake, I thought the world was in essence beautiful and meaningful, if only headaches, real or metaphorical, did not interfere with my appreciation of it, and if only I could stop feeling guilty for revelling in its beauty! I honestly believed I had not had direct experience of darkness and evil. I only flirted with such concepts to stay on other people's good books. I believed there were no ancient sockets in my home.

Then one day I woke up, perhaps after that very dream, and saw that my entire home, together with its inhabitants, was one dark, smoking Ancient Socket.

Mottled with grease, cooking vapours and cigarette smoke, not changed for well over ten years, the wallpaper was yellowing and peeling away. The balcony had a deep crack in the middle and looked just about ready to break up and tumble into the back yard. Our two fridges were rusting; the furniture had lost most of its varnish, and no object, decorative or not, matched any other in the house in style or colour. The flat was full of convenient places to sit down, fuller still of places to lie down and while away the time in pleasant stupor (or just stupor). Places designed to promote activity were precious few.

And this depressing space was full of people sitting down or lying down at regular periods. Michael the dog, ageing fast, also had his places to lie down, which he did most of the time. The sounds we creatures of this space made in it were equally depressing, and the worst of it was that I could anticipate all of them well in advance, including my own.

And the radio always had to be on, but turned down so low that one had to strain one's ears to hear whether it was on or not, because Mama could not stand loud sounds.

She had taken early retirement. She had fallen down a staircase at work — only a stair or two, not the whole depth of it — and bruised her shin. She had taken time off to nurse it, gone back to work, found out that her shin was not yet up to scratch, taken some more time off, repeated the whole exercise, and then given up trying and taken early retirement. Her bosses in Government Administration & Finance were pleased to see the back of her, although she was, as a worker, almost indispensable.

Everyone went to bed very early, while I stayed up regularly till two or three in the morning, writing about Henry the Second. The flat was very quiet at that hour. By and by, I became afraid of it and all that was in it. I felt the presence of Evil, although I was brought up to believe in atoms and molecules. Evil was all around me and, worst of all, inside me as well.

It was in my persisting migraines, my facial tics, acid indigestion, heart palpitations and slightly raised temperature. And I swallowed it every day in the form of diazepam tablets. They used to prescribe diazepam very liberally in those days. The whole nation was, more or less, on diazepam. By my bedside, I always kept an ashtray, a packet of cigarettes, a lighter, a glass of water, a packet of painkillers and a packet of diazepam tablets. Within easy reach was also an orange A4 notebook, into which I wrote down my dreams directly after having dreamt them — the ones to be found in this book, and many more.

Why did I feel there was Evil in that? I was not quite sure then, but it had to have something to do with rejection of Life.

This, by the way, is how I define Evil, now, many years afr the Ancient Socket, in Dracula's Castle which was home, had gone up in smoke:

Evil is when we, *on purpose*, corrupt or hurt others (or even ourselves) in order to avoid pain. Almost always, we tell ourselves stories that convince us we're not doing anything wrong. But deep inside, we always know and *still* do it.

How do I know? Through looking and listening. Our eyes and the tone of our voices give us away. And the words we say.

We hardly ever pause to unpack the neat little parcels of words that readily drop off our tongues. That's because most of us learn from our parents how and when to spew those parcels effectively. But sometimes, sometimes a wrong parcel comes out; or the right one emerges too fast or not smoothly enough. A watchful person might be alerted by such a slip. If alerted, the watchful person might pause to take a closer look. And find oneself staring into a bottomless pit full of swirling fumes of sulphur.

This definition of evil is only applicable to human beings and their doings.

How about Evil as principle, then? Does it, as a principle, exist? (If it does, then Good, as principle, must exist too. If it does, then they are called God and the Devil and we should all go to church every day.)

I'd like to say that it doesn't. Most of the time I cannot detect its presence in the Energy Flow of the Universe. But that may be so Mondays and Wednesdays, while Tuesdays and, say, Fridays, I feel rather more fully awake and in a black mood.

Thus, Tuesdays and Fridays, I remember that there is such a thing as the Second Law of Thermodynamics which is absolutely irrefutable and present in everything everywhere. In simple terms, it says, "Entropy always increases."

What is entropy? It is the gradual permeation of everything by everything else.

Stop here and meditate for a moment. Try and imagine what you've just read.

What does it mean?

In order for *this* to be different from *that*, *this* has to have a boundary, and a structure different from the one of *that*. That boundary and that structure is called Form.

(Mould. Stamp!)

If *this* and *that* permeate one another fully, their form is lost. If everything permeates everything else, all form is lost. Perhaps the disappearance or the weakening of Form makes everything permeate everything else. Whichever be the case, there is an inherent tendency, a Principle, in everything towards permeating everything else at the expense of Form.

If Evil is a Principle at all, it is the Principle of Entropy. It is impossible for me to say at this stage whether this Principle has conscious volition. If not, it should perhaps not be called Evil; maybe it should be called Gloom or Doom.

If it *does* have volition, though, then it is Evil, period. And if that is so, then Form is the Principle of Good. Form is God. Which is the same as saying that Word is God. As is written in the Bible.

Ah, but Mondays and Wednesdays, when my mood is not black but merely bleak, I like to believe that the process of dissipation may somehow be circular and lead back to its own beginning, or that we may have completely misunderstood the Universe and that the Second Law of Thermodynamics only appears to be universal because of our imperfect means of interpreting what we perceive. Maybe nothing is ever gained or lost, maybe everything that exists is merely a kaleidoscope of revolving images behind which there hides... what?

Sundays, when I feel I can face anything, I realise, of course, that there is no more meaning behind one scheme than behind the other. The first one, with God and Devil, makes for a better story; the other one does not engage the heart, but is less contrived and therefore more life-like. But behind both there is an impenetrable grey screen and a silence which even the deaf must hear from time to time.

The only thing one can do given the circumstances, then, is to fight Entropy wherever one can, and that includes things like washing the dishes when one's not in the mood. It appears that it won't make a blind bit of difference whether we do or whether we don't, but we can at least have our fight to be proud of. A fight is a story, hence Form, hence a raspberry in the face of Entropy.

Back then in Agram, I did not know that. All I knew was that the whole business was scary.

My home had surrendered to Entropy, rather too readily, Mama acting as Entropy's Fifth Column. That was why it had become Dracula's Castle.

And I was seriously infected with the blood of Dracula. Wilfrid's championship of Form kept me on my toes to a degree, but, unfortunately, Wilfrid was infected, too. His home – and he knew that – was another Dracula's Castle, different in appearance but similar in essence: Wilfrid's mother was obsessively tidy and anything not forbidden was compulsory[1].

---

1 This superb expression appears in T H White's 'The Once and

Wilfrid's bedroom, which he shared with his father, was full of feminine knick-knacks, embroidery and lace. Wilfrid never, absolutely never ever, invited friends home.

Aunt Olivia was like Wilfrid's mother. She shared a bedroom with Melissa, had been known to hoover the flat at three in the morning and insisted that shoes had to be left outside. And Melissa never invited anyone home, except Daisy and myself. She lives in her Dracula's Castle even now, in mortal peril of becoming a Dracula herself. She is plugged into the Socket.

(She has unplugged herself since! She has sold her old flat and bought a new one! She'll never be Dracula! Well done, Melissa!!)

Suddenly, in nineteen seventy eight, my fear and unease assumed a concrete form. They surfaced, aptly enough, in the form of putrefaction.

One fine autumn day, after having been with Wilfrid to the British Council library, where we borrowed a few records of early music, I accompanied Nan Josephine to the local medical centre, where she had an appointment with her GP because of persistent pain in her right heel and her right toe.

It was quite warm; Nan and I walked slowly, and then settled for a protracted wait at the centre. I mention all this because it was the last time Nan Josephine walked the streets of Agram. I wish to honour that last walk.

Her GP had a quick look at her foot, pressed her leg above the ankle with two fingers and said it was nothing. He prescribed diuretics and told Nan to bind the foot tightly and douse the bandage with surgical spirit. "Bind and douse," he said, "bind and douse."

"But what is it?" asked Nan.

"Bind and douse and call the next patient in as you leave, please."

That was how it was done in those days. Why have a tannoy or make the nurse get up when the patients can call the next

Future King'

one in themselves?

Why indeed? After all, the whole affair is less alienated that way. One gets involved with the process a bit, doesn't one? Like getting the audience involved in a play.

But binding and dousing did not do the trick. The pain got worse.

So I knelt down by Nan and had a good look at her foot. I couldn't see anything out of the ordinary at first, but then, looking harder and harder, I noticed a minute dark spot on her heel, and a similar one on the tip of her toe. I prodded those with one finger and Nan went through the roof.

I had never seen it or a description of it, or known that one could get it at all other than on a battlefield or on a Polar expedition, but I knew with absolute certainty what it was. "Nan," I said, "it's gangrene. You can stop binding and dousing, and we must get you to a real doctor."

Papa made a phone call and that very evening one of his tennis partners, Dr Rustler, came round to see Nan's foot. His verdict was much as I expected: Nan was to go into hospital at once. She would be given one of Dr Rustler's grace and favour beds, because he was Primarius — Consultant in Agramese — at the cardiovascular clinic there. After the visit, in the kitchen over a cup of coffee, Papa slipped Dr Rustler a blue envelope.

'Blue envelope' means bribe. The term was coined in the days when virtually all envelopes in Yugoslavia were blue. Later, when white and other envelopes became available, people continued to use blue ones for that particular purpose. That way everyone knew what was what.

Mama detested blue envelopes but for once kept her mouth shut. Nan Josephine was her mum.

Once in the hospital, Nan had to wait two months for her arteries to be examined. The imported apparatus was out of order and had to be sent to Switzerland to be repaired. During those two months, Nan's gangrene advanced alarmingly. Her toe and her heel turned black and exuded a putrid smell which nothing could dispel.

Retired and thus no longer subject to any kind of

enforcement, Mama never went to see her. She said her nerves could not stand hospital atmosphere.

Papa and I visited Nan on alternate days to bring her clean nighties and underwear and to wash her and clean her dentures. It was another example of DIY patient care. I would bring a thermos of coffee along, sit in the corridor with Nan, share the coffee and smoke a cigarette while we chatted.

Eventually Nan's leg got examined. The news was bad: the artery in her knee was clogged up by cholesterol and eaten up by sugar. It could have been bypassed had she been examined in time, but now the bypass could not help any more: deprived of fresh blood, the flesh of her leg had died and was rotting away. If she wanted to live, the leg would have to come off above the knee.

Nan wouldn't hear of it. The negotiations went on for another month, and then Nan started screaming at night, because the pain in her foot had become unbearable. She was given morphine, to no avail. The Evil Socket was ablaze and nothing could put the fire out. When the morphine dose she received every few hours reached its maximum, Nan signed the form permitting the amputation. It was carried out straight away.

I saw her two hours after the surgery. Drugged up to her eyebrows, cool as a cucumber, she said she was fine. "I don't care what happens now," she said. "The pain's gone. Nice to see you, but do go home." I kissed her, then had a quick look at the stump. It was freshly bandaged and looked neat. The fire was out, even the smoke was dispersing. The Socket seemed to have been rendered harmless.

Why not send a probe down that harmless little Socket? Let's have a look. Nan Josephine, remember, once was that young girl who used to walk about in freezing cold carrying her jumper over her arm and crying because there was no one to tell her to put it on. Further in her life, she went on insisting that everything stay the same. Also, that everything be *nice*. And that no one dare *shout*. And that someone always does something about whatever problem is at hand, someone other than herself. Because she did not know how. And because she simply had *no nerves.*

That last phrase was later picked up by Mama. Whenever something went against the grain with her, in her later years, she would start crying and repeating like a tape on loop, "I have no nerves at all... no nerves... no nerves... no nerves... no nerves..."

But Nan Josephine had *oodles* of nerves and she *did* know how, whenever she got into a tight spot. She would then go and *do* stuff, moaning and complaining and insisting on being helpless and stupid and ill and weak and old (already at forty-something).

She loved good food and merriment. Her black eyes would sparkle in good company. Everyone who knew her thought her the salt of the earth, a fine lady, the life and the soul of the party.

Yet Nan Josephine, with no outsiders about to cast a critical eye on her doings, used to let her hair down in an alarming way. Her housekeeping was loose, greasy and sloppy. In the heat of the summer, she used to go about the house with nothing but her bra, her knickers and her grease-splattered apron on.

We all used to go around with nothing on, only we did not claim to be nice, fine ladies like she did.

For the record, there is absolutely nothing wrong in going around with nothing on.

Nan used to smoke while cooking and drop cigarette ashes into the soup. Then Grandpa Ludwig gave up smoking and told her she had to do the same. She obeyed, happy to have been ordered to.

Nan Josephine craved authority. She had been brought up to believe in God, but the authority of God had always been too dry and remote for her. She wanted authority draped in flesh. Somewhere along the line she lost religion altogether, because under the quivering mimosa skin there dwelled a sharp, cold mind which observed the world and decided that no God had ever created and maintained such a mess. And if in spite of that it were proved to her that there was a God, He would have to be the very essence of Evil. So she got married and passed the buck. Why act when all actions in an evil, meaningless world must by definition be evil and meaningless? Let someone else be evil, she'll just sit back and obey orders.

Come to think of it, the meekness and the niceness of so many people must stem from the same type of conscious or — in most cases — unconscious reasoning. Millions of nice people, perhaps, feel in their innermost selves that the world is evil and that they really want nothing to do with it.

Yet they want pleasure and happiness and *love*. To pass the time comfortably and agreeably.

If you sit back and let the others be evil instead of you (who, presumably, are righteous or at least not responsible), you cannot love anyone. Because they act, see? Because they're evil. (But you still *need* the buggers, to *do stuff* for you and stop you from being alone.) If you are one of those nice millions, you then become *sentimental*. That is what happens when you need to love and cannot love.

And that is how it was with Nan Josephine. She did not love anyone, not even her precious daughter Patricia (who was acutely aware of the fact). The closest she came to loving anyone was with me, when I was little. How do I know that? Because she gave me generously of her Self: she played with me, not to amuse me but really. Mama would have never done that, not to the point of looking silly. And then later, just before she died, Nan loved me again. How do I know that? Because she spoke to me from her innermost being. From the Socket.

No wonder that, not believing in anything and not loving anyone, Nan Josephine became sloppy and greasy and droopy. No wonder niceness and sentimentality turned to sugar in her blood which devoured her eyes and her kidneys and her arteries.

Ready to throw up yet? Reaching for the blood sugar test to measure your niceness? How long before the sentimental bug takes the first nibble at your retina?

Let's descend deeper into the Socket. Listen to this: when

Nan Josephine was a poor young teacher who had just left the protection of her childhood home where others did things and told her when to put her woolly-pully on, she looked around desperately to find someone to whom she could pass the buck of Life. Along came Grandfather Ludwig, a young engineer who had just landed a dream job. He saw her and vowed to have her, the raven-haired beauty that she was. But lo, she would not surrender the cherry unless he married her first. "If that is how the matter stands," said Grandfather Ludwig, "so be it," and married her forthwith.

On their wedding night, he approached the bed where his bride lay amidst embroidery and lace, placed his hand on her virginal body and uttered these amazing words: "May this womb remain forever barren."

Did Josephine throw him out of the window? Not at all. They made love. Read that again: they made *love*. And in that night of love they made Patricia. Bring in the violins, throw the snow!

I heard that story from Patricia herself, quite recently. That means Nan Josephine told her about it at some stage or other. When? At what stage? Before diazepam or after? Above all, *why?*

Shortly after Patricia was born, Josephine developed some kind of feminine complaint and had to have her womb and her ovaries removed. I used to amuse myself with the long, jagged scar as I lay on top of her huge, sweaty naked belly when I was four or five.

The curse had worked. Ancient Evil!

But why on earth did Ludwig curse Josephine's womb? The story is that he felt blackmailed into marriage, coerced into it, pushed into it, entrapped by the voracious womb. On the other hand, he could have foregone the conquest of Josephine's pussy and found one with no strings attached.

He had to have that one and none other.

But there was more to it than punishing the Eternal Female. Little did Ludwig know at the time that Josephine was a willing recipient of his curse. She did not want children any more than he. She did not want to make more evildoers. And Ludwig himself thought that the world was a Garden of Eden, full of beautiful and innocent happy creatures — plants and animals — blighted by the plague of one damned, hopeless species of being: man. The best man could do, under the circumstances, Ludwig thought, was to observe and know the beautiful Universe, try not to do it harm and breed himself out of existence by-and-by.

Josephine did not even admire animals and plants.

Those two smilers produced and raised Patricia.

And raised me, too, later.

Being a consummate actress, Nan Josephine played theatre with me. I would be Dr Kildare[2] and she all the patients, nurses and consultants. I would be a nice dog and she my stupid and cruel master, mistress and their disgusting son. The plot was always the same: I would do right, she wrong. I would suffer for being right but would eventually show her up. Mama thought such games would damage my respect for Nan, but she was wrong. I adored Nan Josephine. I felt at ease with her. I felt she did not want to possess me.

Ludwig the nature-worshipper taught me about animals and plants and other natural history. He taught me so much that I had nothing to do during my first four years at school. The one subject he never mentioned was Man and his doings.

Mama was not too keen on the subject of Man, either. I grew up believing that Man was the one boring, repulsive feature of the Universe of stars, volcanoes, animals and plants. I never played with dolls. I played with toy animals. Dolls were ugly and boring: they looked like human beings. Sir David Attenborough, Bernhard Grzimek, Jacques Cousteau and Haroun Tazieff are still my Four Apostles.

For those who don't know, Bernhard Grzimek, thanks to whom we now have the Serengeti Nature Park in Tanzania used to be the Director of the Frankfurt Zoo. Haroun Tazieff is

2 A 60's American TV series about a junior doctor in a hospital, with Richard Chamberlain and Raymond Massey

the father of volcanology. I have mentioned him before. And everyone knows who Jacques Cousteau was.

Bless them.

Still, I could have done worse. Beats shopping at Harrods any day, I say.

Nan Josephine and Grandfather Ludwig went on living together in perfect harmony and understanding till death did them part. Never did they raise voices at each other, never utter a harsh word in anger. They rose together every morning and went to bed together every evening. They were welcoming hosts, the very embodiment of hearth and home, only they hardly ever invited anyone lest their daily routine got disturbed. They ate well and slept soundly. Their conversations revolved around the next day's meals: what to buy and how to cook it. Ludwig never raised any subject of conversation that could upset Josephine or strain her mind. Never ever did Josephine mention anything personal, like "Do you love me?" Or "Did you ever love me?" They discussed the upbringing of Patricia, later of me, like two good friends working together on the same task. There was no clash of opinions, no rivalry. Ultimately, whatever Ludwig decided went. It was nicer that way, saved breath, left more free time for comfortable pursuits, for another cup of coffee, another slice of cake. Life was soft. And their bodies were soft and white and they both perspired a lot. Nan Josephine slept with a thick woollen scarf wrapped around her midriff. She was worried she might catch a chill on her kidneys. Grandfather Ludwig slept with a handkerchief on his head in case he sweated at night. There was a clammy hothouse atmosphere around them, propitious to growth of blood pressure and diabetes.

I loved living with them when I was little. It was cosy. Nothing ever changed and everything promised an unchanging future. Kids enjoy that when they are little. While they watch the Energy Flow of the Universe.

I did not know then that Ludwig and Josephine never moved because they had nowhere to go and nothing to aim for: in Life, all was bad and all effort worthless, while after Life there was nothing. I thought they sat still because they were happy and comfortable.

They *were* comfortable, and probably quite happy as well.

They also became ailing and then seriously ill while I was still a child, but that, too, was part of the never-changing always. They were Nan and Grandfather, and they were ill and their hair was grey like mine was mousy blond. Medical centres and hospitals were full of ill grandmothers and grandfathers with grey hair. Trees grew in parks. Sun rose in the East.

And now the leg was sawn off, the left one like Frau Margarete's. There were two, then there was one. I'd have to stop letting be and start getting things done.

My fear was that I had postponed getting things done for too long and ended up doing the wrong ones: instead of setting up house with a handsome young bloke and wiping fresh, pink bottoms of babies, I would have to sweep the empty halls of Dracula's Castle and wash Nan Josephine's dentures. I felt I had somehow missed the whole middle part of life and, by missing it, overtaken it and found myself at the decaying tail end of it all, in the same boat with Mama and Nan.

Nan could live for quite a few years yet, and when she eventually died, Mama would be old and sick and need nursing too. By the time I got rid of her, *I* would need nursing. And the UK? And Sean Feeney? And writing? And lemurs, volcanoes, medieval music? Forget it. I was staring at an open grave.

And the worst of all, absolutely the worst of all, I was fat and ordinary and pimply and hairy-legged and could therefore not even suffer legitimately.

I know this sounds petty and stupid but it is probably the crux of the matter. If the crux is petty and stupid, so be it. After all, the only way our essence can manifest itself is in our existence. *Word is flesh.* I disliked my flesh, thus distrusted the word, thus had no confidence to act. Not worthy of action, I was not worthy of suffering either.

It is something psychologists and therapists overlook all the time. *The body.* Even Dr Peck never speaks of the body. Someone ought to draw his attention to that.

The body is all. It never ever lies.

How did I come to dislike my flesh, how did it become unlikeable? Surely it couldn't have been a hand dealt to me by Fate? Surely there had to be more to it than that?

There is the cultural context to be considered. (Stamp!) You know, things like long is better than short, fine is better than coarse, smooth is better than rough, lean is better than fat (less is better than more?). Also, sharp is better than blunt (is sad better than jolly?). All in all, a jolly, rotund, bouncy, hairy creature is fitter to be a puppy than a person. That was how I must have seen things long, long ago while my word and my flesh were still busy moulding one another.

Because word makes flesh but *flesh also changes word*.

Using word to change flesh – and the other way round – on purpose is called *sorcery*. But fear not, hardly anyone is capable of such a feat. Mostly, we do it unconsciously, mirroring the faces and bodies that surround us. That was what I did, to my undoing.

In order to reclaim the fullness of life and avoid stepping directly from childhood into decrepitude, all I needed to do was forego the comfort of the known and step into the discomfort of the unknown; a step I could not take because I distrusted my word as manifested in my flesh which had been moulded in the mirror image of others, equally distrustful of their own word and flesh.

But, dear me, how we self-loathers squeal if our unloved, unlovely, despised flesh is as much as scratched, if our base, boring, ordinary personalities are even mildly criticised! How we howl! Because, you see, in essence, we are so bloody special, so bleeding wonderful, so blooming marvellous that it would be impertinent, nay, insane to criticise us, and our perfection would become evident to everyone, if only this confounded Something that is choking us and oppressing us would let us be.

If only we could be.

Ah, but one day...

MacLear

One day, I dreamt that Alexandra had discovered a wonderful trick: how to make anything green by means of a green clothes-peg. She'd take a green clothes peg and attach it to another peg of whatever colour: this second peg would at once become green. After that, she would add another object to the chain: a key, a toothbrush, a handkerchief. As long as an object touched the previous one in the chain, it would become green as well. The more objects were added to the chain, the faster they changed colour. From time to time, to keep the magic strong, Alexandra would add a clothes peg, green or of some other colour. If she so wished, she explained, she could make the whole world green in this fashion.

Then we were in town, on our way home. For some reason Alexandra was not going to her own flat but to her parents', where Eagerwill was waiting for her. It was late winter afternoon and there seemed to be a power restriction in force: the street-lights were not on although it was past lighting-up time. The sky was greyish-blue, overcast. Trams rattled laboriously through clouds of fine snow swept by the bitter

January wind along the gloomy canyons of almost deserted streets.

Alexandra and I came to the crossroads where she was to turn left and I right. Reluctant to part from her, I suggested we went somewhere for a coffee, but everything appeared to be closed because of the power shortage. Previously, Alexandra would have invited me home, and I suggested something to the effect in a timid, barely audible voice. But it was not to be: politely and coldly, Alexandra told me she and Eagerwill had planned to do something together that afternoon: play a game of cards or draw pictures. Another time, perhaps.

Ah. I produced a rictus of a smile and said, "All right then, another time. Bye!" Alexandra, too, said "Bye!" and took the left turn for home.

I turned right for my home, walking on through the drifting snow and congratulating myself for not having made a scene: I knew very well that "another time" would never come and that Alexandra and I had parted forever.

In waking reality I had coffee with Alexandra the very next day, and many a coffee after that one, but I knew with numbing certainty that we had indeed parted. The fact that it had happened in a dream did not make it any less real.

Why did it happen at all? Because I decided to bind and douse, while Alexandra preferred to cut.

One fine day the hospital informed me that Nan Josephine was as fit as she was ever likely to be under their care and that it was time to move her on. Their advice was to place her for a couple of weeks into a sanatorium in the Croatian Downs where she could build up her strength and learn to walk on crutches. Off I went to collect the necessary paperwork and to find a place for her. I did it all in a day. It was not difficult, but it involved a great deal of legwork and queuing. I did it with pleasure because I was wearing a nearly new pair of boots which Melissa had bought in Trieste but did not like all that much and had subsequently sold to me.

Somewhere inside me pulsated a ball of fear of what was

happening to Nan – and by implication to all human beings – but I was able to ignore it because every few minutes I managed to sneak a glance at my boots and the way the edge of my coat brushed against them.

Nan was taken to the sanatorium by ambulance. I rode with her and saw that she was settled down. Her room was a bit chilly.

When I visited her a few days later, her room was still chilly. She had lost weight. She was not recovering at all. I did not like the colour and the smell of her sheets, and her bedsores were worse.

One week on, I decided to take her out of there. I cannot remember either Mama or Papa having had much to do with that whole episode. And the Manageress would not let her go! She said I was not competent to decide what was best for Nan. I told her that neither was she. I told her I wanted transport for Nan at once, to take her home. She sat there smoking a fag and sneering at me. I said I knew what was going on in her sanatorium and that I'd inform the press, radio and television. Then she signed the discharge papers and ordered an ambulance, but we had to wait until there were more Agram-bound patients to justify the trip.

On the way back, the ambulance stopped at another address first, to deliver an old lady in a nightie and a dressing-gown. No one answered the doorbell because no one was at home. The driver hung around for a few minutes, then hopped back into his seat and drove off. I could see the little old lady through the rear window, sitting on her doorstep in her dressing gown and becoming ever smaller with the distance.

I mention this because no able-bodied person should allow such a thing to happen in his or her presence. I know that my one-legged Nan was in the ambulance. I know that the driver was, at the slightest sign of rebellion, quite capable of throwing Nan and me out on the pavement and leaving us there, *but still.*

The trouble was, no one would have helped us had the driver done so. No one would have stopped to see what was going on. I would have had to drag her home like a sack. *But still*. I should have been angrier, should maybe have written to the papers. Instead, the best I could do was forget my boots for five minutes.

I don't remember how we got Nan up ten flights of stairs. Most probably Papa and the driver carried her in a chair. They could easily have done that; she had lost a lot of weight.

Then we got her eating again by stuffing her full of vitamin B6. We cured her bedsores by treating them every few hours with Jecoderm cream, a very simple ointment most commonly prescribed for chapped cuticles. Anyone travelling to any part of former Yugoslavia should get some. It works miracles on bedsores. It promotes cell growth. Only, of course, one has to apply it and apply it and apply it, and not let the sores fester. One must not be lazy.

One must not be lazy and deserts will blossom. Ask Dr Peck.

To spend all the time working hard does not mean that one is not lazy. With Nan back at home, I was busier than an anthillful of ants, yet I was lazy. How do I know that? Because all that work made me miserable. Every time I had to do something — anything — something inside me said "No." Then I went and did it anyway, largely because Mama and Papa would have been angry if I didn't. The fact that those things needed doing was of no consequence. If one carries on like that for a while, one becomes very miserable.

It is *resentment* that makes one miserable. Remove resentment and you'd be hard pushed to find any real difference between doing something and not doing it. Try it as a purely intellectual exercise. In practice, like hurricanes in Hampshire, it hardly ever happens. Most people resent doing most things most of the time.

This was what needed doing: Nan needed to be served her meals in bed, washed in bed, her sores had to be dressed, and every time she wanted to wee or do a business a bedpan had to be put under her and then removed and cleaned once her bottom or her pussy had been wiped. She had to be given her medication because she would forget to take it. On top of that, there was the housework: shopping, cooking, washing up, laundry, ironing, hoovering, dusting and looking after the animals: the dog, the guinea-pig and the fish.

Papa was working at the time, but he pulled his weight. Still calling her "Madam" and addressing her in the second person plural, he would undress Nan Josephine and carry her naked in his arms to the bathroom twice a week. There he would gently soap her and scrub her, talking and joking as if they were sitting together in a café. Not that Papa was a café-goer. Cafés were, in his opinion, for the riff-raff.

Mama was, of course, unwell and had no nerves at all. That was slowly but surely becoming a fact.

My bedroom was situated between Nan's bedroom and my parents' bedroom. When Nan called at night, I was the only one to hear her. She called at least once a night, often twice or more times. She called very quietly. I had to be half-awake most of the time in order to hear her. If I failed to hear, she would soil her sheets. She could not help it: when one's got to go, one's got to go. Then she began calling me "Mummy".

"I'm me, your grand-daughter," I'd say, refusing to understand or accept the new development, because it was simply too horrible: to have to talk to someone who had always been so close to me and was in the same room with me, but suddenly and inexplicably not in the same universe.

"My grand-daughter?" she'd say while I slipped the bedpan under her. "No, you can't be. You're the nurse, aren't you?"

"I'm not the nurse. I never was a nurse and never bloody will be!"

"But you *are*," Nan Josephine would say, getting upset. "This is a hospital, and you're the nurse. You won't let the people in, will you?"

"What people?" I was angry with the muddle in her brain, and with her for not unmuddling it. I felt it was within her power to do so. "The people in the street trying to get in," Nan would say, exasperated. "There's a war on, isn't there? People are rioting outside. They'd like to get into our hospital. There's a fire in the street." It was her socket, burning.

She was a lot more with it in daytime. She became quite nimble with her wheelchair and was able to shift herself onto the commode which had a bucket under the seat. One still had to empty the bucket afterwards. During her first summer as an amputee, she even made pickles sitting in her wheelchair. I could not believe that she was unable to unmuddle the muddle she fell into every evening. Perhaps she couldn't because as a young girl she needed to be told to put her woolly-pully on? Perhaps I was just being a selfish little shit who will one day get into a muddle myself and won't be able to unmuddle it ever again.

That same amputee summer, Nan Josephine expressed the wish to *go out*. Taking into account the fact that, living on the fourth floor without a lift, Nan had not been out since she returned from the sanatorium, it was not such an unreasonable demand. She wanted to go out only once and have a beer. Nan loved public places, with crowds of people.

Papa and I devised, after much thought and sketching, a way of getting her down the ten flights of stairs. We got my massive wooden sledge out of the attic and tied Nan, all dressed up, rouged and coiffured, to its seat. Then I took up position in front of the sledge, holding it fast. Papa, at the rear, began to slowly release the rope tied to it. The sledge began sliding down the steps with Nan flat on her back, moaning in terror. I descended backwards, keeping the sledge steady. It took us a whole hour and more to reach the street level in that manner, with the whole house cheering us on. Once we were down, Papa ran back up to the flat and brought the folded wheelchair. We untied Nan, bundled her into the chair and off we went.

We took Nan for a spin in the park to see the grass and the trees, and then went to a nearby cafe which had tables and chairs on the pavement. Papa and Nan had a beer each and I had an espresso and a smoke. Papa did not comment, only gave me a look. People stared at us. A wheelchair in a cafe — or, for that matter, in the street — was not a common sight in Agram.

There was no wheelchair access to anywhere. The disabled were generally kept at home.

When I was very little, even before I met Melissa and the socket that had caught fire, Mama took me to visit a friend from work. Her friend's surname was Grass, and I half-expected her flat to have grass floors. What it did have was a Disabled Person At Home: Mrs Grass' fourteen-year old son. I don't know what exactly was wrong with him, but he had been *like that* from birth. Mama told me about him to prepare me; the result was that I had nightmares of a monster living in a grassy cave.

The visit started well. I was given an egg sandwich and cocoa, and I could not see a monster anywhere. Then, after a while, I heard strange moans, like lowing. The monster was probably getting ready to pounce on me.

Mrs Grass saw my fear, smiled, took me by the hand and said, "Let's go see him." I was too scared to protest.

The boy lay in a large cot in a semi-dark bedroom. He could not walk or stand, or even sit up properly. He was blind, deaf and mute. I caught a mere glimpse of him; my imagination supplied the rest: something dark, formless, only vaguely humanoid and therefore even more terrible. He sensed our approach, stirred vigorously and said something like "Mwoooooooo...."

A demon calf! Mama's visit had to be cut short. And I was afraid of the disabled from then on. They were creatures people kept at home in the dark.

That was how it was when I was little. Now I had a disabled person of my own and people stared at us, fearful of the Demon Calf.

I feared the Demon Calf, too. I wanted it to die, to stop saying "Mwooo" and stinking up my comfortable home where I strove to be an intellectual and a woman worthy of Sean Feeney. And, objectively, I could have done with more sleep.

Whenever I could, I went to Alexandra to complain of my ill fortune. I should have known how little ice such complaints cut with Alexandra — even less with Eagerwill — and I suppose I did know, but I couldn't help myself: unless I had Alexandra's sanction, I was not sure that my suffering was real and legitimate. What if it was all sham? I had to find out.

Alexandra did not say, "Poor old you, how terrible it all must be." No such luck. Instead, she said, "How long do you think you can keep it up?"

"Keep it up?"

"Yes, before you go to pieces?"

"I won't go to pieces."

"No? That remains to be seen. In any case, how long? What are your expectations?"

"Expectations?"

"Yes," said Alexandra dryly, a bit angered. "Expectations, hope of the future, plans, whatever."

"Well, I expect it'll all go on till Nan dies," I blurted out.

"Aha. And when is that likely to happen?"

"How do I know?"

"Of course you don't know. You do realise she may live for quite a few years yet?"

"I don't want Nan to die!" I said hoarsely.

"No?" That from Eagerwill who, making coffee, suddenly turned his head and looked sharply at me over his shoulder. He never let anyone get away with anything. He thought there was no time for people to get away with things. He struck like a scorpion, but he was not good at opening discussions. He left that to Alexandra.

"Yes, I do want her to die," I said and started crying.

"And what if she doesn't?" said Alexandra, unruffled by my confession. "What then?"

"I don't know," I said, blowing my nose.

"Are you planning to carry on being a nurse ad infinitum?"

"I can't just abandon her!" I protested. "Dad still goes to work and Mama — "

"Yes? *And Mama?*"

"You know. She's never... she cannot... and her nerves."

"You mean, she'd never forgive you."

"Well, yes, she'd never forgive me —"

"So? Couldn't you live with that? Would you forgive yourself?"

"I can't just abandon —"

"Do you love your Nan?" asked Eagerwill.

"Of course I love her!"

"Do you enjoy being with her? The things you do?"

"Being with her or doing things?" I said. "We're talking of two different things here."

"Not really," said Eagerwill with a slight smile.

"This has nothing to do with love or compassion," said Alexandra. "In fact, it has nothing to do with your Nan. You don't give a fig about your Nan. She is not an issue here. You're the issue, the only one. The rest is an excuse for you not to do anything about yourself and your own life."

"How can I do anything about my own life? I'd love to have time enough to sleep, that would do for the moment!"

"There," said Alexandra, "that's exactly what I just said. You're excusing yourself again."

No, they wouldn't say "Poor old you, have a cup of tea and a good cry."

So I started going where my fur would be brushed the way it grew: I attached myself to Lillian Lagrange.

I met Lillian Lagrange at the Academy. She was in my painting class. She was three years younger than me. Her parents were both officers in the Army; consequently, they had been given an enormous apartment in an extremely well designed block, built along the lines of Le Corbusier's famous 'L'unité d'habitation' in Marseille. They also had a holiday home in Hellhole, some quarter of an hour's walk from where Melissa's parents had theirs. This was purely accidental. Lillian had an older sister, Lara, tall and corpulent, with long, glossy, straight bleached-blonde hair. Lara was all soft and languid, and spoke loudly and fast.

Lillian's mother, Anne, was a stocky, strict, drab, permanently anxious peasant-woman. Her father was quiet, softly-spoken, and reticent. He had amazing eyes, large, black and full of friendly fire. He had killed people in the Second World War. He owned a pistol and ammunition, like Alexandra's father, another kind, softly spoken man who had fought for his country did. Occasionally, he would demonstrate his understated, elegant wit.

Lillian resembled him a lot, outwardly and inwardly.

She was taller than I, and simply the most stunningly shaped woman I'd ever seen — so much so that I didn't envy her. Her waist was small, her curves perfect and flowing into one another without any awkward bulges or corners. No muscle or joint protruded anywhere; in fact, Lillian looked like a drawing more than like a live woman. Her complexion was almost unnaturally white, her eyes enormous and jet-black, her face a perfect oval, and her hair, which she never cut, was thick of texture, abundant and of an extraordinary colour which appeared to be very dark brown, but was, in fact, burgundy. She looked a bit like the Fear Tutor from my dream.

Lillian used to hide behind her hair, emerging from time to time to say something, often with the same understated wit which peppered her father's conversation. She smiled with a closed mouth — to hide her bad teeth which she could never bring herself to have treated — and that close-lipped little smile seemed to be the only expression of her feelings: Lillian smiled when angry, when sad, when embarrassed. In that she was like the Japanese. And in quite a few other things.

Her code of honour — honour! — was Japanese, too. If her honour were ever to be intolerably offended, she would disembowel herself. And she moved like a Japanese woman, touching everything lightly, with respect. That included herself. And she never took off her mask: she slept fully made up.

Lillian was one of those rare people who were born with their eyes fixed on the Ancient Socket. Having had stared at it for as long as she could remember, she knew how dark and immense and powerful it was, and consequently thought nothing of herself. She often gave up on herself because of that knowledge. She found it very difficult to do the Necessary

Things. She was never sure whether they were worth doing, and if they were, whether she was capable of doing them. The only thing she was sure about was her honour, the honour of others and, generally, of mankind. She thought it was the only weapon we had to confront the Socket with.

If honour is understood as loyalty to Form, Lillian was right.

Men, young and old, teachers and students, fell over themselves to please Lillian, to serve her, to be in her presence, to touch her. She moved among them like a benevolent royal, searching all the time for a man who would be honourable, generous of nature, a lover of life, and who would be beautiful.

She found my love for Sean Feeney perfectly normal and in order. She only demanded of me that I paint well. The rest did not matter; she was willing to live and let live. Before the face of the Socket, what did it matter whether I went out or sat at home, whether I was fat or thin, whether I feared my parents or not, whether I could tell reality from dream? Nothing, as long as I did not cheat or give in to self-indulgence when painting.

In Lillian's company, I actually learned how to paint.

We had a marvellous time together. We drank ourselves silly and smoked ourselves sick: these, in her opinion, were weaknesses which, perhaps, were bad for the body but did not injure the spirit. We painted while listening to Manitas De Plata, Jacques Brel, Ravi Shankar and my records of medieval music. We discussed everything under the sun, and, although Lillian turned out to be a peerless abstract thinker, I found it somehow less difficult than discussing the same things with Alexandra: having seen the Socket, Lillian was more forgiving. And, for Lillian, abandon was honourable.

At the time, I merely found it comfortable that she should feel that way. Nowadays I, too, think that abandon is honourable, as long as it is true abandon and not mere laziness. How does one tell one from the other? Acts of true abandon have power and, sometimes, beauty; the other sort is repulsive.

Soon after we'd become friends, Lillian and her sister, who did everything of that kind together, fell in love with two

French lads from Alsace. The four had met in Hellhole, where the two Frenchmen were on a camping holiday. While Lara's love affair progressed steadily over two years to end, eventually, in marriage, Lillian's own faltered. She agonised over the true nature of her feelings for Lucien, questioned his every word, weighed her own responses on the finest of scales and was not satisfied, largely because Lucien's young, open, fiery being still somehow failed to obscure the view of the Socket.

While she deliberated, she abandoned herself to the embraces of a colleague, a student of painting from another class. Hardly anyone knew, myself included, because Lillian and Earl — that was his name — danced a kind of ironic minuet around one another, teasing each other almost cruelly, and were hardly ever seen together.

Earl was younger than Lillian, tall and striking, with blazing eyes and a bone structure alien to Agram, inherited from his great-great grandmother who had been a Peruvian Indian. He was a selfish, small-minded cad, but that was not immediately obvious, because his character was complicated and far less transparent than the simple, earthy personality of Lucien from Alsace. Being opaque, he succeeded in hiding the Socket from Lillian's view. They got married and she bore him two boys in quick succession.

Soon after, Lillian and Earl divorced. Why? Because he wanted her to be wife and mother only. Also, she had to place herself under the command of Earl's mother, even in matters regarding her two little sons. That in itself was common enough and could have, perhaps, been overcome, had not Lillian been told, on top of everything else, that Earl had to be given space for his art, while her own painting did not matter. Painting and honour were one and the same thing for Lillian, and she could not oblige. She took her two boys and returned to her parents.

In Agram, parents do not throw their errant daughters into the street. They roll up their sleeves instead and look after the grandchildren.

In the meantime, Lucien the Alsatian wrote desperate letters to Lillian, married a woman he did not love and took to drink. (That last piece of news came via Jules, Lara's husband.) After that, no more was heard of him.

Lillian had always suspected it, but now it was confirmed to her: it was not worth one's while to try and look away from the Socket; it was equally pointless to seek company in that undertaking. Next she concluded that, since the Socket could be seen from absolutely anywhere and remained unaffected by whatever one did, one did not really need to move around or to do much.

Thus she remained at home, looking after her boys, which was extremely convenient for me: she was always there, and demanded no effort from me or anyone else. She was also extremely short of money. That, too, was comfortable: it gave me a break from Melissa and her glossies.

She painted largely in her mind. Painting materials were expensive, but, even more importantly, no material, no tool and no hand, not even her own, could satisfy the rigorous demands of her mind, or meet the sheer speed with which its concepts evolved and changed.

Lillian quested for the Word. I pretended to do the same, and, as neither of us produced any visible results, she took my phoney notes for real money, making my visits to her a complete holiday from everything.

Lillian even liked Mama. She said that Mama probably had her own reasons for being the way she was (the Socket, most likely), and that Mama, secluded in her den, probably had a richer life than Melissa with her trips to Trieste and Venice. Lillian did not like Melissa. She thought Melissa's square jaw and her shrill voice betrayed the shallowness of her depth.

She did not recognise that Melissa was also tormented by the Socket. Or maybe she did and then saw that Melissa did not have the guts to turn around and face It. Was not honourable.

Melissa thought that Lillian was sweet, helpless and completely daft. She thought her little boys were adorable, poor things. Coo.

But – to be perfectly fair – Melissa did have guts galore and was honourable, only her story developed slowly and took ages to make its point.

Alexandra and Eagerwill never met Lillian. I never dared make the juxtaposition. Luckily, both Alexandra and Lillian were shy, essentially, and, although they'd heard a lot about one another, never insisted on an introduction.

Lillian and I graduated from the Academy together, the only two students that year *not* to do so with top marks. We were punished for insisting that art had its laws which overruled individual genius. We claimed that working under strict discipline actually freed the spirit. Our colleagues and our tutors thought we were old-fashioned and politically incorrect. They thought we lacked courage to express our individuality.

We had no ideas on how to proceed in developing our careers, what to exhibit and where. We were not in with the *it*-crowd, although Lillian, at least, occasionally went to their dos and gatherings. She was always welcome because of her looks.

We knew we would remain at the rear-guard of Agramian art. Lillian was not bothered: she thought it was all a big joke, anyway, and smiled her ironic, tight-lipped smile. I was not very interested because Wilfrid Blake was training me to become a scriptwriter. Lillian was not too happy about that: in her opinion, literature of any kind wasn't abstract enough and provided too much opportunity for self-indulgence.

Lillian read children's books because they were not wordy and dealt only with the essential. She also read 'The Little Prince' who was her absolute hero because he was a child who lived alone on a very small planet and was prepared to die for the love of a Rose, and she read philosophy.

In the winter of nineteen eighty, some six months before I was to graduate, I went to London for a three-day weekend break, to see Sean Feeney live on stage. A ticket had been procured through Eagerwill's ICL connections months beforehand and was waiting for me at the ICL Head Office reception. I had to find out what Sean Feeney was like in the flesh, and be enclosed within the same space as he, if only for once.

I stayed at a shabby Yugoslav-owned hotel in Shepherd's Bush, a place Allbright had told me about. I hardly noticed what it was like, although I later remembered with amazement that my room resembled the hotel room in my dream of meeting Sean Feeney in a place called Farrington, where he was to give a recital of poetry. Remember? I got there in a hurry, with my dog Michael and a packet of biscuits.

It was exactly as in my dream, in fact, bar the dog and the biscuits.

On the evening of the performance, my normal reasoning and perceiving faculties were cancelled. I started getting ready hours before the show, and only minutes later discovered that I had less than half an hour left to traverse London from north to south, find the Old Vic theatre, present my ticket and take my seat. I darted out into the street, got sucked into what appeared to be a meaningless funnel of people, street-lights, cars, tube trains, street names and unpleasant, unnerving wind and was disgorged, without knowing exactly how, at the door of the Old Vic, sweaty and dishevelled. I was fifteen minutes late, but they let me in.

Sean Feeney was already on the stage. He must have had registered my noisy, intrusive, messy, self-conscious entrance, if only at the subconscious level. I sat down, flustered and breathless, and stared at him. He was grey-haired and spectral. Some part of him, a part of his body or a part of his mind, complained miserably against being there. It emitted a kind of a silent creak.

The play was 'Macbeth.' I knew the story, but could not concentrate on having an artistic experience, although I tried, because my attention was busy to capacity experiencing Sean Feeney. I was full of awe. I felt I was in the presence of a being — Sean Feeney or Macbeth, as you like it — who knew Everything. Anything such a being did or said had to be of immense significance, to be treasured and, perhaps, understood one day.

This, by the way, is what is wrong with most productions of

'Macbeth': Macbeth is wise and despairing from the word go, while the play is, in fact, about acquiring pointless wisdom at a terrible price. Who is Macbeth? A Joe Bloggs inhabiting a clean-cut world of dos and don'ts, who suddenly receives notification of having won the Reader's Digest Prize Draw, provided he returns his lucky numbers in the envelope labelled "Yes". When he does so, he wades through rivers of blood to learn that the world is a tale told by an idiot, with sound and fury. At that stage, of course, he is no longer Joe Bloggs, nor is there anything left for him to do but to die: the whole of his life's potential has been used up as payment for this obscene knowledge. And why was he chosen as the winner of the Prize Draw in the first place, instead of, say, Banquo or some other poor devil? Because Macbeth is the sort of chap who can be depended upon to return his lucky numbers. Chaps who return their numbers make the tale told by an idiot go round. That is 'Macbeth' in a nutshell.

I would not have been able to stomach such a Macbeth played by Sean Feeney. I could not see Sean Feeney as Joe Bloggs. I don't think he is the sort of chap who returns his lucky numbers. He respects Fate too much to try and lend it a hand. He does not believe his actions matter in the greater idiotic scheme of things. Sean Feeney knows true humility, like Wilfrid Blake.

After the theatre, I went back to the hotel and straight to bed, completely exhausted by my ordeal, because it was a kind of ordeal. I slept and I dreamt, and here is my dream:

Sean Feeney is preparing the main role in a play which is 'Macbeth' and 'King Lear' at the same time, thus a kind of 'MacLear'. I watch the rehearsal of the climactic final scene in which MacLear delivers a monologue summarizing the experience of his hard, terrible life while squatting on the edge of a cliff towering some two to three hundred metres above the sea.

Sean Feeney looks as if he himself has lived the life of such a MacLear: old, exhausted, barely able to move, bone-thin, with huge, sorrowing eyes and an all-knowing smile virtually unbearable to watch. He is dressed in rags which once might have been white; his arms are naked and his feet are bare. I know he is ill and that his legs can give way any moment. I also know that his life is in danger and that he is not exactly eager to play the role, but has been ordered to and has agreed to do it without a word of protest, knowing it would be in vain.

Who has ordered him to play MacLear on the edge of the cliff? Those very same people who had previously caught him and were trying to make him live in Potter's Bar with geraniums in the window. He refused the geraniums, remember? Well, those who refuse the geraniums must deliver a soliloquy on the edge of a cliff. That's life, one mustn't complain. One must own up, and Sean Feeney does so, masterfully, almost joyfully.

Once the rehearsal is over, I climb onto the empty stage and approach the edge of the cliff. The sight is awesome: deep below, the sea, seemingly stretching into infinity, shimmers in the sun. The tiny ripples on its surface are, I know, huge waves, shrunk by distance. If I were to fall from this height, the surface of the water would be hard as steel: the impact would stun me and I would drown. How can Sean Feeney bear to rehearse his role there and expose himself to such danger? How can he endure such fear day after day? I know *I* couldn't.

Why does he have the strength to come out willingly and face the inevitable while I have to be dragged screaming?

I woke up, although it was the middle of the night. It was pleasant to know that on the other side of the window pane there was London and all its night doings: cars running up and down Shepherd's Bush Road, cats roaming through back gardens, criminals busy with their crimes, night-clubs, all-night shops, late tube trains roaring deep under my bed, night-shift workers toiling away, bare trees standing very still, orange streetlights we did not have in Agram at the time glowing, and Sean Feeney existing somewhere amidst all that, too. I felt no need of him, and that was a new feeling. What would I do with him, or he with me? I had a whole life to live before I could catch up with him. Until that happened, I was not to worry about Sean Feeney again. I felt I could even contemplate going out with a man, although I was not in a hurry to do so.

It was a sort of freedom.

At that moment I heard a voice calling my name, a female voice. It called me thrice, distinctly.

No one could have called my name in the middle of the night in London, especially not a woman. I did not know a single woman in London.

I got up, picked up a chair and propped it against the door. Having done that, I went back to bed and was asleep in seconds.

Upon my return to Agram, I was told that Nan Josephine's sister, my great-aunt Elizabeth, had died — burned to death in her flat in Eszeg. On the timeline of events, this happened before Allbright's death which, consequently, had a flavour of déjà vu.

When did it happen? You win no prize for guessing it was on the night — and at the time — when I heard a female voice call my name. The voice, however, did not sound like Aunt Elizabeth's voice. It sounded more like Mama's, but it was not her voice either.

It could have been the voice of the Socket.

Aunt Elizabeth was a few years older than her sister Josephine. She never married, although she was violently, convulsively sensual. After the Second World War, she qualified as dental technician and was able to carry out minor dental treatments. She lived by herself, and went frequently on holidays by the seaside where she would invariably fall in love with some young local or other, carry on with the affair until it reached the stage of heavy petting, and then run away. She was extremely, extravagantly Catholic. She boasted of having been kissed by various men on every — *every* — part of the body without ever letting any one of them actually make love to her, because she was and would forever remain a virgin. She had been to Lourdes, and to Padua, to pray at St. Anthony's shrine. She was in love with St. Anthony.

She relished extremes: of heat, of cold, violent storms. She gobbled up food until full to bursting, drank pints of water with an ecstatic expression on her face and slept with gusto. She was crazy as a bat and so full of energy that she could hardly walk like a normal person: she would skip and hop and run, driven by sheer exuberance.

When she grew old, her face shrivelled like a dry prune, but her body remained lithe, slim and shapely. She used to sit in the front pew in church, let her short skirt ride up her fine, firm thighs and shiver with delight if the officiating priest looked her way.

By the time I was sufficiently grown up to notice, she had already developed all manner of strange quirks. She carried a bottle of surgical spirit on her at all times, for example, and would never touch a door-knob or a toilet seat without rubbing it with spirit first. And so on.

Recently, I have seen Melissa pull out a bottle of surgical spirit in a restaurant loo and do the same. Socket?

I used to love it when Aunt Elizabeth came to stay with us. She never stayed for less than two months. The most wonderful thing about her was that she was not ill. There was nothing whatsoever wrong with her. She never suffered from anything.

She would probably still be alive and go on until she was two hundred years old, had she not fallen asleep with an electric heater turned on face up under her bed. As she tossed and turned, bits fell out of her mattress straight onto the glowing, red-hot coils and caught fire which spread all over the bed before aunt Elizabeth woke up, because she used to sleep like a top.

The fire remained confined to her bedroom. Aunt Elizabeth was found by the door, charred beyond recognition. She died in hospital a day later, without regaining consciousness. Mama was given a few objects spared by the fire: a small purse full of rosaries and a bundle of photographs taken by Aunt Elizabeth over the years. They were all very small and strange: a corner of a house with weeds growing around it, unknown people seen from unusual angles, smiling young men on the beach, the market in Eszeg seen from Auntie's window, the Energy flow of the Universe. I still have them somewhere.

Nan Josephine did not shed a single tear for her sister. In fact, her sentimental, fluffy, sugary, syrupy mask which had, perhaps, cost her a leg and thus eventually her life, fell off entirely on this occasion. Her voice lost its feminine, submissive meow (yes, we females all meow, only we can't hear ourselves) and her eyes became socket-cold. What was going on? Her other leg was beginning to hurt, and her inner being was busy deciding whether to allow itself to be sliced up like a sausage or give up altogether and die. She could not spare the energy for mourning her sister.

One evening, with Papa and Mama already asleep, I watched a late movie on the box, which happened to be 'Repulsion' by Roman Polanski. At that stage it was no longer possible to sleep and be woken up by Nan calling. Papa had installed an electric bell in my bedroom, but that did not work either: at night, Nan could not remember to press the button. Thus we divided the night into two watches: the first one, till four in the morning, was mine, whereupon Papa would take over until he had to go to work. Mama would carry on till I got up about ten. By then, Nan was again conscious of her surroundings.

Remember 'Repulsion'? It is in black and white, with young Catherine Deneuve as a blonde beautician living with her sister and her sister's husband. When the two go on a holiday, Catherine, left alone in the flat, goes gradually mad. She watches a skinned, oven-ready rabbit decay on a plate, incapable of either cooking it or putting it into the fridge. In her imagination she sees cracks opening in walls and some nameless horror slowly, inexorably descending upon her. What used to be a comfortable, safe apartment is gradually revealed as what it really is: the inside of the Socket. Catherine kills two people who try to help her, because she cannot allow herself to be unplugged once she has plugged herself in. She is mortally afraid of the Socket but even more of the protecting veil we human beings weave over it and call Life. She cannot balance the two and that is her madness.

I watched the movie peering through my fingers. It is one of the scariest movies ever made.

When it was over, I went to Nan's bedroom to have a look. She was awake, and said, "Have you been watching a film?"

"Yes," I said, surprised. She seemed to know who I was and where we both were, which was unusual for that time of night.

"Was it any good?"

"Brilliant." I suddenly felt elated, went over to her and planted a kiss on her cheek. "I love you, Nan," I said.

"I love you, too," she replied, staring at me with cold eyes.

"Isn't it wonderful," I went on, "how we can really talk, you and I? I always believed we'd be able to really talk one day."

"Yes," said Nan, unsmiling. "Pity I could never really talk to Patricia. I often moaned about that to your father. He's a sensible chap. He deserves a better wife." She shrugged under the duvet. "Still, he drew his lot, and she hers."

I did not dare ask her if she knew about Mama's affair with Pierre. I wish I had, though. It is not every day that one gets to talk to Socket Itself.

Instead, I asked: "How do you feel?"

"Fine," said Nan. "Only fed up. Do you think it'll end soon?"

"You mean," I said, "are you going to die soon?"

"Yes."

I mustered my courage and said, "Soon. I think. Are you afraid?"

Nan laughed a dead laugh. "No!"

"I would be," I ventured.

"How can one be afraid of nothing? There's nothing there! Nothing! Never was, never will be, and it is just as well."

"Wasn't there ever anything for you?" I asked timidly.

"No, never."

"And Grandpa Ludwig?"

"Eeeh... Ludwig..." Nan smiled a mechanical kind of smile.

"And Mama?"

"Patricia? I never wanted to have her... but I did what I could for her, one does. She shouldn't have had any children. I told her it was stupid to have children. She went on and had you anyway, silly woman that she is. And now look at her."

"And now look at us all," I said, tuning into her mood.

"Exactly."

"But you do love me?"

"Oh, yes." It sounded a bit facile, but I think she meant it.

"I'm not going to have children," I said suddenly, without premeditation. It simply tumbled out of my mouth.

And I never had any. It's all right. There are kids enough in the world for everyone.

"That's lovely, darling," said Nan. "I'll go to sleep now if you don't mind."

The following morning, Nan had a stroke. She could not speak any more, and had to be given water with a spoon. We were not sure whether she actually swallowed it. Mama and I called an ambulance and Nan was taken to hospital.

I went to the Academy for my lessons. When I got back in the evening, Mama told me that Nan had died.

Papa was truly devastated. He kept bursting into tears. When Nan was cremated, he brought her urn home and placed it inside a cabinet in her bedroom which got converted into a sitting-and-television room. Sometimes, watching TV on his own, he would open the cabinet so that Nan could watch with him. He talked to her, but never in front of other people. How do I know that? He told me about it himself on the last occasion I ever saw him, a year before he died. His inner being was aware of its impending demise and was in a hurry to share its wealth.

Nan's urn remained in the cabinet for nearly a year, until Mama could be persuaded to make a trip to Eszeg, together with Papa, and lay it next to Nan's sisters Julie, Anna and Elizabeth. After that trip, Mama did not venture out of doors for years.

While Mama and Papa were away, I was alone in the flat

with Michael the dog and the fish, the guinea-pig having had died the previous summer. It was a new experience, a first. It made me elated, but as the first day wore on, I became nervous and, with the darkness setting in, positively panicky.

The building was full of sinister sounds, made by old people, sick people, malcontent people inhabiting it. Everyone in the neighbourhood was on diazepam, shooting up insulin, or swallowing drugs for blood pressure. I was on diazepam myself, as I said before.

It was just like in 'Repulsion', only there was no skinned rabbit in the house, and I knew I was not going to go mad, maybe because I had been warned in advance by the movie.

The next day I went to see Alexandra: what else could I do? She made coffee and said, "What will you do next?"

"Next?"

"Yes, what are your plans? You can have plans now, can't you?"

I had to say yes. There was nothing to stop me having plans.

"And what are they?"

"I have to graduate at the Academy," I said.

"That's not a plan," said Alexandra.

"Well, and then... and then... and then I'll make movies with Wilfrid. I'll write, and he'll direct. Movies like 'Star Wars' and 'Conan the Barbarian'."

"No one makes movies of that kind here," said Alexandra reasonably.

"Then we'll go abroad."

"How, and when; and how will you manage to stay abroad, doing what?"

"I don't know," I said, feeling something stubborn and mulish stir inside me, "but I'll do it."

"Don't you want to paint and exhibit?"

"Not really." I didn't, really. I was not a painter. There was something about painters I lacked.

"What a waste," said Alexandra. "All those years."

"Why do we always have to talk about me?" I said.

"Because you want to, and need to. You come here and ask

for it."

"I come to relax, and to see you."

"That's what I mean, you ask for it. And besides, I'm interested."

"Why don't we discuss *you* for a change?"

"Because you didn't ask me anything about *me*."

That was true, I didn't. But what to ask?

"Ask me something about me, and we'll discuss it."

I sat there in silence, smoking, sipping my coffee and feeling awful. I often felt awful with Alexandra, because I had nothing to ask her about herself, yet I wanted to know. I wanted to hear about Alexandra. But what? I could not think of a single question.

"You see?" she said.

I began to cry.

"Eeeeh," said Alexandra with a rueful smile. I wanted her to embrace me and say 'There, there!' but I knew it was not likely she would do so. She lit a cigarette, hunched her back and crossed her arms on the table as she always did when concentrating. "You never plan," she said. "You always blunder blindly into things, as if your life wasn't your own. You don't take responsibility."

I felt terribly hurt. After all I had done for Nan and by extension for Mama and Papa, after all the sacrifices I had made, I felt like a very responsible person. I wanted someone to tell me how well I'd done and that I deserved a rest.

"As if it wasn't real," Alexandra went on, "as if it didn't matter. That's bloody arrogant."

"Perhaps it doesn't matter."

"Don't say such rubbish just to be clever! Would you come here and snivel all over me if it didn't? You're using me and I absolutely refuse to be used. You're availing yourself of my time and my goodwill, so please make an effort! The world does not exist for your pleasure alone!"

I did not understand then, nor years after. I was completely baffled. What did Alexandra want from me? What? What exactly was this fabled responsibility thing? Why should I not be allowed to make 'Conan' with Wilfrid somewhere in the wide world? Where was this reality I disregarded?

Why Alexandra didn't feel she had to please me, while I constantly worried about pleasing her? If I stopped doing that, what would happen? I did not dare to try and find out.

I don't remember how we wound up our discussion. I went home utterly crushed by the realisation that I could not call myself a person until I found out how to colour everything green by means of a green clothes-peg or claim the knowledge of MacLear, preferably both. The peg and the knowledge were probably one and the same thing in any case.

Until I did so I would remain a puppy on diazepam, or Mama's little Kitten.

But what was the first step I had to take?

Tenno

When I got home so utterly crushed, I knew that Alexandra was right: I needed a plan.

I should really write this sentence fifty-two times because our conversation and my realisation that I needed a plan took place on a weekly basis for about a year. During that time Papa retired from work, and I went on looking after Castle Dracula. I shopped, cooked, cleaned, took Michael the dog walkies, went to the movies, had afternoon naps, took diazepam and so on.

In the second year after Nan's death, I hardly saw Alexandra any more. I painted with Lillian from time to time, but most of the time I wrote movie treatments with Wilfrid Blake. We worked together every night and soon had a number of very interesting, original projects for films which were all suitable for Lucas or Spielberg but were of absolutely no interest to the domestic market.

I still have them, if anyone's interested.

We worked in my bedroom, into the wee small hours. For Mama and Papa, Wilfrid had become part of the furniture, or so I thought until Papa said one day, "What are Wilfrid's intentions?"

I said, "I beg your pardon?"

"Intentions," he said. "Is he planning to marry you, when, and on what income does he propose to live with you?"

"He's never asked me to marry him," I said and giggled because the thought was absurd. Wilfrid claimed to have a girlfriend whom he loved (when did he ever see her?), and even if he didn't, I could not marry him. I was grooming myself for Sean Feeney, to be ready and available once I knew the secret of the green peg and became as wise as MacLear. If I married Wilfrid, I'd have to stay in Agram forever and keep house. Wilfrid wanted a traditional family setup, a marriage like in 'The Quiet Man' by John Ford. He'd said that often enough. I was there to write his movies; that was the deal.

"I'll have to broach the subject, then, one of these days," Papa said.

That very evening, when Wilfrid came round as usual, I broached the subject. Because, after my little chat with Papa, I fell head over heels in love with Wilfrid. It happened in a split second. I wanted to hear his voice. I wanted to see his beard, although I hated beards. This is how I set about wooing Wilfrid. Listen:

Once we sat down with sheets of paper, pens and coffee, I said, "Wilfrid, I have an idea. Why don't you marry me?"

"What sort of a stupid joke is that?" said Wilfrid.

"No, really," I hurried to explain. "If nothing else, it would be more practical. You wouldn't have to go home at four in the morning by cab, and no one would pay any attention to us, because we would be like everyone else, married. We'd be able to work much better —"

"Have you been drinking?"

"— without distractions. We wouldn't have to sleep together. We could be like Raisuli and Mrs Perdicaris in 'The Wind and the Lion', there'd be a sword in bed between us... if you wanted it to be."

"Don't even think about it," said Wilfrid enunciating every word with extreme precision which was with him a sure sign of anger.

"But *why?*" I said, panicking. The outlook was poor. "What would change, except for the better?"

"It's never going to happen, so forget it."

"Don't you like me at all?"

"That's not the point. You're a Cancerian like my mother, and it'd never work."

Of course, Wilfrid lived in a Castle Dracula, like Melissa and I. He was on his guard. He did not want another vampire sucking his life's blood.

Alexandra, mother of two gorgeous young women, says that parents ought to be banned. She might be right.

She has actually taught her daughters to talk back and say "no" while they were still children. They seem to be none the worse for that: on the contrary.

"Right," said Wilfrid, "I don't ever want to hear another word about the subject again."

"Okay."

"Let's get back to work."

"All right."

Wilfrid must have been badly shaken by my outburst because he next ordered me to go and find myself a boyfriend. Roger, Gold Leader, I copy.

It so happened that Eagerwill had started bringing a friend from work home from time to time: a tall, willowy young man with a weak chin, sleepy grey eyes hidden behind extremely thick lenses and a mass of long, curly, blond hair. He was polite and affable, but possessed of a merciless wit which must have been to Eagerwill's taste. He was a slow mover and spoke even more slowly, oozing his wry comments like resin. His name was Matthew.

I looked at Matthew across Alexandra's dining table a few times, danced with him at one of Alexandra's ad hoc parties and decided that he was worth a try, especially as he appeared to be willing. Thus, next time Matthew's mum was away for a few days, Alexandra, Eagerwill and I went over to his place to listen to his Frank Zappa records and have a sniff of weed.

Once the ritual of music, coffee, scotch and weed was over, Matthew and I withdrew to his bedroom and got down to business. He complained of the freshness of his sheets: they only smelled right after ten days' use, he said. Had it been a joke, I would have laughed, but it wasn't. I found that disturbing. And Matthew couldn't come. And I didn't help him much. I would have preferred to sit and write with Wilfrid. Still, I stayed the night.

After that, Matthew and I were an item. We were supposed to go to the cinema and disco clubs together, but I hated disco and went to the cinema with Wilfrid, because cinema was there for artistic appreciation, not for snogging.

Snogging bored me in any case, because it was of the body, not of the mind, and therefore belonged to the moment. At that time, I understood the past and the future, but had no use for the moment. I did not understand the moment.

It is hard to understand the moment, no matter how much Eckhart Tolle you've read. I only managed that at my husband's deathbed. He died just before I started this chapter. That is why this chapter is crap. That is why everything is crap now, unless I stick to the moment and nothing else. I can't do that very often.

It has probably been said before, but it won't hurt to say it again: just as all space is made of points which have no dimensions, so is all time made of moments which have no duration. It follows that everything is made of nothing and is nothing. That, of course, is the Socket.

Lillian Lagrange, who had a great head for maths, must have made that calculation when she was first introduced to the concept of points, which would have been in primary school, in a geometry lesson. Years later, when I discussed the subject with her in her drying room studio, she looked at me from behind the screen of her dark hair and smiled her close-lipped smile. "Yes, everything is made of nothing and is nothing. Ha-ha!"

To which Alexandra, had she been around, would have said,

"Good, let me smash this easel on your head, then, and see."
Like everyone else, Alexandra is afraid of the Socket but refuses
to stare at it. In conscious, deliberate defiance, which, she
claims, is the privilege of human beings, she paints the Socket
green by means of green clothes pegs. She also insists that
human beings owe it to themselves and to other human beings
— yes, even to the Socket itself — to make use of that privilege.

There is much to be said for the easel argument, because it
is a fact that some bits of nothing move about and affect other
bits of nothing, while others don't or simply aren't there at all.
Not Being Hit By An Easel is not the same as Being Hit By
One. One tends to disregard such basic phenomena when
thinking globally. Yet the fact remains that the easel, as well as
everything else, consists of dimensionless points and the action
of it being smashed over my head takes place in a succession of
durationless moments. *How can that bloody be?*

Could it be that an absolute nothing is merely the other side
of an absolute everything, the two sides being one and the same
by definition? It sounds trite, like a cheap way out, like cutting
the Gordian Knot. Cutting the Gordian Knot is a cheap way
out, no matter how clever and can-do it appears to be. Why?
Because you lose the *knowledge of the Knot.*

That is why the Sheriff of Nottingham is the looser in
'Robin and Marian', one of Wilfrid Blake's all time favourite
movies. Buy it on DVD if you haven't seen it, it is a rare
masterpiece by Dick Lester. It has no further significance to
this story; I only mention it to bless my book by invoking its
name, and because there is a reference to the Gordian Knot in
it.

The Sheriff's men are fiddling with a knot in the rope
holding up the portcullis of the castle gate. Unless they manage
to bring the portcullis down really fast, Robin Hood is going to
escape. So the Sheriff says, "*Cut it*, for God's sake."

How come that something made of nothing never can exist
at all?

Die and find out.

Lillian did, at the age of thirty-three. This is how it

happened: soon after she returned from Split with her little boys to live with her parents as a single mother, I went to the UK and got married there. Whenever I visited Agram and, of course, Lillian, she was more withdrawn and less inclined to do anything. Yet I could not say that she was depressed. She cared well for her boys, made clothes for them, read a lot, laughed at everything that was funny to a healthy person, she did all that. But she did not go out. Her teeth were in a bad state, she had no money and no clothes because she had no job, and so on.

It was not easy to get a regular job in Agram, particularly if you were a single mother and an intellectual. And Lillian was too beautiful by far to get a job easily. It is as bad as being too plain. Pretty is best, unfortunately, there as here. Was and will be, for a long time to come. Yup. Also, Lillian really preferred to stay in. She said there was nothing worth looking at outside.

Outside, though, the Socket had reached burning point. Yugoslavia was preparing to consume itself, and all the people who wanted nothing to do with the affair generally stayed in: the poor, the elderly, the sick, the ones out of tune. Just before the war in Croatia broke out, in the autumn of nineteen ninety, I saw Lillian for the last time ever. She said it was getting very dark outside, even though it was early afternoon. She was out of tune.

During the war, Earl, her ex-husband, who had in the meantime married a rich woman in Paris, came to fetch Lillian and the boys and took them to France. The boys stayed with him in Paris while Lillian was given the use of a villa in Antibes, next to the Picasso museum. The villa was called Soledad. If she wished, she could stay there forever and paint. Earl, who had many wealthy connections, promised to try and sell her paintings.

Picasso was God to Lillian. She was all alone in a villa called Solitude. The finger of fate had pointed at her — squashed her, in fact — and a booming voice from above had said, "It's you." She had phoned me from Antibes and told me all about it. I was over the moon for her. I was sure she would at last paint all those fabulous pictures she had, over the years, constructed in her mind.

Instead, Lillian stared at the Socket for a few months in the solitude of villa Soledad, then collected her sons and returned to Agram. Her mother was ill, she said, and she had to look after her.

Six months later her mother died. Lillian stayed in Agram with her father and her boys. She got them a Husky puppy she named Vayu, which means wind in Sanskrit. She did not venture further than the grocery shop next door. There was nothing outside to see, she kept telling me over the phone.

I cannot say what it was like at that time in Agram: I did not live through the changes, I was not there. (I didn't have what it took.) But I do know that the world in which Lillian and I grew up had disappeared. There was no Yugoslavia any more.

What, the Yugoslavia everyone including myself wanted to leave because it had not become America? The one with queues for coffee and queues for oil and queues for toilet paper? The one which made you pay tax every time you wanted to travel abroad? The red passport one? The one whose pipsqueak language I did not want to speak, conducting my writing sessions with Wilfrid entirely in English (yes, we actually used to do that, he and I)? The one where Pioneers were gay in May?

Yes, that one. It had vanished off the face of the Earth and was accessible only by means of time travel.

How would we feel, just imagine, if Britain vanished off the face of the Earth and was replaced by Scotland, England, Wales and Cornwall, complete with Immigration Control and different currencies? Would you believe me if I told you that even the very trees growing in front of
your house would suddenly be different, never mind the house itself? You wouldn't believe me, because it ought not to be so, but it is. Even the *sky* would be different.

Very soon after the dissolution of Yugoslavia I dreamt that Agram had been completely destroyed and then re-built exactly as it used to be, in the minutest detail. And there it was, the same as ever, yet profoundly different. It felt wrong and it made my skin crawl. That is exactly how it feels in waking life: all wrong and it makes one's skin crawl, a bit like that perfect replica of Agram and the rest of the world built on the surface of the Sun in my dream of long ago.

Some people cannot or will not take to life on the Sun, not out of conviction or to prove a point, but because their whole being rejects it.

In the early spring of ninety three, Lillian caught the flu, or so she told me over the phone. Once the flu was over, she remained unwell. She felt tired and liked to keep to her bed, but put off seeing the doctor month after month. Then, one day, Mama phoned me and told me that Lillian was dead. She had died of lung cancer which had metastased all over her body. When she was finally taken to hospital, nothing could be done.

Her father told me she must have been in horrendous pain but never told anyone. She just let herself suffer and die, smiling her ironic little smile all the time.

Her sense of honour made her reject Villa Soledad as sham and return to Agram. It demanded that she be true to what her fine abstract mind had worked out and understood: that the Outside, which was not worth looking at, was not limited to Agram, but was everywhere. Once she had fathomed the length and the width and the depth of it, she rejected it with all her being and withdrew herself from it completely. She made like the Oozle-Woozle bird.

My husband told me about the Oozle-Woozle bird. When threatened, it runs around in ever-diminishing circles, finally disappearing up its own fundamental orifice, from which point of vantage it glares at its baffled pursuers.

Not even her two boys could keep Lillian outside. And, when she died, they gave the Husky, Vayu, to a family who lived in the country.

Heigh-ho! Not all of us can practise as we preach. I can neither use the green clothes-peg nor make like the Oozle-Woozle bird.

And, yes, of course it is inconceivable and completely impossible that Lillian got her cancer on purpose. *No one* gets cancer on purpose. But still.

My husband died of lung cancer. I was told it had been developing for some two years before it was finally diagnosed. And lo, some two years before he died, he started feeling that there was nothing for him to do, that he was a waste of space. So he started disconnecting his wires from the space-time network and plugging them into the Socket. One could see all those unplugged wires on the X-ray of his chest. Like Lillian and I, he, too, did not know how to paint the Socket green.

That is why I say "But still."

If I had real guts of steel, like Lillian or my husband, I would not try to mythologise, poeticise, storify or otherwise embellish and meaningfy the workings of the Socket. I would just say "So what" or "Heigh-ho." Instead, I say "But still."

Anyway, back to Matthew. We carried on not going out for a few months, and then I suddenly felt that everything had come to a standstill. I was not finding a job by means of not looking for one, I was not preparing a show because I was not painting pictures, I was not about to have my own home because I was not planning to set one up, and I wasn't planning one because I was engaged in not having a love affair with Matthew which would inevitably not end in a marriage. The only occupation I pursued with interest was my friendship and work with Wilfrid which was leading nowhere.

And then Michael the dog died because his hour had come. And I got rid of my fish. I sold my aquarium with all the fish in it. And I gave away most of my plants. I also gave away a lot of my books and other possessions. Alexandra, who was given quite a few, wanted to know if I was contemplating suicide. I wasn't, of course. Quite simply, the end of one thing led to the end of another until the stream of endings began to flow under its own impetus.

In the summer of eighty three, I went for one last holiday to Vallegrande. Why last? I was not sure, but I knew it was so, if for no other reason then because it made no sense to repeat a pattern ad infinitum. By and by, it made one sick. (The fact that day follows night follows day follows night and so on does not appear to belong to this category because it is not of one's own making; eventually, however, one comes to experience it as an oppressively repetitive pattern of one's own making — and that, I suspect, is the moment to re-wire to the Socket.)

Vallegrande had never been more beautiful, lusher, sweeter-smelling. It was full of new luxurious houses built to let during the summer season. It buzzed with happy, sunburned holiday-makers.

I saw Grandy Andreis. He was married to his Irene and had turned into an old man. His medieval mind had made him age at a medieval rate. He had chronic indigestion. Irene could not have children. The doctors had told her it was because of nerves.

Nerves.

We went out, the three of us, and sat on the patio of a patisserie. We had iced coffee à la Vallegrande: an espresso in a glass and a scoop of vanilla ice-cream in it, topped with whipped cream. Fred Quail passed by. Grandy said "Hey!" and Fred replied "Aha."

Fred was old, too. He dragged his feet as he walked. Bulges of fat wobbled around his midriff. His eyes were only half open. He said he had recently been to Agram, to see a psychiatrist. He, too, suffered from nerves. The psychiatrist had given him diazepam.

I am not being catty. I was on diazepam for fifteen years.

In one of the earlier chapters, I was still on diazepam as I wrote it. That means that it was written five years ago. How time flies! I really should bring this book to some kind of a conclusion soon.

Yeah, because it is now, as I write this, *almost twenty years* since I got off diazepam.

Later that evening, I went for a walk in the hills which began immediately at the back of the last houses of Vallegrande. It was not yet completely dark. The sky was heavily overcast. A storm was brewing in the south-west. The scented air stood still.

I went to bed quite early because there was nothing I could do on an evening like that. There was nothing I wanted to say to anyone, nor did I want to hear anything anyone had to say.

I slept and I dreamt and here is my dream:

Sometime in the nineteenth century, there lived in Japan, in Kyoto, a young painter. He was successful, fashionable and very well off. He shared an apartment in the city with a friend, another wealthy, urbane young man. The apartment was full of paintings covering every square inch of the walls.

One day, while walking home through the hilly suburbs, the painter got thoroughly soaked by a sudden downpour of rain. The rain stopped as abruptly as it had started, and the painter thought, "That's odd; I've always wanted to be caught in a shower but whenever the weather threatened, I ran and took cover. Today I did not take cover, I had my wish instead." The more he thought about it, the more certain he felt that he had undergone a strange inner transformation.

He walked on along the wet road. On his way he passed by a small house with an old woman sweeping the pavement in front of it. At her feet, a strange, fluffy, purple-coloured cat rolled on the paving stones. The painter bent down to pet the cat and, driven by another strange impulse, asked the old lady if she would let him take the cat home. The old lady flashed a toothless grin at the young man and said, "You can have her, if she will come with you." The painter thanked her and bid the cat come along, which she gladly did.

When the painter and the cat got home, his friend was already there, making tea. As soon as she walked through the door, the cat turned into a young woman, neither pretty nor plain, dressed in traditional Japanese costume and sporting an elaborate hairdo. She approached the painter's friend, pointed at the paintings on the walls and said, "Take the paintings if you like them. Take them all and keep them — they are yours." Then she turned to the Painter. "You probably think that I, whom you've only just met, have no business giving your paintings away. But I know that you were about to do it yourself. Were you not?" The painter nodded, then said to his friend, "I'm going away." He told him about the rain. "I looked at the sky — *tenno*[1] — and knew it was time for me to leave."

He spoke no more and packed his bag straight away, refusing his friend's offer to help. He packed some dirty clothes together with the clean ones, insisting that was how it had to be. He glanced around his nice flat for one last time, took leave of his baffled friend and departed, followed by the woman who, once in the street, became a cat again.

They strolled through the city. It was evening and the windows of fine restaurants glowed with friendly light, the restaurants where the painter had eaten many a time in good company. The walls of the houses were covered with posters for Kabuki theatre and other events the painter loved and regularly attended. Looking at all the wealth and sophistication which could be his for the asking the painter began tearing his hair out and moaned, "Why am I doing this? There is no reason for me to leave my home, my friends and my lifestyle, none at all! I could go back right now and everything would be as it was!" But even as he said that, he walked on, with the cat trotting at his side.

Eventually they reached the suburbs and passed again by the house where the painter found the cat. Her old mistress was still there, sitting on the porch. She nodded at them knowingly as they passed by.

Finally, the painter and the cat found themselves alone in the wilderness of the mountains. The evening got darker. They decided to stop and spend the night where they were. The moment they got off the road, however, the cat turned into a woman again. Together they arranged blankets on the grass.

"I must be mad," said the painter. "There is no other

---

1 'Sky' in Japanese. I heard the word in my dream and found out later that it really meant 'sky' in Japanese...

explanation for it. I could be tucked in my lovely warm bed at this very moment, instead of trying to sleep in the wet grass." But, while saying that, he looked again at the sky — *tenno!* *tenno!* — where the last red rays of the sun touched the very rain-clouds which had made him leave his home. That blessed rain was still somewhere on the horizon. Gazing at the clouds, the painter knew he would never change his decision.

As he got ready to lie down, a wandering samurai came by. He took a good look at the painter and said, "What are you, a soft city slicker, doing here in the wilderness, trying to sleep by the road?"

"I am seeking my salvation," the painter replied, finally able to put his decision into words.

At this point I began waking up, but before I was fully awake, I knew how the story would end: the painter and the cat-woman would become lovers; much later they would fight a duel with scythes, the scythe being the cat-woman's weapon. She is a woman-samurai, and more than that, she is Death, who has become the painter's companion on the road. I did not know who would win.

I swear by the Socket and by everything anyone might care to name, I did dream all this. And when I woke up the storm was in full sway, raging over Vallegrande.

I know, it all sounds too pat and to the point to be true, but life is sometimes corny beyond belief.

Corny and pat (a good title for a movie) as it may have been, I acted upon it. I packed my towels and my suntan lotions and got on the first boat to Split. Luckily, there were still a few seats to be had on the Agram train, not the fast one I would have liked to have taken but the slow one, which stopped at every hamlet along the way.

Yes, but listen; this is what happened on the slow train:

A young woman of my age entered the compartment and sat down opposite me on the seat she had previously booked. She read a magazine and so did I. We read for an hour or so in silence before the train condescended to depart. From time to time, I glanced at her. She was amazingly beautiful, yet her beauty was strangely dated. In spite of her contemporary clothes and make-up, she belonged essentially to a Hollywood movie from the fifties. She had a fifties chin and very fifties cheekbones; her eyebrows, unplucked, were naturally fifties.

Half an hour later, as the train laboured up the slopes of Mt Mosor, I thought she looked the image of Alida Valli in 'The Third Man'.

An hour later, while trundling through the moonscape of Lika, I thought, "This is the sort of girl Wilfrid would fancy."

Another hour passed, and I thought, "This *is* Wilfrid's girlfriend. She has to be. Don't know how or why, and it is madness to assume that I might be right, but it is she and no one else."

The afternoon turned into evening and, while chugging through Bosnian mountains, Alida Valli and I began to talk together of this and that. Eventually and inevitably, we told each other bits of personal information. It turned out we had many mutual acquaintances. She was an actress, fresh out of drama school. And her boyfriend had just graduated film directing.

When I started studying painting, Wilfrid started studying film directing and had graduated at the same time as I.

"His name wouldn't happen to be Wilfrid Blake?" I said. Alida Valli nodded. "You are Pearl, then," I said, choking. Pearl muttered my name. She knew of me, too.

Once we'd recovered from the shock, we were able to maintain civilised conversation until we got off the train in Agram. We made arrangements to meet but, of course, it never happened.

Never take a fast train when you can take a slow one!

Is there a point to this account of a meeting on the slow train? No. The meeting happened just so, as a gift from Fate. An electric shock from the Socket. It put paid to my comfortable relationship with Wilfrid. It was a herald of change.

Back in Agram, I told Matthew as nicely as I could that we ought to stop our not-going out. He took it casually, hiding his face behind his blond curls much as Lillian used to do.

Matthew, I hear, is still single and arranges his dates and other pastimes around his mother's absences from home. It has nothing to do with me. He is one of those people who inhabit Dracula's Castles, like I did, like Wilfrid did, like Melissa still does. (Doesn't! Doesn't any more! Whe-hey! Yippee!) It's a very Agram way to be.

Even my solicitor in Agram, little Donny Horvath, one of the inner circle of secondary school wits, still lives like that, in spite of his huge black BMW and Savile Row suits.

Again, I'm not being catty or ratty. I was like that too, in spite of living two thousand miles west of Dracula's Castle and in spite of being married to my husband whose quicksilver person never gathered moss. I only broke out into the open when, in nineteen ninety six, I packed Patricia Prochazka's personal effects and moved her to a care home. On that occasion I stayed on in Agram for another month and dismantled the Castle once and for all. I sold and gave away virtually everything that was there, then sat down on my own, in the empty flat, with a bottle of wine and celebrated, while outside an almighty storm shook the tall poplars in the courtyard. Tall poplars abound in Agram.

But listen: I kept the wooden chest in which Mama used to put dirty washing. I cleaned it and placed a few things inside: some knives and forks, an old electric iron, a poker, a ceramic bowl, and so on. I stored the chest in Alexandra's cellar, because the flat had been sold.

From time to time, that chest emits a faint siren call. Woooooooooo...ooo...ooo...

If one tied a string to that poker, and held the other end of the string in one's ear, and then hit the poker gently with something made of metal – say, a fork – one could hear a loud "Twannnnnng!" right inside one's head. That's why I've kept it.

Mama, Patricia Prochazka, showed me that trick. I am grateful to her for that.

Having disposed of Matthew, I looked around me and saw that everything around me had been swept pretty clean. It would be fatal, I felt, to disturb all that cleanliness. Whatever I could attempt to do would re-introduce the old mess which I could never ever hope to clean up again.

Alexandra doesn't mind cleaning up the same mess a million times. But then, she has a lot more stamina than I. She is in the business of showing two fingers to the Socket. I'm not. Once I clean up, I move out. I cannot make myself pick up the same burden twice. (When I run out of places to move to and find that everything everywhere has been cleaned up, it'll be, I suppose, time to re-wire.)

Alexandra would say that the burden is different each time, but I've never been able to confirm that, because I cannot work the clothes-peg magic.

So one evening, shortly after my return from Vallegrande, I said to Wilfrid, "That's it, I'm going to England."

Everywhere on the continent, people call the UK "England".

"When?"

"I don't know yet," I said, "but not later than this autumn." I suddenly became all hot and sweaty and my pulse speeded up. That was how it felt to make a decision, then. Because five minutes earlier the decision had not yet been made. Now it was out. I said it, aloud. It would have to be done.

Wilfrid rubbed his hands, lit a cigarette, rummaged through his attaché case and produced a yellow hardback book. "You must consult the I-Ching", he said.

I asked my question silently, cast the coins and constructed the hexagrams. Wilfrid interpreted them for me. He was very good at interpreting the I-Ching. He did it respectfully.

I have forgotten what the Book had said. I only remember that I was to make like a fox crossing a freezing river. If as much as the tip of my tail got caught in the ice, all would be lost. I was also told that I had to find a wise old man: everything hinged on that.

I still don't know whether the tip of my tail has made it across. I did find the wise old man and married him. He was more than twice my age. Only I didn't know he was wise until, at Death's door, he taught me what a moment was, how to understand it and how to make use of it. Then I knew he had been wise indeed, and remembered all the other wise things he told me, like the one about the Oozle-Woozle bird.

I'll tell you how he taught me about the moment, although it won't work second-hand. But still.

He — my husband Edward, that is — and I were alone at home. He was mortally ill and could have taken a turn for the worse at any moment. I knocked the telephone over; it fell on the floor and the line went silent. The set was damaged and I needed it to work, as we didn't have a mobile.

I dropped whatever I was holding in my hands there and then, fetched a screwdriver and opened the set. I compared all the bits and pieces inside that came in pairs and found a disconnected bit. I re-connected it and screwed the set shut. I lifted the receiver and listened: the line had come to life. The whole operation had taken less than ten minutes. I grinned at Edward. "Phew!" I said, "I enjoyed that."

"Of course you did, darling," said Edward. "You *lived* just then."

What he said was like a flash of lightning. I stood there gaping. I felt like Saint Paul on the road to Gaza.

"Wait," I said, "you mean, *that is it*? THAT IS IT?"

He nodded and smiled.

"So that is It. Do you realise I've been waiting for this all my life? Why didn't you tell me before? The time I've wasted!"

"It didn't happen before," said Edward.

He must have been a patient man, to have waited full fifteen years to see me live for a moment. Soon after that, he went down the Farewell.

Can you imagine a lifetime of such moments? I can just

about faintly taste its flavour. It is an awesome concept. It is a constructive way of dealing with the Socket.

Don't gloss over this sentence. Don't assume that I said, 'denying the Socket', 'defying the Socket' or 'defeating the Socket'. I said, *dealing* with the Socket.

It might even have something to do with that famous reality Alexandra is always on about. It certainly makes one feel one is standing on the ground and not being blown around. It gives one the feeling of *substance*.

Wilfrid was pleased with the Book's pronouncements. The augury was good. He stroked his moustache and beard, rubbed his hands and smacked his lips. That was how he used to summon the Intent of Pleasure. It is actually a very clever thing to do. Try it sometime. It works, albeit for a moment, but everything is made of moments and points, remember?

Alexandra was sceptical about my leaving. She thought I was attempting to solve my identity problem by means of space when I should have been using a different, more appropriate medium. She pointed out, very correctly, that I would be taking myself along. For me, the important thing was I would not be taking Patricia along. That, said Alexandra, was only partly true. Even that was something, I retorted. To this she did agree.

Melissa thought I was incredibly brave, if a bit silly. She was looking forward to having a close relative and friend living within a short hop on the tube to Harrods (she assumed it would be a short hop — hell, *I* assumed it would be a short hop).

Lillian thought I would have a hard time of it but believed it was important to follow the call of one's Destiny. If that was what it was.

Papa, amazingly, shrugged his shoulders and said, "You'll see it'll be a waste of time, but there's no use my saying that. You never would be told. You were and always will be mule-headed like your mum. So go ahead and find out, you can always come back."

I would have liked to have told him I couldn't, but he'd never have believed me.

Mama cursed me. I was so amazed to see an act of cursing being performed in our day and age that the actual curse did not penetrate very deep. She raised her right hand — whether instinctively or because she had read Greek tragedies — and shouted so loudly that the whole flat reverberated with her voice: "Bad daughter, may you be damned! May you have a child of your own and may she treat you as callously as you have treated me! May you suffer at her hands as I suffered at yours!" Then she just stood there, her chest heaving.

"Shut up, Patricia," said Papa, a bit belatedly. He, too, was nonplussed.

Papa hated everything that was over the top. (So did Edward.) Mama, on the other hand, only came to life when the top was transcended.

She could not have been very good at cursing, because, as I said before, I am childless.

I wondered whether we could eat dinner that day and get up the next morning as usual and have coffee and breakfast. We did, and continued to do so, for the next three months, and then it was time for me to go. Wilfrid paid for my ticket. He said I was his scout.

Wilfrid is married these days. Not to Pearl; to another girl. She has borne him a daughter and a son. Both Wilfrid and his wife work hard to provide for them. He has thus kept true to his word (to his Word). Remember? He wanted a traditional family. Keeping true to one's Word does not come free. His life is full of strife and so it should be.

I am not his scout any more. This, too, is how it should be.

Wilfrid accompanied me to the airport. It was the end of November and the airport was snowbound. We sat in the cafeteria for five long hours waiting for the snowstorm to stop and the planes to be de-iced by glycerine jets. During the first hour I realised I did not have the foggiest idea of what to *do* once I landed, how to live. I was to stay with some people Wilfrid knew, a married couple. I had an expensive giant salami in my suitcase for them, and a bottle of grappa. They were to be my base from which I would venture forth in search of work and a place to live in. That was the plan.

Can you imagine? In spite of the fact that London was made of points and moments no less than Agram, I preferred to embark on a mad adventure of moving there rather than to look for work and a place of my own in Agram where it would have been a lot simpler to find both.

I could not handle simple, sober stuff. I only performed once the top had been transcended, like Patricia.

But I wasn't going to see Wilfrid any time soon, or Melissa, or Lillian, or Alexandra and Eagerwill.

I howled for the duration of the other four hours. I could not stop.

Once on board the plane, I stopped like a turned-off tap. I felt fine, only it seemed that the flight had lasted a mere few minutes before the plane began its descent towards Heathrow. That was because the babble that normally went on in my mind had quietened down to near-silence. It is the babble that makes the time.

Staines, Stanwell, Bedfont, Ashford, Feltham, Shepperton, Sunbury, Twickenham, Kingston, Richmond were rising to meet me, a web of orange streetlights and streaming cars and gleaming reservoirs and wet roofs of suburban semis. I thought, "This time I don't have to go back and see it all fall away from me again."

As the plane touched down, 'there' became 'here' and Agram's tentacles snapped back beyond the drizzly invisible night horizon. At least it seemed so. But that is the most I can say about anything.

Don't tell Alexandra! For her, "it seemed so" would never do.

4. What Happened to Sean Feeney, or: As You Like It

Sean Feeney Commits Suicide

I never met Sean Feeney. (Or so it seems.) I don't know what became of him, but I can offer two options.

Remember how Government agents had him against the wall? How they offered him to live in Potter's Bar with a windowful of geraniums and not make waves? And how he had to play MacLear on the edge of a precipice? This is what happened next:

I dreamt that, walking along a grey, joyless street of a grey, dull city, I heard people talk about an explosion which had just happened in one of the houses. Everyone around me had their noses in the evening paper, reading about it, although it had taken place only minutes before. Sean Feeney had died in that explosion, the paper said.

Horrified, I rush to see the place. It is easy to find: people are constantly streaming in and out of the building, eager to see what there is to see, with no one stopping them. The house itself is damaged inside and outside by the force of the explosion.

Upstairs, Sean Feeney's flat is completely destroyed. Suddenly, I understand what has happened and realise that I must have been expecting it to happen for a long time.

It is the flat with geraniums. Sean, no longer quite sane after MacLear, had been brought there to live against his will. Tormented by some terrible knowledge which he desperately wanted to but could not impart to others, he finally decided to blow himself up, believing, rightly or wrongly, that the explosion and its consequences would be such that everyone would immediately understand everything.

He must have been at least partly right in his assumption, because, looking at his wrecked flat and imagining his death in the explosion, I suddenly do understand everything. Many other horrified spectators must have felt the same knowledge descending upon them like Pentecostal fire.

When I woke up, I did not have a clue of what I had understood or what 'everything' was. I've been trawling for it over the years and some residue may have, indeed, got caught in this book as if in a net. If not, then it is lost. Sorry, Sean Feeney!

On the other hand, Sean Feeney may not have blown himself up at all. Instead, this could have happened next:

Sean Feeney Goes to the Desert

I dreamt that Sean Feeney had set off for 'the desert' (in the Biblical sense of living in a cave and eating locusts in order to grow closer to God). I somehow know he wasn't going there to mortify his flesh but was simply leaving the world of people and their affairs in order to perfect his understanding of... everything, what else? No one was forcing him this time, it was his own free decision made in joyful anticipation, although it was clear that he would miss being with people and loving them.

There he is, then, walking along a dusty road, dressed like a monk, or, rather, like a Biblical Patriarch: in a greyish-brown robe, with a simple string around his waist, and the whole outfit is not exactly clean. He looks beautiful: his face is beautiful and his body moves in a beautiful way, in spite of an overall appearance of illness and emaciation, which, nevertheless, does not mean that he is in danger. Sean is fully in command of his material existence and is going to be ill only if he wants to be.

The road takes him past an inn, with the Innkeeper, a portly, calm, benevolent man, standing in the doorway. Taking an instant liking to the Innkeeper, Sean Feeney stops and strikes up conversation with him. "You look like a good man," he says, beaming.

"I am," says the Innkeeper, "a very good man."

"How do you manage to be so good?" Sean wants to know.

"Easily," the Innkeeper replies. "After a lifetime of tribulations, I have found the courage to respect myself. I have stopped treating myself like a spoilt child or a moron and started demanding of myself what I demand of people whom I respect. That is why I am a good man."

"Why," says Sean Feeney with an expression of utter delight, "that is brilliant! By Jove, I must be on the right road if people like you keep inns by its side!"

"And you," says the Innkeeper, "aren't you a good man, too?"

"No," Sean Feeney replies, shaking his head in a most graceful way, while the wind tosses his long, greying hair. "No, sir, I don't believe I am. The trouble is, I don't really give a damn because I don't respect myself at all, not one bit. That is why I'm not a good man and don't demand anything of anybody, least of all myself."

"Don't you respect anything at all, then?"

"Oh yes I do," says Sean Feeney and his eyes are suddenly filled with awe. "Oh yes, sir, I do. I respect the road. I demand absolutely everything from it."

Off he goes, his feet barely touching the ground, to the desert and out of our story.

And I, at this point, bow out of it too.

Goodbye.

3431964R00172

Printed in Great Britain
by Amazon.co.uk, Ltd.,
Marston Gate.